POSTMORTEM

POSTMORTEM
The Murderous Legacy of
JOHN WAYNE GACY

COURTNEY LUND O'NEIL

MIRROR BOOKS

MIRROR BOOKS

© Courtney Lund O'Neil

The rights of Courtney Lund O'Neil to be identified as the author of this book have been asserted, in accordance with the Copyright, Designs and Patents Act 1988.

All rights reserved. No part of this publication may be reproduced, stored in a retrieval system, or transmitted, in any form or by any means without the prior written permission of the publisher, nor be otherwise circulated in any form of binding or cover other than that in which it is published and without a similar condition being imposed on the subsequent purchaser.

1

Published in the US in 2024 by Citadel Press. Published in Great Britain and Ireland in 2025 by Mirror Books, a Reach PLC business.

www.mirrorbooks.co.uk
@TheMirrorBooks

Print ISBN 9781917439039
eBook ISBN 9781917439046

Printed and bound in Great Britain by
CPI Group (UK) Ltd, Croydon, CR0 4YY

To all the boys

"Don't you, forget about me."
—SIMPLE MINDS

from *The Breakfast Club*,
filmed in Main North High
School, Des Plaines, IL

CONTENTS

AUTHOR'S NOTE	9
PROLOGUE, 1997	11
1. W. SUMMERDALE AVENUE, 2017	13
2. EXPOSURE, 1978	25
3. DES PLAINES, 2022	36
4. WOMEN'S INTUITION, 1978	59
5. KIN, 2022	80
6. DECAY, 1978	97
7. COMMUNITY, 2022	114
8. WINTER, 1978–1979	128
9. ALL SAINTS, 2022	148
10. WITNESS, 1980	161
11. POST-TRIAL, 2022	203
12. CALIFORNIA, 1994	217
13. THE RIVER, 2022	234
14. A FIGHT FOR GOOD, 2011	243
15. INHERITANCE, 2018	250
16. WHAT SURVIVES, 2022	259
17. REFRACTION, 2023	270
ACKNOWLEDGEMENTS	284

The Des Plaines River, taken in the summer of 1978, by Kim Byers.

AUTHOR'S NOTE

When we sift for items on the shore of a beach, we may surprise ourselves at the mix we find: slivers of shells, slimy seaweed, sea glass and stones, decaying crustaceans, a plastic bottle cap. It's in the unfolding of our hands that ignites a sort of wonder, at both the macabre and marvellous. This approach, of opening my hands and letting the water of this story carry in its pieces, is what has guided me in search of truth. This book is based on layers of truth, from archive materials, newspapers, published books, public records, yearbooks, oral histories, documentaries, and interviews. I spent seven years conducting research for this book, looking closely at what I held, and constructing a narrative based on my findings.

This is a work of researched creative non-fiction, and therefore common techniques of the genre have been employed. Names and identifying markers have been changed to protect identities of some people in the book. Composite characters may appear as a means of protecting identities while holding tight to emotional truths. Timelines have been condensed and altered in places of the text for narrative effect. Descriptions are as accurate as possible but, in some cases, rely on a reimagination to fit time and place. I have adhered to this ethical oath, of truth and story, to the best of my ability.

I chose to focus on one of Gacy's victims with the hope that going deeply into one crevasse of the story reveals a larger picture. All the victims of the Gacy murders were in my heart and mind as I wrote this book. They always will be. I cannot speak for everyone involved in this murder case, but I can speak for what I have seen, felt, believed. I hope you too can find yourself in the journey within these pages. I hope that together we might write a new story about who holds power in events like the one I'm about to tell.

PROLOGUE

1997

THE PALM TREES WHISPER AT night. The stars sleep in the sky, and the moon does not shine brightly enough. My mum startles awake in her beach town home in southern California. The snap of branches echoes from the backyard to her first-floor bedroom. Outside in her double-fenced-in property filled with gardens, rabbit hutches, and children's swings, she senses an intruder.

She lifts her head from the pillow, my dad asleep next to her. A familiar chill of anxiety creeps across the back of her neck. Although she is a million lives away from the murder case that overturned her life, she can never shake that feeling, something grisly can happen at a moment's notice. She wraps her dressing gown around her athletic body and tiptoes through the dark house. In the garage, she grabs a metal baseball bat from my T-ball bag and lurches outside.

She's barefoot under a basin of stars. Her ears perk up as a bush near the rabbit hutch rustles. The animals are awake, and she notices their eyes glowing in the darkness. She bangs the bat in her hand. "Who is that?" she yells, swinging toward an overgrown bougainvillea. Purple-pink petals flicker and flutter to the ground. The bat makes contact with the chain-link fence, behind the hutch. The crash of metal against metal is sharp.

The rabbits shoot around in their homes, fearful. Pellets of sweat rise on her neck.

The outline of a tanned man with black hair emerges. He stands from his crouch behind the bush she is swinging at. His hands flattened open, showing he is not holding a weapon. She screams for my dad and the sound of her voice wakes me. I trail my father outside in my *Little Mermaid* nightgown. My mum is crying, still holding the baseball bat. My dad holds her head in his hands. My breath picks up. I look around for the stranger she claims to have seen. I don't see anyone.

She tells us that her scream made the man run away, over the fences, into the shadows of the alley. I don't remember if the police were called. I cannot recall them being there. But I remember that something was wrong, something was different about my mother.

In the morning, she tells me she had a feeling someone was in our yard. I'm getting dressed for school, loading the lunch she made me into my backpack, exhausted from the night's interruption. After I went back to bed, I pulled the comforter over my head, worrying over a new, stifling feeling. That man could have taken me. Because I didn't glimpse the man, I wasn't sure if he was a figment of my mother's imagination. Or if he was real.

Standing in the kitchen, my mother sips her morning orange-flavoured cappuccino while she gets ready to take me to school. She matter-of-factly tells me what I need to know. Safety is an illusion, no matter how many fences and locks we have. Always keep your ears up. We hear before we see.

What haunts my mother will also come to haunt me.

CHAPTER ONE

W. SUMMERDALE AVENUE

2017

She'd never stepped on John Wayne Gacy's old property, but for some reason, on the last morning of our weekend trip to see her family, my mum agrees to come with me. The car zooms down the road, as though the faster we get there, the faster we can leave.

I gaze out the window as my mum drives down the bare highway. My eyes lock on the horizon of the Midwest, blanketed in grey. Grey strip malls. Grey sky. Grey highways. Illinois in the summer is buoyant and green, but today the state feels stark and cold. I take hold of my mother's free hand, her skin warm against mine. I could go to the property alone, but it feels better to have a witness for this journey, a partner. I'd been yearning for this visit ever since I became a mother, 11 months ago. Something about having a boy of my own made the murders more real, more palpable.

I don't remember the exact moment I became consumed by my mother's role in the John Wayne Gacy murder case. Some of my early memories are of cuddling with her on the couch while devouring *Unsolved Mysteries*. We always hoped someone would call the phone line publicised at the end of each episode to help solve the case. We hoped the families who experienced tragedy could get answers, find an ending.

Back then, I didn't know why my mum was so invested in strangers' losses. I didn't know about her own loss. I didn't know that when a mystery is solved, the heartache never fades completely. I guess my obsession had many beginnings.

My mum's teenage co-worker and friend, Rob Piest, lost his life just over 39 years before we took this drive to W. Summerdale Avenue. The house had no more room for Rob's body. The man who murdered him dragged his body into the Des Plaines River, where he remained for months under heavy ice. That morning, on my run, I noticed the frozen surface of a pond near my grandparents' place. The ice was solid, leaves and twigs crushed under its weight hovered in time. I halted, looking for a face in the ice as I always did. Some primordial part of me sought the story of this place and the gruesome murders it agreed to hold in its belly until a spring thaw.

When I returned from the run, I peeled off my gloves, kicked my tennis shoes to the side, and slid off my ear warmers. In the kitchen I pulled a white coffee cup from the cupboard and let the fresh brew warm me from the inside. After pulling out a chair, I sat with my mum, my sisters, Danika and Sydney, and my 11-month-old baby. My son crawled to the chilled sliding glass door. His face pressed against the cold surface. Warmth fogged, creating a halo effect. I felt the urge to visit the last place Rob walked, to pay respect to the boy he could have been and the girl my mother was before a murder stopped time. When my grandparents asked what my plans were for the day, I asked my mother if she felt prepared to take the drive with me.

My entrance into this case begins with my mother. As her eldest child, I was her confidante, the person she opened up to as she grew in her motherhood. When your mother shares something as devastating as living through a national murder trial involving one of the most horrific serial killers in modern history, it stays. Her part in this story evolved as a mystery unto itself with its own clues. They included our shared investment in true crime; my mum's name appearing as the first two words in a weathered book, *Killer Clown*, I pulled from a bookshelf in her bedroom; and then, her diary stitched with silk cherry blossoms. By no means did she keep a regular diary in the years she was my mother. As a physician, army reservist, and mother-of-four, her free time was limited. But when I became a mother, she handed me this diary that seemed to have come from some sort of time capsule. I read it and was changed. It was the diary she began writing at age 17, in the fall of 1978, into some of her early college years, and a few notable times in her adulthood, when life would challenge her again.

WE PULL INTO Norwood Park Township. W. Summerdale Avenue seems like a pleasant suburban street, in a neighbourhood on the outskirts of Chicago. Ranch-style homes covered in Christmas lights line the streets, a perfect setting for children learning how to ride bicycles on short winter days. From the outside, the area seems like a quaint location to raise a family, perhaps even a safe one.

This unremarkable place is where serial killer John Wayne Gacy murdered 33 innocent boys and young men.

Snow has yet to cover ground in the Chicago suburbs. We park a street away and walk to the address where Gacy once lived. The house has a two-car garage, two storeys, and was built with chestnut-coloured bricks. I stand next to my mother in silence, unsure what to say. The wind is thin, the street quiet.

Our reverie is interrupted by the rumble of a mail truck driving by. My mum whispers, "Don't talk to anyone." I ignore her, waving to the driver. I want to confirm that this two-storey Tudor, which does not fit in with its neighbours, is correct. The mailman pulls over. He nods, as if he knew I was going to ask if this is the location where Gacy once lived. He confirms it is.

"People still send mail addressed to him," he says, "to Gacy."

We pause in the middle of the street, in disbelief as the mailman drives away. My mum and I look at each other as if we have just experienced the beginning signs of food poisoning: upside-down stomach, slightly light-headed.

"Too weird," my mum says. People still send mail to a man who has been dead for over two decades. I feel sorry for the mailman. The way his tone hardened and his eyes widened when he said "Gacy" made me think he was just as disturbed. I look for signs of the missing boys. A "Beware of Dog" sign hangs in the front window, a well-loved Ford Probe is parked in the driveway, a tree without leaves shoots up in the front yard, branches latticed like a witch's hand. There is no memorial or remembrance of the boys who died. It is an erasure.

Goosebumps rise over my mother's skin as she backs away from the house. But the property's energy pulls me closer, and I snap a photo with my Canon Rebel T6. It is full circle, to be here, with my camera. Film had played such a crucial role in the ending of those murders. I put my camera in my bag. Later, I will look at my photos from Gacy's old lot, and one would be smudged. An orb floating in the centre, in front of the house.

"We shouldn't be here. It's too creepy," my mum says quietly. I want a ticket inside her mind, to watch her film reel spin images from the past. I want access to a version of her I can never meet: a brave girl who stood up to a murderer because she felt she had no choice. She dashes toward the rental car, breathing heavily in the driver's seat. The engine rumbles. She tells me, "Get in the car," in a warning tone.

Turning to the house one last time, I imagine a brick house, the one I've seen from photos in 1978, wrapped in crime-scene tape, the semicircle driveway that was once here jammed with police cars, the ongoing investigation, as detectives and police dug up the bones of 29 young men who never got their full turn at life. The stretchers, carrying out skeletons.

The bones were black, dirty, and brittle, decomposing at abnormally fast rates because the quicklime Gacy threw on them sped the decaying process. But they were still humans, easy to recognise, close to each other, like guests at a packed slumber party. The coroners knew they were teenage boys and not girls because the collarbones on the skeletons weren't fully formed. Collarbones are the last bones to mature in a young boy's body. And many of these boys and young men, sleeping in the dirt, did not have fully developed clavicles.

I pull open the passenger door, take my seat, fasten my seat belt, and turn on the heaters. My mum's foot drops on the gas pedal, and we leave the neighbourhood.

Her role in this story has been overshadowed by police and

legal narratives, and the evolution of people's obsession with the killer himself. But the woman next to me, hands tight on the wheel at 10 and two, is a living testament to a feminine perspective, another entrance into these murders. Our visit back to Des Plaines is meant to fill the holes in a larger story of what remains after the killings. The myth of Gacy continues to rise, and the smaller, more human stories sink under the weight of his monstrosity.

I want to ask my mother so much. What she had lived through bled into me. Understanding these murders through her eyes feels like it might help me to understand myself more fully. Why I run toward danger to better understand. Why I worry about keeping my boy safe. But she is processing something in the driver's seat. Instead of poking her with questions, I ask if we can stop by Nisson Pharmacy, the last place she saw Rob alive.

THE PHARMACY NO longer exists. We walk into Touhy Liquor, a low-ceilinged store where my mum thought the pharmacy once was, in a strip mall. The businesses have changed names and outer appearances. Much of the old red brick from the 1970s has been replastered and painted white. A bell rings as we enter, and two women speak Russian behind the counter. I walk through the short aisles, brushing my hands across shelves filled with rum and tequila, wondering if my mum and Rob once moved across these same floors while at work.

"Do you think this is it?" I ask my mum.

"I don't know," she says. "It was so long ago."

We ask the two women if they remember Nisson Pharmacy. They've never heard of it. We exit and stroll through the small strip mall, pausing at the business directly to the left, double the size of the liquor store. My mum sees, or rather feels, something familiar in the double-door glass entry. These are the same doors she walked out of toward the rest of her life on the last night she saw Rob alive.

Angel Town is the private children's school that replaced Nisson Pharmacy. The name on the sign is painted in chunky, large, pale letters. A wood awning covers the original brick. No bright orange sign urges patrons to see Santa Claus here. But this was it. The path to the back alley is the same one Rob walked through to speak with Gacy at his vehicle. Angel Town. An ironic name.

My mum presses her face to the glass doors. She is no longer an army doctor officer. She is 17 again, behind the cash register. Long blonde hair, a gymnast, swimmer, member of the Marmosets, an aerial gymnastics team named after the flying monkeys in *The Wizard of Oz*, and high school senior whose largest concern is acing her physics test. There she is inside, lolling against the front counter, tossing a film receipt into the wastebasket, pausing to reconsider, picking it up and placing it in Rob's parka pocket. There is Rob, with his vulnerable hazel eyes and boyband brown hair, stocking shelves with pharmacy products nearby: Barbasol shaving cream, Ban deodorant, Vicks VapoRub. And a reverberation of Gacy, lurking on the outskirts of the building as he readies himself to enter the scene, smelling Rob out like prey.

I walk out back, by the dumpsters, where Rob met Gacy to speak about the summer work. The job that falsely promised a future. The worn concrete ground, the same cracks, but wider now that time has passed. I wonder what would have happened if Rob had said no to going to Gacy's house to sign new hire paperwork. He was 15, a child.

And what if he did say no? How many more would Gacy have killed?

I step up on the crossbar of a six-foot-tall wooden fence to peer behind Angel Town, where children are playing on a new playground. I squint to make sure I am not seeing things. Perched in the window of a house behind the playground is a mummy-like corpse with a human skull covered in a grey-haired wig. It looks like the decomposing body of Norman Bates in *Psycho*, glaring down at me from a second-story bedroom.

Although Norman Bates comes to us from fiction, an invention of writer Robert Bloch, he was an archetypal killer. Norman ran his mum's motel. He was sometimes charming, handsome in certain lighting. Something might be wrong with him, but the audience doesn't foresee it, not completely at least, until he stabs Marion Crane in the shower. Norman Bates was like Gacy in that sense.

Gacy was a real person who blended in with the world. He held down jobs, threw backyard summer block parties and was involved with the Democratic Party. He had posed for a photo with First Lady Rosalynn Carter. The shot was taken in 1978 during a private reception in Chicago, in celebration of a major parade Gacy helped oversee. It would become famous after the news of the murders broke.

When I return home from this trip, I will research why killers kill. What made Gacy kill? Was there a recipe that made him a killer? Was there a scientific and psychological explanation?

My research leads me to a neuroscientist named Jim Fallon, a professor of psychiatry and human behaviour and emeritus professor of anatomy and neurobiology at the University of California, Irvine, School of Medicine, who studied Gacy's brain, along with the brains of other serial killers. Through his research, he concluded three components make up many murderers' brains. One, genes – MAOA is the major violence gene that serial killers carry; two, brain damage – if there is trauma to the orbital cortex, the part of the brain that sits above the forehead, the chance of turning out criminal increases, because the damage affects the part of the brain that regulates empathy; and three, environment – if you experience trauma, like abuse or neglect, before the pubescent years, you are much more likely to act out violently. Fallon's research suggested having the combination of all three equated to a disaster. Gacy had all three.

The skeleton peeking from the faraway window is too much, even for me. I step down from the crossbar on the fence and look for my mum, who is pacing in front of the old Nisson Pharmacy. "There was some sick skull peeking out a bedroom window back there," I tell her. "Want to see?"

She raises her eyebrows, shakes her head no. The truth is that she didn't need to see. I had done the seeing for us.

ON THE DRIVE out of Des Plaines, my mum and I stop for coffee. When we are back in the car, we agree no one should live on the land where all those boys were murdered and buried. No matter how different the house looks, the cemetery that once was cannot be forgotten. At the time, some victims remained unidentified, and this plot of land was the last place where they were known, their identities soaked into the soil. It seems like the town tried to forget. But those boys deserved to be remembered, and we are not convinced they ever were. My mum and I want to raise awareness and money to set up a memorial, either here, on this property, or somewhere in town. We'd have a remembrance for every boy. Their names. Their photos. They'd never be forgotten again.

As our car parallels the Des Plaines River, I ask my mum, "Do you know where Rob is buried?" She does. She went to his funeral service, where Mr and Mrs Piest gave her a plaque she keeps in the shelves in her garage, a small acknowledgement of thanks for helping to put an end to their son's killer.

"He's in a drawer," she says. "In a mausoleum." She points out the window in a general northwestern direction, toward All Saints Catholic Cemetery and Mausoleum. Mr and Mrs Piest chose to have Rob's body stored above ground. Her son had been dead, floating in a freezing winter river for nearly four months, gummy and ballooned and wet. I assume his parents opted for him to be in a drawer because he'd be preserved. Nothing more could be taken from him. Elements and people could not touch him.

While staring out the front window, my mum lets herself think about Rob. The windshield wipers flap as light rain flutters against the glass. Her voice cracks through the cloudy atmosphere of the car. "He was just a kid."

My chest tightens. He was just a kid. Often, that is forgotten. Much of the narrative about Gacy centres on this ordinary-looking man targeting vulnerable men in the LGBTQ+ community. However, this was a generalisation made by the media and retellings. Some victims had clear ties to the community, others did not. Rob did not fit this narrative. He was a kid at work, saving money to buy a Jeep, a new camera. He had recently had a girlfriend. On the night he was taken, his mother was waiting to pick him up. It was her birthday.

I ask my mum what she thought her role was the night Rob disappeared.

"I was a conduit that night, I was there as part of a bigger plan." She pauses. "I paid attention to feelings, messages. And followed them."

"Like intuition?" I tap my fingers on the window, watching them form foggy miniature ghosts on the cold glass.

She says it was something more. She sips her cappuccino, becoming distracted by the faded yellow arches out the window. Des Plaines is home to the first McDonald's, and the original restaurant is a museum now. She used to go here as a Brownie Girl Scout. The original sign is still up, promoting 15-cent burgers. My family has a name for this type of convenient distraction: squirrelling. I tell her she is squirrelling, going off topic. We both laugh.

A fuzzy glow seeps into the car, the sun slicing through the clouds. In my mum's diary, she wrote about a dream in which she saw a body in the trunk of a car on the night Rob disappeared. From December 13, 1978, she wrote: *I feel like going away and leaving this all behind. But I know I must soon face reality.* In these early days, her diary told a story of hope, the possibility that her friend was only missing. A belief that he would be found living. She pictured him locked up somewhere in a basement or adrift in a forest where no one could hear him scream for help. For her, it was possible to hold the worst at bay.

She also recorded that she felt something important would happen on the 19th day of December in 1978. And it did.

That was the day the police found my mum's receipt in Gacy's house. In her entry on December 19th, she wrote: *Well, I guess my hunches were right. I came home after school to get something to eat before I went shopping. The phone rang. They asked me questions about the film slip. My guess is that they found it. Will pray for Rob.*

The Siri with its British accent interrupts, telling us to turn right and pass over a bridge crossing the Des Plaines River. My mother's eyes lock with the thrashing movement of the water. "And why do people dump a body in the river?" she asks, speaking to herself as much as to me. "To wash it away. Send it away. As if it didn't happen."

I place my hand on hers, look out the window into the murky water, and consider the stories that water carries. The run-off from the Des Plaines leads into other rivers, eventually heading south for the Gulf of Mexico. Water molecules make their way to the ocean and can live over three thousand years, travelling all over the earth, through surface currents. Eventually, water molecules evaporate and return to the atmosphere. One day, the water that held Rob would return to the sky, but for now, it lives in its liquid state. I want to go down to the river, place my hands in it, pay my respects. Feel the coldness Rob floated in until my fingertips crease egg white. I want to stay in this moment, stretch it out, tell Rob I wish it didn't have to be this way. But we have a flight to catch back to California. I tell my mum I love her, let go of her hand, wipe my eyes, and find the river and bridge in the rearview mirror.

CHAPTER TWO

EXPOSURE

1978

On a warm summer day in Des Plaines, Illinois, a young man walked into Nisson Pharmacy on E. Touhy Avenue. He was there to pick up some milk for his mother. The store was only eight blocks from their family home and had become a quick mainstay for errands. A birthday card; a place to cash a check; where everyone could develop photos. It was the town's one-stop shop. The boy's mother waited in the car while her son ran into the Nisson Pharmacy. She rolled down her windows. "Don't forget the change," she said.

"Got it, Mum!" the boy said, a pep in his step. He was happy and looking forward to Cub Scouts activities coming up that summer. He was 15, and the school break was a time for swims at the Iroquois Swimming Pool, hikes in the woods, days canoeing on the lake.

In the store, by the fridges, the boy wiped his hand on his Levi's before pulling open the silver moon handle of the large glass door. He wore a Wrangler tee and pulled out a jug of chilled milk. At the checkout counter, he rested the item. Across from the boy was Kim Byers, almost 17. She had long dark blonde hair. Her skin was olive, warm, freckles sprinkling over her nose and onto her blushing cheeks. She smelled like fresh linen and lilac. Her lips slightly opened, and she had the aura of a carefree, jovial spirit, common of kids in the 1970s.

Something about the boy appealed to her. His effortless smile, his cool charm for someone so young, his thick cedar hair that curtained his face.

Kim rang up the milk at the register. "That will be 91 cents," she said. He pulled a dollar out of his pocket and slid it toward Kim. "You looking for a job?" She didn't ask everyone this, but she could tell he might make for a good co-worker or friend. The store was two years old, with new management, and the owners were looking to hire more help. Most of the employees were highschoolers who would go off to college, so the turnover was high.

"What's your name?" she asked, warmly. Rob Piest was 15. He wanted his own car. He'd get his licence in March, when he turned 16.

Kim handed him a piece of paper and pencil to write his information on. Soon enough, the pharmacy owners, brothers Phil and Larry Torf, called Rob for an interview. He was hired by the end of September.

Rob's daily shifts began at 6.00pm. His mom picked him up from high school gymnastics practise at 5.30pm each day with a hot dinner and thermos of milk. She drove him to Nisson Pharmacy while he ate in the passenger seat next to her. Rob was the youngest of the three Piest children. The baby, always extra special.

IN PHOTOGRAPHY, EXPOSURE is defined by both the intensity of light and duration of its presence through the aperture. In many ways, exposure became an embedded metaphor for the events that were about to take place, as the light slowly receded in the fall and winter of 1978. Throughout the season Kim, Rob, and Rob's neighbourhood friend, Nathan, developed a close Nisson Pharmacy friendship. Nathan worked at the pharmacy doing local deliveries. Rob restocked shelves and checked new items into the store, placing price tags on Pond's cold cream, Danish rings, Puretest Epsom salt, and other sundry items. Both boys developed crushes on Kim. Sometimes she was clueless to this fact. Sometimes she wasn't.

After some shifts the trio would go to the movies or take nature photos in the Algonquin Woods. Other times the three would head out to Big Bend Lake and the boys would drink and flirt with Kim. She loved being with them, one of the boys. Even if they flirted with her, she did not reciprocate. She, too, felt like the whole world was ahead of her, the in between of childhood and adulthood. The magic of what life would be like after high school felt as real as the fall chill. When Kim wasn't around, Nathan and Rob, both talked about how they wished they could be her boyfriend. The two boys were especially enamoured with her athletic ability, always checking out her shoulders: tan, athletic, symmetrical. "You do have the best shoulders of any girl I've met," Rob would say. Nathan would add, "He's right, Kimmy."

Kim's cheeks would bloom rose-pink. "It's what happens when you work out in the pool twice a day right after gymnastics season." Rob, Nathan, and my mom were all gymnasts. Nathan, the oldest and a recent high school graduate, had been invited to join a circus as an acrobat. He planned to leave for Texas in December.

Nathan and Rob would have asked Kim out, but they couldn't. Rob had an on-and-off-again girlfriend. My mom had a boyfriend, Cory, who was a gymnast like herself at Maine North High School. Nathan and Rob went to Maine West High School, part of the Maine Township District. The separation of their school lives allowed Kim to show a different side of herself. With them she didn't have to be hemmed in by the way people at school saw her: a smart, social, pretty jock, in a million different school organisations and clubs. To them she was just a Nisson Pharmacy co-worker. In a way, the reduction of herself in this friendship made her walls fall more easily.

In October 1978 Kim Byers began writing in a diary. She was a senior in high school, and this journal was going to be a way to record and remember her senior year. At the end of each day, no matter how late, Kim would sit in her room with a little lined notebook and reflect on her day in the quiet of the night. The diary had been an August birthday gift. She was very much a Leo: a born leader, energetic, and loyal. But maybe there was some feeling deep inside, telling her: Keep some things for yourself, write. On entries leading up to December 11, 1978, Kim writes in blue pen. The writing is half cursive, half not. It reveals a sense of her searching for the woman she might become. Dipping in and out, her thoughts and reflections swerve and drift.

October 13, 1978

Friday the 13th. What a day. I started the day off on the wrong foot. I told Cory I would pick him up at 7.30. Didn't make it till 7.50. He was a little upset. He had an awful day: a fight with his parents, school was bad.

He'll be better. I went to work then out with Nathan. We went to a lake and talked. I'm going to try not to see him anymore, Cory's more important.

October 21, 1978

A very busy week. On Wednesday had a dance class with Cory. If it wasn't for that one hour a week, I'd go crazy. It's a time for me to forget everything. Thursday night we had our first Marmoset show. Also got my new Canon AE-1 camera. It cost $263. A LOT of $$. The show was okay. Thursday and Friday I went to Cory's after school. Saved a bird which flew into the basement window. Went home around 5pm.

Today I worked at the pharmacy from 9-8. I'm exhausted. Came home and Cory had brought over a bouquet of flowers for our anniversary, just a few tears. Being in love is scary!

On October 29 Kim attended the homecoming football game. She and her friend Peggy dressed up as clowns. This was before clowns had become a symbol of a trickster, someone not to be trusted. From the 1950s to 1970s, Bozo the Clown was a popular, joyful entertainer. Kim hoped to spread joy among the crowd with her red wig and polka-dotted body suit. The two girls painted their faces white with big red noses and sold balloons as a fundraiser for the yearbook. Rob and Nathan were working that night, or they would have gone to the game to see her all dressed up.

When Kim was not around Nathan and Rob had their own

friendship. They were friends as children, living across the street from each other. But as they grew, the age difference set them adrift from one another. At the pharmacy they reconnected. One evening in the fall, the boys took a canoe out onto the Des Plaines River. They were in the rushing water, not yet frozen, when the canoe flipped over, trapping Rob inside. Rob shrieked under the canoe, not because it had flipped, but because spiders were crawling all over him. Tiny legs pitter-pattered across his wet skin, through his thick, damp hair. His arms thrashed, shaking off the insects. He had a phobia of spiders. Nathan grasped the canoe and flipped it back over, witnessing little black specks wiggling across his friend. Rob dunked his head underwater and slashed his hands through his hair. He came up for breath and the boys both laughed. It was the kind of memory only two best friends can share, a memory Nathan would never forget.

ONCE DECEMBER CAME snow piled down on Des Plaines. Many activities were moved inside, as the season was one of the coldest and had the heaviest snows in the town's history. Nathan, Rob, and Kim went to the movies to see *The Wiz*, a musical based on the novel and film *The Wizard of Oz*. Nathan and Rob spent their afternoons playing on Rob's new pinball machine, whipping the silver ball up and around, getting buzzed from drinking Mad Dog out of paper bags. Kim had her nose to the grindstone, finishing her senior year strong, and enjoying it, before heading off for college.

On December 11, 1978, Kim arrived late at Nisson Pharmacy for her five o'clock shift. The storefront had a bright orange sign that encouraged customers to come back on December 18th so that their children could take a photo with Santa. A vertical yellow sign on the window advertised gifts for him: Brut, English Leather, Old Spice, Canoe, Vetiver. To the right, a pink vertical sign, gifts for her: Jontue, Chanel No. 5, Nina Ricci, Charlie, White Shoulders, Intimate. A Presto Hot Dogger for toasting weenies was also advertised on the glass window for $7.66.

The wind twisted loose strands of Kim's hair as she entered through the store's double doors, to the right of the advertisements. It was 31 degrees when she arrived. For her shifts she wore black pants and a short-sleeved shirt, keeping her jacket on a hook in the bathroom in the back of the store. Her hair was pulled into a ponytail with a middle part. Rob came to work shortly after her, wearing brown pants, a beige shirt, and his favourite blue parka. She worked the register, and Rob busied himself pricing and checking in new items to be shelved.

A new person was working in the store that night. He was a large man, overweight, his slightly receding brown hair laced with silver. The man did not acknowledge Kim and she did not say hello to him. They bumped into each other in the aisles of the pharmacy. The two looked into each other's eyes. Kim's, light glacier blue. The man's, dark omen indigo.

"Who is that guy?" Kim asked the owner, Phil, at the pharmacy counter.

"A contractor," Phil said. "Larry and I asked him to take measurements for the store. You know, a possible face-lift." Phil said it like the contractor was a family friend.

Halfway through the shift, the wind chill nipped at Kim by the front door. Rob had set his parka down on some boxes next to the front left checkout counter.

"Hey, Rob," she said. "Mind if I borrow your jacket?"

He handed her his blue parka, and she was snug in it, the warmth immediately allowing her shoulders to slump. The goosebumps on her arms lowered.

Midway through her shift Kim decided she wanted to develop a roll of film. They were actually reprints from the homecoming dance. She had gone with Cory and loved how the pictures turned out, how they captured young love. For Christmas, she wanted to give a print to her older sister. She stood at the counter and slipped the film roll into a red and white envelope.

She filled out the envelope with her name and address, in her own writing. It took her a couple tries to get the envelope just right. Once it was correctly filled out and sealed, with the film safe inside, she tore off the top receipt. In her right hand, she went to discard the receipt, but then paused and slipped it into Rob's parka pocket instead. Nervously, she thought maybe Rob would find it and ask to see her photos. She wanted her cute friend to see her all dressed up at the homecoming dance.

But she also placed the receipt in the pocket because she had an instinct that this is what she was meant to do. A small, faraway crevasse of herself she did not have daily access to had opened. Something, someone telling her to save the receipt.

The rest of Kim's shift dragged on. She cast around, ringing up guests and listening to conversations her boss had with the strange man in the store. He estimated the cost of the remodel would be $1600. The contractor left around 7.15pm. He also left his coffee-coloured appointment book on the pharmacy counter.

Around 8.00pm it was nearing the end of Rob's shift and he needed to take out the trash. "Hey, mind if I take my jacket back?" he asked Kim.

Kim slid out of the blue parka and handed it to Rob. He zipped it up to his chin to keep out the cold. Rob looked like a bright blue cloud, Kim thought.

As Rob carried the plastic bags to the dumpster in the back, he noticed school-age kids playing in the snowbanks. A girl noticed him and flirtatiously chucked a snowball at him. It left a light powdery residue on his parka.

"Hey!" Rob said. The girl laughed and ran down the alley, back into the dance at the Iroquois Junior High School. He would rather have seen Nathan, who sometimes passed by the pharmacy when he was headed to a friend's house. It was his night off, and Rob missed him. He was anxious to get as much time with Nathan as he could before his friend left at the end of the year to join the circus. Rob kept an eye out for Nathan's car but never saw it. In the wind and snow, Rob hefted the trash over his shoulder and into the can. He brushed the snow off him, then wiped his hands together, blew on them to keep them warm, and headed back inside.

Sometime in the last hour of Rob's shift, the contractor returned. He grabbed his forgotten appointment book. But he didn't leave. He lingered, noticing Rob. He noted the kid's good work ethic. He often hired highschoolers with good work habits to help him on various projects. It wouldn't elicit suspicion if he offered this kid a job. The contractor meandered; irregularly walked the pharmacy aisles, pretended to eye the shelving again.

At 8.55pm, Elizabeth Piest entered the store. She was lean, with short hair. She greeted Kim, she greeted Rob. She did a bit of shopping, browsing up and down the aisles, and then leaned against the Fannie May chocolate counter, waiting for her son. Boxes of See's Candies were for sale, too, perched behind her on a shelf. The night was supposed to be special. Elizabeth was turning 46 and anxious to get back and blow out candles. She had a birthday cake waiting at home. The whole family was waiting for her and Rob at the house.

Rob was finishing his stocking job while his mom waited and he approached Kim around 9pm for a final time. "That contractor wants to talk to me about a summer job that will pay me $5 an hour. Mind watching the front for a minute?" The minimum wage was $2.50, so the contractor's offer made him light up at the possibilities the money could offer.

Kim looked at Rob, and his image imprinted in her mind. Loyal, handsome, strong. The blue parka was made for him. "Okay," she said. "See you soon."

Kim watched Rob slide his hands in his pockets and thought of her receipt. He would notice it at any moment now. But as he stopped on his way out of the store he didn't seem to notice. He looked from Kim to his mother and said, "I'll be right back."

"Okay, honey," Mrs Piest said. "I'll be right here."

The door shut behind him and she thought nothing of it. But for the rest of her life, she'd see his departure, the closing of the door in slow motion.

Rob never came back into Nisson Pharmacy. After about 10 minutes, Kim went out back to look for him. He was gone.

She saw footprints in the icy snow, tyre tracks of the contractor's car. The wind was mean in its chill, and she shuddered, her arms wrapped into her body. Her eyes scanned the ground. But she didn't see anything abnormal. Kim went back inside and said she didn't see him.

Rob's mother went out to look for him as well and saw nothing. She would have waited outside for him to come back, but the wind chill was below freezing. The two women waited in the store. The long hand on the clock ticked and the seconds and minutes marched by. Instead of immediately worrying, the two women thought Rob would return within a reasonable amount of time. But deep down, a rock immediately formed at the basin of Elizabeth Piest's stomach. Where could he have gone?

"Kim, will you call me when he comes back?" Elizabeth Piest asked. "Of course," Kim said.

Mrs Piest drove home. She called Nisson Pharmacy every few minutes to check if Rob had come back to the store. Every few minutes Kim ran to the back to answer. "Kim," Mrs Piest breathed. "Is he there?"

"He's not here," Kim said, feeling more and more confused. She knew he loved his mom more than anything. He'd never miss her birthday.

Rob's disappearance would not hit Kim until the next day. At school a youth officer visited her and told her Rob never came home.

12/12/78

Today was an absolutely miserable day... he never came back to the store and he never went home. Rob would never run away, he had no reason to. And this guy Gacy claims he never talked to Rob... I can just imagine Rob lying out in some empty forest, alive but unable to move, crying for help with no one answering him. It is just not fair, Rob never did anything wrong to anyone... I can't talk about it anymore -my heart is being ripped apart.

CHAPTER THREE

DES PLAINES

2022

"Welcome to Chicago, where the local time is 9.08pm. We hope you enjoy your time in the windy city," the flight attendant intones through the phone at the front of the aeroplane. The sun had set long ago when I land in O'Hare Airport. Under the industrial lighting of the rental car centre, I hand the woman behind the desk my identification. She moves her long pink acrylic nails across the surface of my driver's licence. "Happy birthday," she says.

Technically, my birthday was a couple of days ago. My 35th. I celebrated it with my family by going out for Mexican food by our house. I didn't feel 35, whatever that is supposed to feel like. But I did feel a sense of privilege to be alive, to have a birthday. People often notice my birthday: 9/11. "I'm going to upgrade you, honey," the woman behind the desk says.

I blush. I've never been upgraded for a flight or a hotel room or anything. I take it as a good omen for the trip. The woman taps her pink nails over the keyboard, changing my rental to a chrome full-sized SUV, a Toyota 4Runner. Being higher up off the ground, in this tank of a car, I will feel safe. I thank her and climb into my birthday gift, headed to the suburbs of Des

Plaines, Illinois, and the landmarks that make up my mother's memories.

It has been almost five years since I first began my excavation of this place and its history. When I began researching the Gacy case, my firstborn son, Bennett, was an infant. Now, he is a kindergartener. I have another son, too. Cal is just over a year old.

Five years have led me down an untraditional path: a restaurant server turned PhD student as a new mom; four years of research and writing in the academic world. This is my first research trip as a postgrad. My doctorate was not easy, but the degree, the research, the writing, the long nights and even longer weekends: they mattered. Just as motherhood had swept me into a beautiful and brutal new world, so did the work of asking questions and uncovering meaning.

On many weekends I would hole up in the library and my husband, Nick, would bring Bennett when he was just a toddler to visit me. Bennett always remembered our tradition, to press the buttons on the vending machine just right so a Rice Krispies Treat could fall. I was lucky to use some of my time over the past four years to explore the rhetoric of grieving mothers, inherited trauma, the trickle-down effects of murder on both cultural and personal levels.

A lid opened on that trip back here in 2017 with my mom. This place, these people, Rob, my mom at 17, it all became an itch I couldn't quite dig my nails into. As I saw bad TV shows and tabloid-like books and podcasts erupt about John Wayne Gacy, telling inflated half-truths about some clown who killed kids (spoiler: he killed, but it is unclear if he ever did so while dressed as a clown), I felt angry. It was often a story choreographed without nuance. Often the same angle, with Gacy at the centre, and men telling the story of the murders. I craved something more. I wanted to see my mom in these stories. It was a national murder case, but it was also my mother's life. How had this shaped her? Shaped my family? Affected me?

Women aren't often central to murder narratives from the 1970s unless they were the victims. Their voices are largely omitted from the retelling of the narratives around serial killers because usually they are the ones being killed. But my mum was not killed that night Gacy came into the pharmacy. I guess you could say that was my door in. It was as if this case was trapped in time, in the black and white photos of the 1970s, but now we had colour, and the story was waiting to be revealed.

I'd learn during my trip to Des Plaines, Illinois, where this story was born, that a grief-stricken silence wore down the families, friends, and acquaintances of Rob and other victims. Silence was a form of survival. But so much time had passed, this place had an energy. A current of stories, of memories, fighting to be heard. I first planned this trip to better understand what happened to Des Plaines and how the murders by John Wayne Gacy still infiltrated this place today. I hoped to learn about the evolution of my mum's life based on these murders.

Des Plaines is a suburb of Chicago in Cook County, Illinois, with a population just over 60,000. It's situated north of O'Hare Airport, the centre of Chicago's northern suburbs. The neighbourhoods and small-town businesses spin out like spokes on a wheel. Anywhere one drives around Des Plaines, and down to where Gacy lived, one can see aeroplanes overhead. Jet engines sputter and tilt in the sky.

The city of Des Plaines took its name after the Des Plaines River, which runs right through it. The river rushes, carrying anything miles away. Like the aeroplanes the river can frequently be spotted when driving to, from, and within the Des Plaines area. In many ways, even in the silence of the outskirts of Des Plaines, the river and jet planes remind you that you are not alone.

ON THE DRIVE to my hotel, a Hyatt Place west of Des Plaines, in Itasca, I stop at a Jewel-Osco grocery store to pick up some food for the week. My car pulls into a spot next to the cart return. I open my door against the warm wind. The raspberry-red Jewel-Osco lights are blurry in the proof-of-life photo I snap on my phone to send home to the boys. While I'm busy looking down on my phone, a car door shuts behind me. My eyes scan the parking lot. I keep my ears up for footsteps around me. All clear.

A row of red carts is parked to the left of the entrance. The wheels spin wildly on the cart I select, but I don't want to waste time returning it. Grocery stores are like Savasana in yoga for me. A place to relax, think, decompress.

I grip the red handle on my cart and select miniature glass bottles of San Pellegrino, spicy beef jerky sticks, miniature chip bags, vegetarian sushi, and Pinot Noir.

It's midnight by the time I pull up to the Hyatt Place. Nick and I met while working as restaurant servers at a Hyatt, and we still have friends who work there. Hyatt hotels feel like another home to me, I know what to expect.

I park my 4Runner, stack my grocery bags, and pull my luggage with my left hand. Sliding doors open. Someone at the front desk tells me about the breakfast in the morning and points me toward the elevator.

It is early fall. And I am here. In the flesh. Fall seemed like a good time to immerse myself in Des Plaines. Fall had been the last good season in 1978 for my mom, for Rob. The season of high school dances. The season of curious walks in the woods. The season of photography. Winter changed all this goodness. Winter became the season of disappearance. The season of desperation and despair. I wanted to visit Des Plaines during the last good season.

During breakfast, I brainstorm how to divide my day. There is the factual history of this place and the oral history of these people, two paths to the truth that should be a straight line but aren't always. Once in the rental car, I plug my phone into the centre console and pull up directions to the Des Plaines History Center. I know it is close to downtown, near the police station. In all my trips back here, I had never stopped at the Cook County Sheriff's Office. My hope is that somewhere in the midst of these two buildings I can gain a better understanding of what it was like to live through the discovery that the town was harbouring a serial killer.

I park on a shady street next to the Des Plaines History Center. Trees with low-hanging branches shade the curb. Charming. That's how I feel as I approach the building, with its brick wall covered with a colourful Des Plaines mural.

Inside, history blooms everywhere. I read about the city's beginnings with the early tribes of the Potawatomi, Ottawa, and Ojibwe that inhabited the Des Plaines River Valley. Remnants of life in Des Plaines throughout the decades are displayed in photos dating back to the farmlands before the area became sprawling suburbia. But there's history closer to my mum's era: an old pinball machine, Lincoln Logs miniatures, a Girl Scout sash. A photo of O'Hare, taken in 1979, the same year American Airlines Flight 191 crashed, killing 273 people, commemorating one of the deadliest accidents in local history. The winter and spring of 1979 was rimmed with death for the Des Plaines community.

I have the urge to run my hand over the pinball machine, try and play. I know Rob enjoyed pinball in his teens. Nathan had shown me a photo of the one he and Rob used to play on together at Rob's house.

A woman in her 80s in a pink fleece stops by and asks if there's anything she can help me find. I place my hands behind my back, nervous that she noticed my hands itching to touch the pinball machine. I want to show her I have good museum etiquette and am serious in my research. When I ask her for any historical references of the Piest family, or my mum's family, or Gacy, she smiles and slides me a piece of paper. I write down my name and email, and I thank her. "This will give me something to do," she says with a laugh.

On my way out of the centre, I buy a shirt to take home to my husband. In bold type, it reads: **"Can Someone Des Plaines It to Me?"**

The rest of the morning I walk around downtown. Next to the police station is a old movie theatre, the Des Plaines Theater, a historic brick building, built in 1925. The sign is embellished with thick block letters. It is the place my mom went to view *The Wiz* In the fall of 1978.

I stand out front of the police station and imagine the first calls from Elizabeth Piest, her voice travelling quickly from her house, across town. The sharp worry in her tone about her missing son. The station is about three miles north of E. Touhy Avenue, where Nisson Pharmacy sat. The Piest home was only 0.7 miles from the pharmacy, a quick three-minute drive. I pictured a thin, triangular shape on a map, the route the Piest family must have made that night.

The police station, 1418 Miner Street, is a white multi-level building. A glass revolving door appears original to the building. The Piest family must have swung through, a certain slowing down required when asking for help at the front desk. Could someone go over to that contractor's house?

A suited detective pushes his way through the doors now, giving me a curt nod before heading to his patrol car. He might be on the job, aware that the full picture is available only outside of the police station. The answers the Piest family searched for that night couldn't be found here or in the history centre. It feels like a false start.

SHORTLY INTO THE trip, my mum flies out to Illinois to meet me. From 100 yards away, I spot her, standing outside a breezy sidewalk at O'Hare. She is in a black dress with black flats, with a white sweater wrapped around her waist. I roll my window down and wave to her.

It is nearing 8pm, a little late for any big adventures.

We grab dinner in the hotel lobby. "I can't believe I'm back here," she says. The hotel lobby has moody, dim lighting, and we are tucked away in a corner.

"I'm happy you are here," I tell her. "What do you want to do tomorrow?"

She thinks about it, biting a piece off a chicken wing, but it is too spicy, and she sets it down on the plate. "I would love to show you where I grew up," she says. "And some of the places we would go to as kids. And… to see my mum."

I had travelled to Illinois many times in my childhood, and she never mentioned visiting her mother's grave. Her mother was buried here, even though none of my mother's family lived nearby anymore. My maternal grandmother, Barbara, had been dead almost 35 years, as she died when I was just a baby. My mum had flown out from California to Chicago to see her mother, one more time, before she died. She wanted her mother to meet me, her first granddaughter.

Barbara had suggested for my mother to name me Courtney. She would meet me with my chunky cheeks and orange-coloured hair. There was one photo I had seen in an old photo album, of my tummy lying warmly on hers, in the hospital bed. In the photo, my grandmother looked visibly sick, with grey circles around her eyes, but she had a smile. She had my mum's smile. Of course, I had no memories of the trip, just stories passed down from my mother to me.

Mothers pass down much to their children, and it begins with a story. My mom would tell me the story of the night my maternal grandmother died. I was asleep in an open drawer next to her. In the middle of the night she said, out of nowhere, I screamed. She said I shrieked so loud it was a volume and pitch that did not normally come from a baby. Startled, she quickly jumped out of bed to check on me, and I was still asleep. She wondered if it all had been a dream.

My mum went back to lie down in the bed. A minute later, the phone rang. Her mother had died in the night. My mum tells me she thinks her mum's spirit passed through me, causing me to scream.

THE SUN CLIMBS through the space where the curtains meet. After the free breakfast, we buckle up in the rental car to begin our day. I order us coffee at a shop in the heart of Des Plaines, then we are off.

My grandmother is buried in Arlington Heights, at Memorial Garden Center. My mother remembered that the family had got a good deal on the burial plot. My mum walks into the visitor centre while I sit in the driver's seat. She comes back with a paper map. Showing me the location, my mom points to the far back wall of the cemetery, the veteran's memorial section. My grandpa was a veteran from the Korean War and was offered some plots at this local Des Plaines cemetery. It was a good deal.

Who could have predicted that the whole family would not live in Des Plaines forever?

We park the car. Our feet shuffle through the thick grass. My eyes scan the gravestones, some have grass completely overgrowing the bronze plaques.

"I'm worried the grass has completely covered her," my mom says. We brush dirt and grass off gravestones, by the back wall. "Here she is," my mom says.

My mom stoops down. She takes the sunglasses off her head, onto her face. A sadness pulls over her. "I should break her out and bring her with me," she laughs-cries. My legs bend and I sit down in the cool grass with her. Grass grows through the bronze surface of the flat gravestone.

"What do you mean, break her out?" I ask. I imagine my grandmother's casket and body being exhumed from the ground.

"She's cremated under here," she says.

"Oh." I pause. "Why haven't you ever come back here?"

"I don't know," she says. "It makes me think a lot about my own death, and what I want." She pushes her sunglasses back onto her head. "I don't know if I want to be buried. Maybe I want to be cremated and thrown into the ocean. Me and your dad have those spots up in Miramar reserved."

She is referencing the US military's plots provided to active duty and their family in San Diego County. "We should have brought flowers," my mom says.

My shoulders slump. My mom hasn't come here in three decades and we brought no flowers, no offering. I should have done a better job anticipating that we should bring more than just ourselves.

"I have an orange," I say. I run back to the car and bring the waxy orange from the breakfast buffet this morning. I turn it in my hand. "It's better than nothing."

I brush the orange against my lips. A brisk kiss. I hand it to my mom. She does the same. She rests it near the broken spot in the gravestone, where the grass peeps through.

OUR NEXT STOP is to meet a very old acquaintance of hers, someone who had long lived in the community of Des Plaines. We'd meet him at Sunrise Café, an unpretentious eatery deriving decorative inspiration from Tuscany even though the food is solidly Midwestern. We order some iced teas, food for the table, and wait. Michael first reached out about the writing I was publishing about the murders. We chatted over email, and I found him to be interesting and insightful.

Many people messaged me over the years, but his outlook was unique. He stood both close and far away from the case. He was friends with my mom when she worked at Nisson's and was acquaintances with the Torf brothers' kids. He lived in an apartment complex over from my mom and worked at a store located near the pharmacy. Although he had lost touch with the Torf family, he remembered how the disappearance of Rob impacted the store owners.

At around 2pm, Michael slides into the booth across from my mom and me. The way Michael brings his fingers to his mouth when he speaks makes me uncomfortable. He seems to not trust himself or what he'll say, attempting to physically keep words in his mouth. His eyes dart toward the kitchen, then the front door, every few minutes, like a man being watched.

I try to keep my face neutral. Sometimes it was difficult for me to decipher the level of my guard, my own protective mechanisms. When meeting new people, especially men who are older than me, I feel a certain defensiveness. I don't know if this is a mere effect of being a woman, or if it is some errant thread in my DNA connected to Gacy. Maybe both. I am happy to not be alone.

Michael appears to be in his early 60s with thinning grey hair. His collar bone protrudes below the thin weave of his black cotton T-shirt. He is petite, the same height as my mom when they embraced. My mother tells me later she thought he smelled of alcohol.

"It is so great to see you," my mom says.

And at first, it is. They recall old neighbourly memories: throwing a ball around in a field that no longer exists, across from the pharmacy. It's been developed now, apartments filling the once-open space.

"The pharmacy is a day care centre now," my mom says.

"Once the Wal-Mart set up shop on West Algonquin, a lot of the mom-and-pop stores packed it in," Michael says, tipping his Diet Coke into his mouth. His straw sits still in its wrapper on the table. "People don't know the owners of places like they used to. Everything is corporate."

Nisson Pharmacy had been a joyous place to work. People stopped in and out, grabbing daily necessities. In a scrapbook my mom put together in the fall of 1978, she created a section dedicated to the nice folks at Nisson Pharmacy. There was a sticker in this section, which read: "Work is fun!" In some photos, she is with co-worker Linda Mertes, who would also go on to testify against Gacy. The Torf brothers seemed like decent bosses and owners. The brothers did not come from a lot, and Larry Torf and his family lived in the same complex as my mom, in Section eight housing. She babysat for Larry Torf's two sons, too. In the winter, the Torf owners let the Nisson staff take a day off and head to the mountains to ski. A common place for skiing was Wilmot Mountain, on the Wisconsin-Illinois border.

Funny photos in the scrapbook show my mom at work, with about five pairs of cheap plastic sunglasses stacked on her face. In a Polaroid shot, she is dressed in a bunny costume, presumably for Easter. The pictures tell me she felt comfortable at work, and that she could be herself. I recognise the mom I know with her easy smile. Even with what was to come, I see some solitude in the happy faces in these photos. It was not all bad.

In the way he slouched, in his general nervousness, Michael seemed not to have recovered his joy the way my mom did after the Gacy trial. Maybe if my mom stayed in Des Plaines the way Michael did, she too would be acting as if she were being hunted.

"What happened to Rob really destroyed Nisson Pharmacy," Michael says. He takes a long sip of soda. "Did you know they were sued?"

We had known. My mom wrote about the suit in her diary.

<u>9/3/79</u>

We (Nisson) are being sued by the Piests for 85 million dollars.

AS AN ADULT looking back, my mom thinks it is funny that she wrote "we". She often saw herself as part of Nisson itself, a part of a team. She cared about work. But on every other page, the diary also reflects how much she cared about Rob. This March entry, unlike the others, is only this single line. I imagine it being an emotional day, trying to walk the line for both sides, the Piests and the pharmacy. She felt the stress from her bosses. She felt attached to both parties. She expressed no anger for the Piests, of course not. Rob's body was still nowhere to be found when my mother wrote about the suit.

"The whole pharmacy was gutted," Michael says. He pauses, as if he is stepping into a dangerous world of 40 years before.

"It just changed the whole community," he says. "The Torf brothers had big dreams. To be the new Walgreens of pharmacies. They got that dream stolen from them when Gacy took Rob."

Shortly after Rob went missing, the pharmacy shut down. Once a venue for work fun, for envisioning a different kind of future, its appeal dissolved in the months and years to follow. Floors were torn up because Gacy had been there, authorities were unsure of a connection between the owners and Gacy. But no bodies were found, and therefore nothing was further pursued.

Michael takes another sip of his soda and discloses that Rob wasn't the only missing boy the Torf family knew. In 1991, years after my mom moved to California, six boys who attended Maine East High School headed out to Waukegan to swim in Lake Michigan. The site was off-limits for swimming, because of a power plant nearby. Signs were posted everywhere. But it was a popular place for fishermen because the discharge pipes from the plant created a heated pond that attracted many fish. However, the pipe from the power plant also created dangerous currents in the water.

The boys, many from the varsity baseball team, enjoyed the day out on the water until, at about 3pm, a Torf boy went missing. A riptide effect. The current pulled him under water, then offshore. Another boy went unconscious in the lake from being yanked around, but he recovered in hospital. Authorities and friends searched for the missing boy all night. The next morning, they found his body on the beach. He had drowned.

During the funeral all the boys from the lake placed matching black-stringed necklaces into the coffin. It was a way to keep a pact, a friendship, in life and in death.

"If Rob going missing from their store didn't destroy the family," Michael said, "then losing a child of their own did."

Before meeting Michael, I had wrongly imagined the two

pharmacists expanding the store until old age forced them to sell. To have one of them lose a child seemed unfathomable.

"That's all so sad," my mom says. Her response feels measured in the moment, but later that night I see she's Googling the incident, searching for articles and an obituary for the Torf boy.

She tells me that this was Larry Torf's son, the one she babysat.

Michael is jittery and excuses himself to smoke a cigarette outside. I pay the bill and meet him outside with my mom.

Outside, early fall hangs in the humid air. The hot, dangerous summer lingers. My mom gives Michael one last hug. I thank him for his time.

"One more thing I should say." He moves the cigarette away from his face. "I heard that one of the Torf brothers was close with Gacy. Used to go to Gacy's backyard summer barbecues or some shit like that." He takes another drag. "Weird to think they couldn't bring the Piests to Gacy's house that night, isn't it?"

The way he spoke was so certain, as one might sound when holding on to a very buried truth. Indeed, this was something my mom and I had wondered but never heard spoken aloud. We drive away. Who was protecting who the night Rob went missing? If one of the pharmacy owners was a friend of Gacy's, how might that have diverted the course of events that night? Were the pharmacy brothers thoroughly investigated about their possible connections with Gacy? The place was gutted, sure. But just because no bodies were found on the location, that doesn't mean there was no foul play. The story was beginning to reveal itself. Of the many ways murder can raise questions. Create waves in a family unit, in a business, a neighbourhood. Murder touches everything.

THE FLASH OF green. A click with the turn of the door handle. We arrive back at the hotel room to change. "How about we go check out your old neighbourhood before dark?" I slide on my suede boots and grab my Canon camera to take photos. Running a comb through my hair, in front of the large mirror, I note that my mom and I look like we're in uniform together, both in black pants and white tops. When I was a teenager, sometimes people mistook us for sisters. Even with our 26-year age gap, my mom carries an aura of youthfulness.

I drive the hire car toward Gregory Lane, where her apartment complex still stands. She points out the general direction of where Larry Torf and his family once lived, too.

"There it is!" My mom points toward a doorstep a few doors into the large housing complex. "My home."

I park and we walk to the front address. The township holds more than a hundred units, carbon-copied townhouses linked together, touching walls. They were designed as long rectangles, each with three bedrooms. A few steps lead up to the front door, and behind each complex is a small backyard space, probably nothing more than 20ft. But it is enough for residents to make this space their own. Many gardens and seating areas are set up in the backyards. Families outside enjoy the end-of-summer heat, watching their children splash in kiddie pools.

When we arrive in front of her old front stoop, the third one in the long rectangle, my mom's face glows. She is a teenager, with long blonde hair, running up the front steps indoors and up to her bedroom, where her diary awaits.

"There is my window!" she says. I look up, picture her writing. "And out there behind the apartments is a field I used to walk through on the way to school." She tells me that she and Cory used to stand under the electric wires and rub forearms. The hairs on their arms would become static and they would get small electric shocks. "Sometimes we would kiss and we could feel the shock in our lips."

I look out to the fields where the high-tension wires loom. Black, crackling. They are nothing I would want to hang out under. She convinces me to try.

Just beyond the front stoop of her old apartment, the fields flow with tall, dry grass and hiss from the electric wires above them. The scene reminds me of *Stranger Things*, a show about a group of friends in Indiana in the 1980s who each season battle a new sort of dystopic monster from a parallel universe. It looks like the real world but is more deadly. The show depicts the trauma bond that forms when young adults must face the unthinkable: gore, murder, loss.

After watching this first season, my mom was hooked. It didn't take me long to understand why. She saw herself in the characters, specifically Will Byers, who has a certain type of sixth sense. As a survivor of the Upside Down – the dangerous other world the monsters come from – Will experiences visions that flicker in and out of his psyche. He holds a connection between both worlds: the Upside Down, where the monsters roam, and the reality he finds himself in, where sometimes the monster visits.

My mom has voiced her feeling of intuition many times. A knowing without knowing; the flicker of images. Will Byers helps Kim Byers better see herself.

She pushes her forearm into mine, now, moving her skin against my own, waiting for a spark. She looks up to the wires. It feels silly, but in a way helps me see her more clearly, as a girl.

"Slower," she emphasises. We rub our forearms together gently. I do not sense any waves of shock. Maybe the electric currents are better grounded, safer now than when my mom was a child. "Keep going," she says.

With nothing to preoccupy my mind, it wanders to a study I read about boredom in children. Conducted by sociologist and professor at MIT, Sherry Turkle, for her book *Reclaiming Conversation: The Power of Talk in a Digital Age*, the study left kids alone in a room with nothing to do. If the children were bored or curious enough, they could administer small shocks to themselves. No one made them, it was just an option in the room.

The psychologist reported that most children chose to administer the shocks. With our arms rubbing together I picture my mother as a kid. Kids will try things that often adults will not.

The wind coils our hair as we continue to search for a shock.

The cicadas sing in the trees and the sky turns a deep grey. The Midwest sky is like an ominous mood ring, changing colours with little warning. The horizon can go from blue to deep grey and back to blue in a moment's notice. The wires spit from above. "I guess it's not working," my mom sighs. "Let's head over here."

Skipping across the field, my mom travels effortlessly. I follow. We crouch through an old fence and find ourselves in the back of a cemetery.

"We went from trying to shock ourselves to sneaking into a cemetery?" I laugh. "What if someone catches us?" My belt hook on my black jeans catches on the fence, and my mom frees me, pushing the black denim off the metal rung. "No one is watching," she says.

She crawls under some bushes to a corner of the cemetery

and rubs her hands in the dirt, the same dirt she carried back home with her after playing until dusk. A twig pokes out, sticking into her back, and she snaps it off, tossing it farther into the woodsy area beyond the graves.

"What would you do back here?" I ask.

"Play," she says simply. I watch her sift dirt between her fingers, and try to remember the last time I was free to be joyfully dirty. I grew up with a barefoot childhood full of catching roly-polies and playing in mud, I had an imagination like her. But adulthood had removed me from that past version of myself. Becoming a mother, a wife, so fast. My mom did it even faster than I did when her adolescence ended at age 17. Watching her now is like witnessing magic. If we spent time with our old selves, we could really tend to them, love them, not forget them.

Between the cemetery and her apartment, the field with the electric wires travels for miles. It led right to Maine North High School. And when she went off exploring, which she often did as a child, she'd come to this cemetery and pick wild lilies for her mother.

"Speaking of play," she says. "Follow me."

We speed out of the cemetery, under the electric storm, to the centre of the apartment complex: the community park. The place where she played with local children.

The playground's theme is *The Wizard of Oz*. It makes sense, as one of the story's central messages is: "There is no place like home."

A statue of the Tin Man stands sturdy, over 40 years old. It holds up two swings. We each sit on one, kicking our feet up. Pumping our legs. Forward and back. Forward and back.

Growing up, my mom read me *The Wonderful Wizard of Oz*.

I can remember times that she helped me dress up as Dorothy for Halloween, as she had many Halloweens before. During my childhood, my dad also dressed up as Scarecrow. Perhaps, subconsciously, my mom had seen herself in Dorothy, trying to make sense about the time during her face-off with Gacy. Because the deeper message of the literature, beyond there being no place like home, is that good triumphs over evil.

We walk around the community and search for old holes in the fence she used to crawl through to get to other complexes to see friends. We find one, and it leads to an original pool, most likely built in the 1970s, where she had one of her first jobs as a lifeguard. I picture her sitting in the lifeguard chair, twirling her whistle. When I was 16, my first job was as a lifeguard. I wore my own red bathing suit and pushed a whistle up to my lips to warn, protect. Reliving her childhood made me appreciate how painful the stripping of her youth must have been.

My mom did not grow up with much. Her dad worked in a factory, and her mom began staying home shortly after my mom was born. My mom would often say this made her mother depressed and she wished her mom had returned to teaching, for her mental well-being and for the addition of financial resources. Her parents loved her, though, even if they did not have a lot of material objects to give. And whatever my mom would make out of her life was because of this place.

AFTER GREGORY LANE, we stop by Mil-Green, a furniture store that had been around when she was a kid. My mother tells me that when she was four, she stole a child-sized folding chair and walked it all the way home. Her dad made her walk the chair all the way back to return it.

We drive to Maine North High School, which closed shortly after my mom graduated. It is an iconic building, the set where *The Breakfast Club* Was filmed. We walk to the back of the school and push our heads to the glass wall to catch a glimpse of the indoor pool where she competed in her swim meets. The lights are off. How easy it is in my mind to turn on the lights, hear the whistles blowing amid the splashing and flip turns. Although the stands are now abandoned, I can see them full of friends and family cheering on the swimmers. I, too, swam and dived in high school. My mother living on in me.

We pass by Rob's old house together, and she can visualise herself sitting at the dining room table in late December, talking to Mr and Mrs Piest. Worrying about where he is.

As the sun sets, I ask her if there is one more thing she wants to do. "Let's go to the nature reserve," she says. I know why she wants to end there. It is the place she and Rob and friends would go to practise their photography skills. I drive down a gravel road, parking the 4Runner under the overhang of a large tree. Lawn chairs are scattered in the grass near the pond. Geese waddle nearby. I hand my mom my Canon camera, an updated version of the one she had when she was 17.

A long feather blows past her, nipping her feet. She picks it up for me and smiles. I take her photo on my phone. The pond is behind her. Leather crossbody bag looping across her chest. A child-like smile. One that is both proud and in awe at all the nature around her. She has passed this wonder down to Bennett, to me, to find a spiritual connection to nature, to the world, when finding a feather. Feathers are our lucky charm in my family. I watch her twirl the feather between her fingers and notice the wrinkles by her eyes. With all the luck in the world, death is still a certainty. I take the camera back from her and hold it close to my chest. I tell her there's one last stop we should make before we pack it in for the day.

NANCY'S PIZZA IS one of those places you wish you stumble into as a tourist when travelling. It's not showy. It's in a strip mall. The signage is near original. Inside, a small section offers digital gambling. To the left, the dining room. When you are greeted, you are greeted by someone who feels like a descendent of the original Nancy.

The hostess leads my mom and me to a booth near the kitchen. Her husband takes the to-go orders on the phone, in the corner of the restaurant. A server greets us and tells us about the deep-dish pizzas, which they are known for. My mom orders one, and I offer to share it with her. She tells me to order my own. The pies come out steaming and huge, enough for four to six people. My mom takes her fork and slices into the thick, cheesy pie. Her eyes close. "Mmmm."

A taste of home.

"Now I get why pizza is your favourite food," I say.

"Me and Cory used to come here for date nights or to study," she says. "It is just like it was back then." Cory remained her form of security and safety as the murder case unfolded.

"How is everything?" A woman stops by our table, the owner of Nancy's.

"Perfect," I say.

"I used to come here as a kid," my mom adds.

"Oh, really?"

"Yes, we are here visiting. My daughter is investigating some of the effects of the John Wayne Gacy murders from the 1970s," she says. "Oh, my husband's cousin was a victim," the woman says. "Awful." She points to the man by the takeout counter, who looks too busy to bother.

We share condolences.

The case has created a wave, less than six degrees of separation, and it seems everyone has a story, a piece to the puzzle.

CHAPTER FOUR

WOMEN'S INTUITION

1978

At 9.20pm, Elizabeth Piest had been waiting for over 20 minutes for Rob to come back inside the pharmacy. Kim told her that Rob asked her to watch the register at the front of the store, near the door, while he talked to the construction guy outside. Elizabeth decided to leave the store just after 9.20pm because she did not think much of it and her birthday celebration was soon to begin back home. She asked Kim, "Do you mind calling the house when Rob comes back?" Kim responded that she would.

As Kim finished her shift, she wanted to know who that man was that Rob was meeting. "Who is that construction guy?" she asked Phil Torf.

"John Gacy? He's a good guy," replied Torf.

Arriving back home, Elizabeth glanced at her birthday cake, suspended in time on the dining room table. "Anyone from Nisson's call?" she asked her husband. Harold shook his head and Elizabeth's pulse rushed. She grabbed the telephone, hoping Rob had returned to Nisson Pharmacy and Kim forgot to call.

Kim answered the phone. "Not yet," she said. Mrs Piest detected worry in the young girl's voice.

"Who was he talking to outside? Who was that man?"

Kim repeated what Phil Torf told her.

Another 20 minutes passed and the whole family, including Kerry, who was six years older than Rob, and Ken, who was a premed student and the eldest of the Piest siblings, paced and huddled. Elizabeth clutched the phone, nervously pulling at the curls of its cord in her other hand. She called again.

"Kim, is he back?"

A pause. Elizabeth could make out some chatter from the other end of the line. Was Rob there? Was Kim grabbing him to put him on the phone?

"Phil Torf wants to know if you have a Christmas tree yet." Kim seemed confused as to why she was asking Elizabeth Piest this question.

Elizabeth scoffed. "What does that have to do with Rob?"

Kim replied, "He thinks John Gacy may have taken Rob to his Christmas tree lot in town to pick one out." Perhaps this made a sliver of sense. Rob might have wanted to give his mom a tree for her birthday. It was exactly two weeks until Christmas.

Elizabeth hung up. Harold rifled through the phone book, trying to come up with a number for John Gacy. Kerry and Ken hunted in older versions of the White Pages. They could find nothing.

When Elizabeth called back a final time, the store was closed. This time, she spoke to Torf. She wanted to hear an inkling of concern from the store owner, but so far, the only one concerned at Nisson Pharmacy was Kim. She had gone home for the evening.

"What is his phone number?" Elizabeth demanded. Elizabeth scribbled down the number. "Do you have his address?"

Elizabeth asked. Torf hesitated and then said no, he did not. Elizabeth did not feel he was telling the truth. She wanted to drive to the house herself, to look for her son.

"What I can do is have someone keep an eye on the building," Torf said. "If he slipped and fell and is lying unconscious on the ice, we will find him." This was not comforting to Elizabeth Piest. Was he insinuating that Rob was unconscious somewhere? Bone-chilled, on slick ice? Before Torf hung up, Elizabeth had one more question. "Why would he be talking to a 15-year-old boy this late at night?"

Torf got defensive. "Wait a minute," he said. "This Gacy guy is no bum."

Elizabeth slammed the phone into the receiver. Torf seemed to defend Gacy, as though the contractor was indeed a friend. Her throat tightened, as if she was choking. She knew something was wrong. While Elizabeth paced in the living room, then the kitchen, Harold called the number she had written on a slip of paper. But no one picked up. It was Gacy's answering machine.

The family's thoughts were in agreement: If Rob had the means to get home by now, he would have. It was his mother's birthday. His mother. Who he loved, who he loved, who he loved. The family decided they would all go to the police for help.

The Piests grabbed their coats, slipped on their snow boots, and packed gloves. They did not know how long they would be out of the house or where they would go. They only knew Rob was missing, and they needed to find him. Before the Piests drove out of their Des Plaines neighbourhood, they pulled into the driveway of Rob's friend Nathan.

"Have you seen Rob?" Mrs Piest asked.

Nathan brushed his hands through his thick coal-coloured hair. Elizabeth Piest's breath hung in the freezing air. Nathan remembered Rob was working tonight. He had driven by Nisson a couple times on the way to another friend's house.

"I haven't," Nathan said. "What is going on?" His eyes squinted at Mrs Piest's. Her bottom lip quivered.

Nathan felt his heart tank as Mrs Piest explained why the whole family was bundled up and headed to the police station. Once Nathan had left for the night without telling his parents and Rob gave him crap for weeks. Rob would never not come home. Nathan knew as fact.

"Call if you hear from him?"

"Absolutely." Nathan slipped his keys in the car engine and went on to search, screaming out Rob's name through his driver's side window.

After leaving Nathan's house, the Piests stopped by Nisson Pharmacy. Though it was closed for the evening, Phil Torf was still there talking with a man. Presumably a friend. But it was not John Gacy. The family parked near the front of the pharmacy, on the ice-glazed blacktop. Elizabeth left the car running while she ran inside. "Any word?" she said, with warm tears surfacing.

"Nothing," Torf replied. "I called Gacy's house, too, and only got the answering machine."

The thought crossed Elizabeth Piest's mind again, that Torf knew the address to Gacy's house. Was he protecting Gacy because he had hired him? Was he covering for Gacy because they were friends? Phil and his brother Larry, Rob's bosses and the pharmacists who owned Nisson, knew her son. They should know he wouldn't just take off. Why weren't they worried?

"Take my home phone number," Phil said. He scribbled it on

a scrap of paper and handed it to Elizabeth. "Call me if you get an update."

Elizabeth took the piece of paper and hopped into the family car. Her heart thumped, as if it had left her chest. She could hear its rocket-fast beat.

Harold drove them to the Des Plaines Police Station. The Des Plaines River Road they took ran parallel to the Des Plaines River. Elizabeth watched the water, ominous and swift, from the passenger cabin of the car. The trip took about 10 minutes, but for her, the car could not go fast enough. "Go, go!" she shouted.

Downtown Des Plaines was nearly empty, filled with a chilly Christmas cheer. Red, green, and white lights adorned the buildings. The business district was basically one street with a couple of convenience stores, an old movie theatre, and a police station that was nearly brand new. The station sprawled at the northern end of a four-block strip. From the outside, it looked like a fortress – inaccessible, cold, looming – something impossible to break into, or out of.

The family rushed to the counter to speak to the watch officer George Konieczny.

Elizabeth breathed in, out, trying to centre and focus, but her fear was making it nearly impossible to relax. "My son, Robert Jerome Piest, is missing," she gasped.

Elizabeth and Harold Piest were not the first nor the last parents to report a missing teen. It was common in the 1960s and 1970s for young men to hitchhike off for adventure or slip away for a night or two, then turn up. This type of event had jaded officers like Konieczny, but he could tell, in the tone of Elizabeth Piest's voice, that this was likely not the case for Robert Jerome Piest.

"I'm so sorry, ma'am," Konieczny replied. His eyes locked with hers, she could sense he was genuine. "But there is nothing I can do at this hour." Police stations like the Des Plaines one were not staffed like those in the bustling city of Chicago. In fact, very little could be done, just by the mere lack of warm bodies available to help the Piests. Konieczny asked her to state her missing son's statistics so he could take them down for a youth officer to be assigned the case in the morning.

He is "male, white, age 15, wearing tan Levi pants, a plain T-shirt, brown shoes, and a blue down jacket."

Rob became missing persons case number 78-35203, one of around 72 missing persons cases for the department in 1978. When the Piests left the station, they were told to get some rest, although Mrs Piest couldn't imagine how that would be possible. Konieczny called Phil Torf himself. He got no answer. Then he brought the report to his commander. He explained that the parents were really concerned, which made him concerned, too. He was then able to notify the radio room upstairs. At 1.54am, a message was sent to all police jurisdictions across Illinois. Finally, Konieczny's report was placed on the desk of Lieutenant Joseph Kozenczak, commander of the Criminal Investigation Division, where he would consider it over his first cup of coffee in the morning.

The Piests made the drive back home, with outside temperature at freezing under a mean windchill. They knew they would not be able to rest as Konieczny had told them to do. What they would do was search. Stand watch. The family divided up. Harold decided he and Kenneth and Kerry would bundle up and head outdoors with their German shepherds and look for Rob. Elizabeth would stay home, near the phone, and stand watch. If Rob was hurt and trying to make his way back home, she wanted to be there, to meet him. Heat him up milk, make a bologna sandwich for her son.

Around the same time the Piests arrived back home, Kim Byers was writing in her journal about the events of December 11, 1978. She wrote about swim practise after school and before work, where each swimmer planned their own 3000-yard workout. She wrote the entry at midnight after finishing some English homework. She had no clue what was unravelling over at the Piest home. Kim Byers went to sleep thinking Rob had made it home. At the end of her entry, she recorded she needed to get some ZZZs!

Kim's mom, Barbara, said she could sleep in and go to school late the next morning. Her mother sometimes let her do this, and December 12 was one of those days.

Through the darkest hours of the night, the Piest family searched. And searched. Every street in that small town. They walked over ploughed snow, as the snow banks became bunkers. Seven inches had fallen that day. It wasn't until the sun rolled over the plains that they decided to call it quits. Rob might already be home, warm and asleep in his bed.

When Harold and the Piest siblings arrived back home, Elizabeth was still standing vigil, in her same clothes as the day before. No one had slept. The cake the family was supposed to eat together on Elizabeth's birthday still sat untouched.

On December 12, authorities contacted John Gacy. Ronald Adams was the youth officer assigned to the case. Adams got Gacy on the phone and asked if he had been in the pharmacy the previous night. Gacy confirmed that he had. "Did you speak to Robert Piest last night?"

Gacy was firm, "No, I never spoke to him."

After Adams hung up, he called the Byers residence and spoke with Kim before she went late to school, asking if she had any idea where Rob was. He told her Rob had not come home. The officer visited Maine West High School, Rob's high school. A friend of Rob's told Adams that Rob had no problems at home or at school. However, he did disclose that he had broken up with his recent girlfriend, Carrie, around homecoming.

After leaving Maine West High School, Adams continued his search for answers. He drove to the strip mall where Rob often bought sodas, next door to Nisson's at Wall's Liquors, owned and operated by Stanley Wall.

The door pushed open, and bells rang at the front. "You Stanley?"

"How can I help you, officer?"

"A young man named Robert Piest often purchased bottles of A&W Root Beers." He slid a photo of Robert Piest, one Mrs Piest had given to him, onto the counter. "Perhaps you or someone from the liquor store saw the boy last night?"

"Sorry, officer. I've seen him. But he did not come in yesterday."

Adams called the Byers home again at 1.34pm, only to find out from Barbara that her daughter was at school. He wanted to ask her more questions. Maybe she had a clue as to how he could find Rob. Adams parked at Maine North High School at 1.57pm. It had been less than 24 hours since Rob went missing. Everything was still so raw, so fresh, so uncertain for Kim. She felt like she was walking in a dream as she left class to meet with Adams in a small, windowless room. The Dean of Girls perched on a desk nearby to act as her guardian.

Adams pulled his chair closer to the desk. The legs made a screech across the floor. Kim looked at the time, worried about a physics test she would have to make up if this took very long.

"Could you describe what Rob was wearing last night?" She described his shirt, pants, and, of course, his blue parka, which she had borrowed. "Do you know if he had any items on him, or anything in his pockets?"

Kim replied, "ChapStick, a pipe, my film receipt."

"Did Rob speak to the contractor that was at Nisson Pharmacy on the night of the eleventh?" Adams asked.

"Yes, Rob spoke with him and went outside to speak more about a job," Kim responded.

"What time?"

"Between 9.00 and 9.02pm," Kim answered. "I'm pretty sure because he said, 'Come watch the register. The contractor guy wants to talk to me. I'll be right back.' I looked at the clock, and it was just after nine o'clock."

"Are you sure?"

"I said I'm sure," Kim responded, agitated.

"Do you think anyone over at Wall's Liquors may be of help with finding Rob?"

"Don't bother. Rob didn't go there last night."

This confirmed what Adams had already been told.

Adams's questions dragged on, and she felt an anger warming inside her. Wasting time asking about what was in Rob's pocket or where he liked to buy soda didn't seem like a good way to find him. Toward the end of the school day, Kerry and Ken Piest visited her to ask if she had seen Rob this morning or knew anything. She said she didn't. After school, she cuddled up with her dog, Jiffy, in her bed upstairs and wrote about how she felt.

12/12/78

Today was an absolutely miserable day. It started out good. I got up at 9am and took a bath. Then I got a phone call from a youth officer, he never came back to the store and he never went home. Rob would never run away, he had no reason to. And this guy Gacy claims he never talked to Rob. I can't believe Rob would have lied to us. But someone is obviously lying. Kerry and Ken (Piest) came to see me at school. They're pretty upset too. I held my cool for the whole day. But right before we were supposed to leave for the meet – I was talking to Mr Tanner (school counsellor) and I just started crying. I feel so scared, worried and helpless. I can just imagine Rob lying out in some empty forest – alive but unable to move – crying for help with no one answering him. It is just not fair, Rob never did anything wrong to anyone. I pray he has just run off somewhere and is at least safe! Kerry will call me and let me know any new news. I can't talk about it anymore, my heart is being ripped apart. By the way, we lost our meet.

Kim fell asleep that night scared. Her dreams were vivid. More vivid than ever. And they were full of Rob. Similarly, Elizabeth Piest could not sleep. She felt her mind slipping, moments from the night before overlaying her present reality. She replayed every detail. "He's probably just gone to a friend's house," the officer had reported to Mrs Piest on the night she declared her son missing. "There is nothing we can do, not until 24 hours." Nothing, nothing, nothing. The nothing hung heavy in her mind. It encapsulated everything.

Twenty-four hours had now passed. For Elizabeth, to imagine what could happen to her son in 24 hours was otherworldly. He would never just go to a friend's house or run off without telling his mother. He had nothing to run from.

On the second night of Rob's disappearance, Mr and Mrs Piest searched with some neighbourhood friends and their other two children. They checked the Christmas tree lot supposedly owned and operated by Gacy. But Gacy was nowhere to be found. Instead, snow piled onto Douglas firs, ready to be brought home and decorated for Christmas cheer.

While the Piests searched, authorities visited Gacy's house. They asked him about Rob Piest. He said he had been at Nisson Pharmacy but never talked to any kids working there. Authorities then asked Gacy to come into the station to fill out a statement. Gacy said, "I'll get there when I get there."

On the night Rob disappeared, his mom imagined bringing him home for birthday cake. But in the deepest ravines of her being, Elizabeth knew something was gravely and horribly wrong.

Kim shared this intuition. As more time passed, Kim would consider that strange pang in her heart. Was it her soul talking to her? Was it God? It sounded like a whisper and felt like a punch. Pick up the receipt. She listened. She put the receipt into Rob's parka pocket. The receipt, unbeknown to Gacy, rode in the car and travelled through his front door.

13/12/78

Well, no word about Rob yet. I feel worse and worse as time goes on. It's the not knowing that's ripping me apart. I called Ken (Piest) at 2.30. He said they have Gacy under surveillance. Tailed him and then lost him after two blocks, I could do better than that. I had a really morbid dream last night (had it twice). We found Rob in a trunk of a beat-up old gold car. Any significance?

Gacy finally came into the station to give a statement at around 3.20am, early on December 13, which was about 30 hours after Rob was last seen alive. He was filthy, covered in thick mud. Later, authorities would learn the mud was from trying to push his car out of heavy sludge near the Des Plaines River by the I-55 bridge. Kim would not know it at the time but her dream about her friend being in the trunk of a car did have significance. On December 13, Kim Byers could hardly function. Officer Adams called her at her home to question her.

Adams said he spoke with John Gacy. "He says he never spoke with Rob, like you say. And doesn't know about his whereabouts. You sure about what you saw?"

Kim hardened. Officer Adams made it seem like Gacy's lies triumphed over the truth. Gacy was spinning a narrative that went like this: Why is anyone listening to this 17-year-old girl when we have this upstanding adult? And Gacy's lawyers would feed the same narrative, and then the reporters would catch wind of it, too. Kim felt her age, her gender, and the power this man named Gacy attempted to exert over her. And it made her full of rage.

"We're going to keep some surveillance on you, too," Adams said.

Kim opened the front door into the chilly air and saw a cop car by the curb. Officer Adams made it seem like this surveillance was in her best interest. If she witnessed what she said she witnessed, she could be in danger. Someone working with Gacy could potentially cause her harm. Come after her.

Cory tried to get her to smile the whole day. Kim felt helpless, disassociated from everyday life. A desire surfaced. To leave her body, this town and run away. The fact that Rob was missing and something bad plausibly happened to him ate at her, twisting her guts. She had no interest in what made her happy: photography, swim meets, school, Marmosets, and gymnastics.

That same day the police obtained their first search warrant for Gacy's house. Terry Sullivan, the supervisor of Cook County State's Attorney's third district office, wrote the warrant. Lieutenant Joseph Kozenczak had made the call to Sullivan, to give him a rundown of Gacy's prior convictions, including an outstanding charge against Gacy in Chicago, and then the kicker. Gacy had been charged in Waterloo, Iowa, for the sodomy of a 15-year-old boy. Same age as Rob.

On the phone, Kozenczak stated, "I want to get a search warrant because I think Gacy is holding Piest captive in his house."

Terry Sullivan agreed that the sodomy charge was enough of a red flag to get a search warrant. It would take time to call up Waterloo to get more details, and during this wait, Harold Piest fumed. He threatened to storm Gacy's house himself to rescue his son. The Piests now knew Gacy's address but felt it was too late. Mr Piest considered it absurd that no one had set foot inside to look.

Terry Sullivan learnt that in Waterloo, Gacy had managed a KFC restaurant, where he had bound and handcuffed employees. He had sex with one of them. These were innocent teenage boys. Although Gacy was sentenced to 10 years of imprisonment for what he did, he served only 18 months. During his incarceration, his wife filed for divorce and sole custody of their two young children. She was successful. Within 24 hours of being released Gacy fled to Chicago to start a new life. There, Gacy's mom helped him buy the house on W. Summerdale Avenue.

The search warrant allowed police to search anywhere on the property. They were to be on the lookout for signs of Rob – his clothing, strands of hair, blood. Sullivan also made it clear in the search warrant that if officers were on the fence about seizing an item from Gacy's house, they should just take it. They would worry, later, about whether a piece of evidence might be inadmissible in trial.

On December 14, Terry Sullivan talked to Kim Byers. Her first impression of Sullivan was that he was non-threatening. Someone doing his job. She was relieved he was looking for her friend and taking the disappearance seriously. And that he hadn't brought up her age or gender.

During their meeting Sullivan wanted to know what happened. What she remembered. Was there anything "off" about Gacy? Officer Adams took notes. In a C.I.D. continuation report from the Des Plaines Police by officer Adams, he documented:

She described Rob as being an all-together guy and feels that Rob would not have run away or, as she said, split. On Monday, the evening in question, she worked from 5-10. When asked by assistant state's attorney Sullivan to describe the encounter, the man who was working in the store, she described him as wearing a brown or greyish jacket with a reddish coloured shirt... this man was Gacy. She said that Gacy bumped into her several times. She said this may have been intentional. Kim saw Gacy in and out of the store several times. She is not sure of the last time she saw him leave. Kim left the store to go into the liquor store during the course of the evening to get something to drink. The drinks she purchased were three bottles of soft drinks. The last time she recalled seeing Gacy was approximately 30-45 minutes prior to the time she observed Rob leave the drug store.

Kim stated that Rob had argued about his job that very night. That he thought an employee by the name of Tom was getting a $3 raise and he was angry that he was not getting one. Rob also stated that he was going to quit his job and, when Kim stated to him "that you'll probably get a Christmas bonus," Rob said, "Yeah, but I need the money now." Mr Gacy promised to give Rob a job that paid approximately $5 an hour. Kim ended the interview by saying that although she and Rob had gone out several times, they were not boyfriend and girlfriend. She felt very close to Rob and that they had a personal relationship. Rob had broken up with his girlfriend approximately in October, I believe she stated, around homecoming time.

Kim felt more confident after her talk with Terry Sullivan. Even if the days yielded no concrete answers, she could tell Sullivan was someone she could trust. But the moment she felt confident was the moment the first wave of reporters began calling her house. The phone rang nonstop, as her mom and dad took turns answering the line like factory work, saying "No, she is not here."

Kim felt trapped within the walls of her life. A panic built in her, the feeling of being watched. When she was 14, she babysat for the neighbours next door. One afternoon, the dad of the children came home early. He was drunk and she asked for her babysitting money and to go home. Instead of paying her, the man sat next to her on the couch and ran his hand up under her shirt and across her jeans. She ran out of the house screaming. To be a girl in the 1970s required patching one's skin for survival. For the rest of her life, she had to see that neighbour, share a wall with him and his family. If she'd had to be cautious after the incident with the neighbour, she now felt like she had to be more cautious than ever.

14/12/78

Well, still no sign of Rob. Went to school as usual today, a pretty fair day. I was still depressed. Cried twice. Then Nathan came over from 10.45pm–2.15am. He is supposed to leave for Texas soon. We had an excellent talk. They (police) have a theory! I hope they find him soon. Also, they put the case up to the grand jury – he says I'm the key witness. I'm scared, say they come after me?!! Yuck.

15/12/78

Slept till 10am, went to school only for my physics test. Talked to my mom, she too feels helpless... I can't wait till this is over. It's damaging my family relationships + my relationship with Cory. Went to Rob's. Stayed at Rob's to about 2.30, it was good for us all to talk. Mr Piest was worried about me so he was glad I came over.

18/12/78

Mondays, yuck. Got up, took a shower, Mom took me to school. Was called into the office to speak with Mr Adams and another detective. They found a pendant but I can't remember if Rob had one on. I wish Rob would show up. I have a strange feeling something will happen tomorrow, call it women's intuition. But first of all, the film stub I put in Rob's coat pocket Monday is number 36119, the 19th (the film is not back yet) is tomorrow. We had tentative plans for tomorrow nite – I was going to introduce him to Cory.

From the outside Gacy's home looked like all the rest in the neighbourhood: a 60-foot lot, single-story, built in the 1950s with a two-car garage, shadowy hedges lining both sides of the residence. Inside, authorities found creepy oddities: the strange Tiki-style bar, the gallery wall of clown paintings, a hallway that looked like it was out of a haunted house with bizarre yellow and brown zigzag lines on the walls, and then, a trap door that accessed a crawl space. They found startling mementos: a Maine

West High School class ring, a 6mm pistol, handcuffs and keys, an identification card that was not Gacy's. A film receipt.

Kozenczak found the film ticket sticking out of a trash bag on the floor. It was from Nisson Pharmacy, with the serial number 36119. He assumed the receipt was Gacy's but picked it up and slipped it into the evidence bag, just in case it wasn't.

19/12/78

Well, I guess my hunches were right. I came home after school to get something to eat before I went shopping. The phone rang. They asked me questions about the film slip. My guess is that they found it. Will pray for Rob.

An officer smelled the scent of decay while in Gacy's house. It was the scent of old sewage; the smell of deterioration; something deathly. Investigators jumped down into the crawl space to look for the source of the odour. They had to advance on hands and knees, with little to no room to move about in the wet mud. They crawled over what they could make out as yellowish powder. It was everywhere. They thought it might have been lime, something to help cover the scent that permeated the air. But they left the first search with no Rob and no body.

THE POLICE CALLED the Byers residence when they got back from Gacy's house. They wanted Kim to come to the station and write an official statement. After dinner, Kim's father, Buddy, drove Kim downtown, both of them blissfully unaware of what was discovered in the crawl space of Gacy's house.

It was gloomy outside. The weather remained freezing, and

the snow kept piling up. Cars were buried under icy hills. Kim walked into the Des Plaines Police Station and was asked once again about the receipt. She thought about being the key witness and wondered whether this was a first step toward that role. She didn't want to have witnessed anything. She was handed a pen and paper and asked to write about the film she developed on December 11, 1978.

Kim had a saying, one her mom taught her. It was, "Always tell the truth." That saying would become her internal compass.

Des Plaines Police Department
WITNESS STATEMENT
DATE: 19/12/78 TIME: 8.29p.m. **PLACE:** Des Plaines Police Station.

I, Kimberly Byers, am 17 years of age and my address is 8704 Gregory Lane, Des Plaines, IL 60016.

On the night of December 11th, 1978 I worked from about 5.20-10pm. I brought in with me an envelope of pictures and negatives from homecoming 1978. My sister wanted copies of some of these pictures. I decided it would make a nice Christmas present (they were pictures of me and my boyfriend). So I would have to have them done soon. So about 7.30 the store was kind of quiet, it would be a good time to put my order in for the pictures. I went to my bag and got the envelope out. I walked over to the counter, took an envelope and began to fill it out. The order I wanted was confusing (1 of #3 and 1 5.7 of #3). Normally you put the order in different envelopes but I couldn't cut the negative. Anyhow – I ended up having two envelopes because of explanatory mistakes. Finally I was satisfied with the way I wrote it (envelope #36119). I then recorded it into the logbook, took the tab off + put the envelope into the bag on the side of the counter. I stood there for a second dumbfounded, not knowing what to do with the stub. I would normally either throw it out or put it on a hook behind the counter. But these pictures meant a lot to me for some reason. I thought I shouldn't throw it out. I started to stick [it] on the hook. I hesitated, then stuck it in Rob's pocket of his jacket, (The Rt. One). (I was wearing his jacket because I had a short sleeve shirt on and was very cold – I really don't know why I did – maybe I meant it as kind of a joke – or maybe just to put responsibility on him, not to lose the ticket. I think the most probable reason I put it in his pocket was that I intended him to find it, ask me about it + I would remember to take it home. Anyway I had second thoughts about putting it in his pocket, thinking he would say something like, "Kim, why did you put this in my pocket?"

But for some reason I decided to leave it there. A while later Rob came to the front and asked for his jacket to take the garbage out, I gave it to him. Then the next time I saw the jacket off of him was when he was working the front. It was on top of the cases of cigarettes. Then of course when he left he grabbed it and walked out. X K.B.

I have read the two pages of this statement and the facts contained therein are true and correct.

Kimberly Byers
(Signature of witness)

OVER THE FIRST weekend of Rob missing the case dominated the news. Kim and her parents collected newspapers in an old Marshall Field & Company shopping mall box. She would try and save all the articles of Rob. Headlines with his face appeared on newspapers across the state: "Missing youth last seen with middle-aged man"; "Hunt continues for missing teen".

Toward the end of the weekend, the Piests and friends of Rob traversed the town with missing persons flyers. The picture of Rob was a black and white school portrait. His mouth is shut, hair framing his face, covering his ears. The flyer's signage was in all caps:

> MISSING SINCE MONDAY, DECEMBER 11,
> AT 9PM: ROBERT PIEST,
> MAINE WEST SOPHOMORE,
> 15 YEARS OLD — 5'8" TALL — 140 LBS
> BROWN MEDIUM-LENGTH HAIR WEARING A
> LIGHT BLUE SKI JACKET HOODED,
> A TAN T-SHIRT & TAN LEVI PANTS.
> ANYONE IN THE VICINITY OF NISSON
> PHARMACY, 1920 TOUHY AVENUE, AT THAT
> TIME, PLEASE CONTACT THE DES PLAINES
> POLICE AT ONCE.

Kim kept one of the missing persons flyers in her Marshall Field & Company box. She saved everything, because if Rob were to come back, she wanted to show him how much he was loved. If he never came back, she had a responsibility to her friend. If she was the key witness, she needed to know what was occurring in the case.

CHAPTER FIVE

KIN

2022

It rains on my mom's final night in Des Plaines. The 4Runner pulls into the last open spot in the parking lot at Beacon Tap. Live music from the patio area greets us, an Irish celebration in progress. Children and adults perform joyous Irish jigs. My mom's eyes brighten. She loves anything and everything Irish.

We're given a table outdoors. My mom, in Ireland-Des Plaines heaven, claps along with the performers. A dampness settles in. I swipe lukewarm mist off my forehead. The late-summer rain does not stop my mom from leaving the table to be close to the music and dance. In addition to the Irish performance, a woman is celebrating a 50th birthday with friends and neighbours; young adults are sharing a tower of nachos and a bucket of beer; mothers and children are playing Uno at another outdoor table. Tonight the Beacon Tap is a reminder of how close a small-town community can feel, everyone's life on display in both big and small ways.

I think about how the community reacted after the news of Gacy's crimes surfaced. Parents became worried. Kids had less freedom. There were earlier curfews and less playing after dusk. The nuclear family became the norm. The community, in shock, mourned and feared how something like this could happen in their unsuspecting town. If these crimes happened in Des Plaines, Illinois, they could happen anywhere.

Looking around at Beacon Tap tonight, an unassuming person wouldn't know this place's shared history. A certain scarring happened on this town after the murders, but the scar is different on each person. And often not visible to the unsuspecting eye.

Before I flew out to Chicago for this trip, I spoke with various people involved in the case, detectives, prosecutors, police, and folks who knew Rob from the community. In one of my calls, I spoke to Nathan. I looked him up on LinkedIn. In his photo he wore a long-sleeved business shirt and an inviting smile. He was in his 60s now. He still can't get over the fact Rob is gone.

The loss that Nathan and my mom experienced was unique. Often they had nowhere to turn but to each other. Back then, few communities for grieving friends existed. No Reddit, no Google, no conversation forum on Facebook was available for those whose friends went missing. This was a time before a more nuanced conversation surrounding the complications of grief.

In 1989, Kenneth J. Doka, PhD, an expert on grief and Professor Emeritus at the Graduate School of the College of New Rochelle, coined the term "disenfranchised grief". It's a grief less discussed in mainstream cultural responses after loss. For example, when a child disappears, sympathy is offered to the immediate family. However, the same level of empathy is not often bestowed on the disappeared person's friends. I think disenfranchised grief is what my mom began carrying on the night her friend disappeared.

Another example of disenfranchised grief may be a survivor

of a mass shooting. This survivor may feel unsettling grief, but society may see them as lucky. Of course, survivorship is not that black and white. It's as though the grief holds diminutive value, to the person experiencing it or larger society. This shouldn't be the case.

This form of grief is what happens to every child who has lost a friend or classmate. This disenfranchised grief is a real grief. It stings, it burns.

Nathan's grief means he keeps a photo of him and Rob as the lock screen on his smartphone. He tells me this the first time we talk.

I WAS WITH my mom in my house the first time Nathan called.

"You won't believe who is calling me back," I said.

She smiled when she heard his voice on my phone's speaker. He called her Kimmy. Our conversations with Nathan were intimate in the way of a close friendship. He was filled with stories of a childhood when people left their doors unlocked. Stories of catching pheasants, swimming in the summer at the Iroquois Swimming Pool, kayaking down at the lake, riding bikes through the neighbourhood, drinking cans of Mad Dog together, feeling the burn of cheap alcohol on the back of their throats.

When I asked about what changed between Nathan and my mom after Rob disappeared, he became shy, then open to pulling up that chapter. "Losing Rob brought us closer together. We had both lost one of our favourite people. We were so lucky to have each other, really."

I asked what this closeness led to. He said she was the one

who got away. In a dream life, he would have dated her, maybe even married her. I asked him to explain.

He said, "Your mom was different than me. She was going to work really hard to not let this define her life. And, well, I knew I didn't have that kind of strength." After a silence on the other end of the line, Nathan told me he never wanted to become a parent either because losing Rob had been too difficult. He couldn't raise a kid when there was a possibility of losing them.

I've thought a lot about how the disappearance of Rob shaped my mother. The easy answer is it changed her. But the real answer is more complicated. The murder also made her. Losing Rob framed her twenties, staining her early motherhood. It became the scaffolding on which she built her military career, the reason she made so many decisions about who to spend her time with and how long. It would form the foundation of the way trauma lived and flowed through her.

My mom returns to our seats at Beacon Tap, away from the stage area, where men in kilts dance and sang. We drink our red sangria out of plastic stemless wine cups and our water out of Miller Lite ones. As we clink glasses, I feel a deepening between us.

When I graduated from my doctorate program, my mom gave me a necklace with three stones stacked on top of one another. She told me they represented the past, present, and future. She wanted me to always be reminded of the fluidity of these spaces. I wear the necklace tonight, grab it, feel the three stones brush against my fingertips.

BACK IN THE hotel room, we sit together on the couch. My mom eats barbecue pistachios, and I have a beef jerky stick. We had been so into the performance and the rain, we had forgotten to eat. "This will be quite the story you are writing," she says. "And I wouldn't trust anyone but you with it."

When I originally expressed interest in travelling to Des Plaines, the first thing she said was: I'll go. Her enthusiasm now is refreshing, different from when I first started digging into the case in 2017. Back then, I had felt more fear. The past was kept so separate from the present on purpose. But as she began to revisit Des Plaines in her memory, she told me she felt lighter. She understands now the way the story drives me. That I am here because I want the story of this place. I want the story of who she was at 17.

I turn on my voice recorder and ask her to speak about what it was like to come back to Des Plaines. "What is it about this place?" I pull socks over my feet to keep out the fall chill, which has crept in as the rain continues to fall outside.

"Hard to come back," my mom says, popping a shelled pistachio into her mouth. "For some people, including myself, after the event was over, I wanted to shut the lid, tack it down. Lock it, bolt it, move on, never come back."

I inhale. "And what is it like coming back?"

"It's been stressful, anxiety-provoking."

We both laugh uncomfortably. "Sounds terrible."

My mom continues, "But it has also allowed me to see this as an adult, not as a teenager. Which allows for a different type of processing and reflection." I ask her what kind of reflection she means. "A parent's eyes, an employer's eyes and a police officer's eyes. Instead of raw teenage eyes, which were very short-sighted. However, as an adult and a parent, you process it through a different sort of response." It's a relatable moment, the desire to live through a painful experience and move on. Her new-found reflective mode is different. It's as if the mom I grew up with operated in a perpetual state of moving forward, with a fear of the past catching up. But we grow through difficult experiences by revisiting, in safe conditions, both metaphorical and literal.

I sip my water. "What has been a beautiful moment for you?"

"Spending time with you," she says without hesitation. "You have been prying the lid on my box, which has been well tapped down. That's... that's been great for me. Therapeutic."

I thank her. I thought, hard and long, about my role as both researcher and daughter. What did it mean to revisit the past of a major event in history with my mother? What would I learn about her? Would she feel safe with me?

I pull my legs up onto the scratchy couch. "What has been a more difficult moment for you?"

"The flashbacks," she says. "Names, places, things that have been tucked away. As soon as you stand somewhere, from the store to the neighbourhood, all of a sudden, names you have not thought of in 40-plus years just pop in your head. Full names! What these people looked like. That has been enlightening. You think that all these memories are gone, but then being in this place is like a stimulus. And films start rolling in your head."

"Did you have any flashbacks of Rob?"

"Absolutely," she says. "When we stood in front of the store, I could see us back in the day. Him squatting, stocking, breaking down boxes. Us chatting in the parking lot."

"Any fun memories?"

"We used to do a lot of goofy stuff. We both loved photography, so we would go out to Beck Lake, look at those woods. We both took a lot of photos in those places. If you are nice, you can have one," she said, joking. I pause the recorder to take a break. Sometimes being recorded can feel forced and I want it to feel like a regular conversation. We FaceTime my dad and brother back home.

When we come back to the conversation, she seems more relaxed. "What are some of the lessons you gained from that time period?" I ask.

The lamp casts a shadow on the side of her face. She thinks about it. "I think that if something does not seem right, it is not right. People should never hesitate. Because I will always agree that the delay in going to find Rob probably cost us his life."

This was the first time she has said something like this to me. I hated to admit it, but I had begun to feel the same way.

"You thought about that more after this trip?" I touch my phone to check the time. It's after 10pm. She will want to go to sleep soon.

"Absolutely," she says. "I learned some stuff I didn't know. And his parents knew. Back in the day, there was this power of scepticism that every boy wanted to run away and join something. But this did not apply to every boy, especially boys that were well-loved. On the flip side, I was reminded to enjoy every day."

She looks tired, and it's a good place to end the impromptu interview. But when I lean forward to switch off the recorder, she presses on. "Some people, too, will never return to the people they were after an event like this. And it is sad for the observer, but it becomes a way of life for the survivor." She turns her face to me. "How do you feel? Is this going the way you hoped it would?"

I think about her questions and pick up an empty snack bag

to throw in the trash. "I try to come in with no hopes," I say. "I already had an inkling that the murders have been challenging and strange for every single person. But it has been clarified that this experience is unique and there is a snowball effect on people's lives, their own family lineage that you don't know."

I would be completing the remainder of this trip without her. She had to get back to her medical practice, her patients. But I was grateful for her time in this place with me.

"I'm going to go to bed now," she says, and reaches across the couch to give me a hug. My nose buries in her hair, which smells of aloe vera from the free shampoo and conditioner in our room.

LOOKING AT HER asleep, a part of me wonders how this would bring us closer together. When I gave birth to my second child, we had gotten in a fight. The fight had spread out for months, almost a year until we felt comfortable enough to talk. I mean, we talked. But not deeply. Not in long, stretched-out conversations.

The fight was about how we spoke to each other over one June day in 2021. I had just given birth to Cal. I had also moved into a house in the same area as her and my dad. I was in the middle of two life events: purchasing a first home and bringing a second child into the world with Nick. It was Father's Day, and Cal was less than two weeks old. We went to my parents' house to wish my dad a happy Father's Day. It was such a small, familial gesture.

Out of nowhere, from a couch across from me, my mom asked, "Can you watch the animals when we leave, or should I ask someone else?" My family were going on a week-long trip to Minnesota: my two sisters, my brother, and my parents.

I looked to my husband, a little overwhelmed.

The animals included ducks, chickens, three dogs, and the cats. Nick or I would have to come over twice a day to feed them, let them out into the yard, put them in for the night. It was a simple but time-consuming task. We had done it many times before. But Nick had only two weeks off for parental leave. I had no official maternity leave, as I was entering the fourth year of my PhD program. Nick and I wanted all the time we could get with each other over the next two weeks to rest, to move into our new home, and to begin to figure out this new chapter.

If my mother was in the mental space to consider my first post-partum experience, which left me in a thorny place, she would not have asked. She'd know to give me my space to heal, to find my footing.

"Someone else would be great," I said. She nodded, and that was it. Or at least I thought that was the end of it.

My family went on the trip, and I would learn soon enough that most of the talking my mom did on that trip revolved around me. How I had deserted her; how selfish I was. I could not do something as simple as feeding a few chickens to help her. When they came back, I heard about what was said on the trip. I was heartbroken and felt like trust had been broken between us. All I wanted was a peaceful post-partum experience, and for my family to share in the love and welcoming of a new baby. It seemed so silly, so odd, what one small conversation could do.

Her fight with me, I'd later learn, was a tipping point for her.

Many private issues were ongoing in both her personal and professional life and she broke. Feeling deserted by people in her life surfaced was a common theme. Soon, she sought out therapy and learned that Rob's disappearance was the foundation for so much pain. And thus, she began to untangle the rope of her life and learned the string began to knot in 1978. Me saying "no" was not the problem, the 40-something years before our fight had not yet been unravelled to reveal the larger canvas.

When I asked her a year later why she became so mad at something so simple, she said she could not see more than a few feet in front of her. She said she could not think of anyone else's experience but her own. Everything weighed so much, too much. Looking at the past allowed for an expansion of vantage point.

The silver lining of all this confusion was gratitude for a mother who cares about self-reflection, who can apologise, who does want to change when she is not her best self. We had many conversations to repair the divide that occurred between us, to rebuild trust. We are all capable of repair. Capable of repairing ourselves and our relationships.

On the trip to Des Plaines, my mom brought her therapy journal along with her. It is the second journal she kept in her life, a purple one I gave her for her birthday. I had her other one on the desk in our hotel room, the cherry blossoms on the cover fading but still visible.

SOMEONE WHO I think will help me better see my mom at 17 is her boyfriend from that time, Cory. I meet him at Elly's in Elk Grove Village. When I was dropping my mom at the airport that morning, she said she was both excited and nervous for me to meet him. He had met me once before, when I was a baby, while he was visiting San Diego. Everyone in my family knows Cory. He was the gymnast who was in love with my mom in high school, who wanted to marry her. But she chose my dad instead. When I asked her about why she stayed with Cory so long- more than six years – through high school and college, she said that what she went through bonded them. Cory could see her at her best, her worst, and love her.

I pull open the door to Elly's and spot Cory in an olive green sports polo. He smiles. I smile. I hug him. He hugs back. It is one of those it's-so-good-to-see-you firm hugs, not the flimsy one-armed kind. He exudes a generous energy, pushing a menu toward me, and later he will insist to buy my lunch. He is fit, sporting only a sprinkle of grey in light brown hair. I can see the gymnast in his slight build. It was easy to picture him even now as the base of a stunt or tumbling across the floor. I felt that I knew him.

"Do I look like my mom?" I ask. It seems like the right ice-breaker to get him thinking about her. I mean, I am older than when Cory dated her, but I was curious.

"You look just like her," he says. I smirk. When I was a teenager, I did not like it when people told us we looked like sisters. I wanted my own identity, unlinked to anyone, especially my mom. Now that I am older, I am pleased when people say we look alike. I love my mom and I know who I am. When I was a teenager, I don't think I did. It's an honour to look like the mother you love.

Cory tells me about their relationship between the years of 1978 and 1979. They were teenagers. The world stretched so far ahead. The two of them tried to make their relationship work through their senior year, into college, and after college. Cory moved out to California to be with my mom for a few months after she moved there post-college graduation. She felt immediately at home in California. But Cory did not feel the same. He was close with his family in Illinois, and he couldn't quite land a job he liked. When he got the call for graduate school at Northwestern, his dream school, he moved back to Chicago.

The woman Cory ended up marrying was a widow whose previous husband died in a tragic accident. Her husband died on the day of their child's baptism. He was swimming in a lake with other men when a boat raced toward them and the captain was unable to see the heads bobbing above the surface. The men dove deep to avoid a collision. All came up except for one.

Cory adopted his wife's baby, stepping in as a father. He is good at handling other people's tragedy. He steps in, saying "I'm here," offering comfort. The way Cory tells his wife's story, the attention to detail and focus on care, helps me imagine how he must have been with my mom during the Gacy trial.

"Did you notice a personality shift in my mother after Rob went missing?" I ask.

"She seemed stressed." He leans back in the booth as if to counterbalance her past anxiety with his own ease. "Your mom distinctly remembered Rob leaving to get in the car with Gacy," Cory says, scooping a bite of yoghurt. "There was a lot of 'he said, she said'. People would call her, saying, 'Are you sure your facts are accurate? Are you sure you remember that correctly?'" He says that the whole experience took her innocence too fast.

"What did you think when this questioning from authorities was happening?" I ask. My mom never spoke about a loss of innocence. I knew she was deeply bothered by Gacy telling people she was lying, but I didn't know that other people questioned her reliability at the time. It is the first time I considered how fighting to keep your memory of something so important might corrupt other parts of yourself, so much energy going toward preserving one memory.

"This was grown-up stuff, big-time stuff," Cory says. "There were adults saying she was lying. A large part of the shift in her personality was this. It was the authorities; it was attorneys for Gacy." I imagine her writing in the journal at the end of each night, every pen stroke stoking her anger, her frustration. "But," Cory went on, "the receipt was the physical piece of evidence to back up her truth." Cory remembers the story of the receipt in fragments. In our conversation, I can tell he misremembers where the receipt was found. He thinks it was Gacy's car. But after so many years he has not forgotten the weight of this small piece of paper on my mom, on a country. It isn't his lived experience, but he was linked to this story in his own way, just as Michael was, and just as all of Des Plaines was. People joke about six degrees of separation, but in a town as small as Des Plaines, I'd argue it's closer to two degrees.

I ask Cory how Rob's disappearance altered his life. He says his kids ask him about it. Say the name John Wayne Gacy and ears perk, people listen. Cory keeps quiet about what my mom shared with him, but he's happy to talk to me, her confidant in the second half of her life. My mom kept a few close girlfriends but did not have an extensive amount. Rather, she devoted herself to her family early on. Because I am her eldest daughter, she treated me like a close friend. Someone with whom you shared secrets and hopes and dreams. Cory and I are kin in this way, binary stars, her secret keepers.

When I look at Cory, a grown man, now a grandfather, it's hard to imagine him as the father I might have had. I think that Cory served a deep purpose in my mom's life, and because of that, she found it impossible to break up with him. Someone so good, so loyal. It was as if she knew he was not "the one" but could not bring herself to end their relationship. Because of the murders and because of the trial, they had abnormal connective tissue harden between them.

If they had married, the case would have become even more of my childhood, something rooted in the story of both my parents. When Gacy was making headlines around the country, my father Sam was on a one-way bus ride to California. All-American swimmer at Kenyon College who needed an intermission from college life, my father was searching for a new start. After he met my mom, she forced him to finish his degree, and he would go on to have a full career as an educator and administrator. He received his degree from the University of California, San Diego, where I would end up teaching. Walking through campus, I imagine what the trees looked like from his perspective, wondering if he could hear the ocean waves and whether he, too, walked next to the cliffs off Torrey Pines Road when he needed a break from the workday.

My dad describes my mother as a fighter. When he first learned of her role in the murder case, of how she lost her friend Rob, he knew that she could handle what life would throw her way. She thrives in the way he sees her, the strength he recognises but will never fully understand. Their marriage works. But I wonder what her life could have been with Cory, now just a dear friend from another life, but someone who fell in love with her soft girlishness before Gacy.

My father offered my mother a new start. She saw a fantastic father in him, someone devoted to her, and someone who believed in her. At one point my father wanted to go to medical school, too, but he decided it was in their best interest as a couple if she went. He told her he would support her through it all. When she grew tired of fighting, he'd step in for her. My dad walks my mom to her car every morning, handing her a cup of coffee for the road, and giving her a goodbye kiss as she sets off to treat patients.

When I think about what my mom captured of Cory in her diary, he is solid. Present. A friend does not leave when the world opens and life feels like you might be swallowed by its wrath. A friend throws the rescue ring into the stormy waters, says hold on. Even if he has never saved anyone before, a friend does not stop trying. They are alike in this way, my mom and the man sitting across from me now.

Cory wants to know about my life, so I tell him about myself, how I ended up here at Elly's sharing brunch with him. How Rob's story became my own piece of family history to explore. How fear shot through my bloodstream during my first pregnancy when I realised I was having a boy. My mind couldn't shake the horror of what it would be like to lose my son to an unthinkable man like Gacy. My own anxieties led me to wonder what kind of effect the history had on the town even after so much time had passed.

"This remains part of a community's history," Cory says. "All anyone needs to say is his name or the street. It becomes part of the DNA of a place. Time does not wash that away. Nothing makes it disappear."

"It becomes the undercurrent," I agree.

"Exactly," he says. "And if you are a parent or grandparent to young boys in the area, it strikes a different chord in you."

I ask if I can take Cory's photo and he says yes. His smile is unchanged from the ones in photos my mom keeps in old albums. Her love of nature photography also carried over into her love of portraits, her love of people and their smiles, the backs of their heads, of kissing and hugging. An album I have in my office back home includes a multi-page spread of fall 1978. The Marmosets' fall act was called "With One Last Kiss".

Cory wears blue shorts and a baby-blue cotton shirt, holding my mom as she leans back in his arms, kicking a leg up. The homecoming 1978 photos are in this same album.

These are the photos she developed on December 11, 1978, which made their way back to her without needing the receipt in Rob's pocket. Trapped in time, Cory and my mom pin boutonnieres, pose on her family stairs, laughing. The photos are good, the composition clear without an errant thumb on the flash to overshadow the memories with darkness.

In our conversation, Cory spoke of my mom's innocence, but in these photos, I also recognise his innocence. Rob's disappearance made him grow up too quickly, having to support my mom through a national trial. When we hug goodbye, I want to tell him thank you, thank you for sticking with my mom, carrying her trauma with him. I want to tell him it means the world to me for us to meet today. I want to tell him how I wish these murders had never happened. Cory told me something at the end of our conversation that planted an image in my head for the rest of the day. He said his wife had lived nearby when authorities exhumed corpses from underneath Gacy's house. She could walk right down to the scene and watch the unthinkable unfold. The terrible truth of what happened. When bodies exited on stretchers, covered in white sheets.

CHAPTER SIX

DECAY

1978

In Gacy's house on W. Summerdale, one of the officers following Gacy was secretly looking around for evidence. Gacy had invited them in as a gesture to get out of the cold. Officers were assigned to follow Gacy's every move after the first search, when the film receipt and other oddities were found at the house. The officer excused himself to use Gacy's bathroom while Gacy made him and another officer a drink at his Tiki bar. In the guest bathroom, Officer Schultz unzipped his trousers and urinated. When finished, he zipped up, pressed his finger down to flush, and heard the rumble of the furnace as it kicked on. The smell was unforgettable: rancid flesh liquifying in the summer sun. Except this was December. The pine trees outside were coated with ice, the snow so thick it blocked in cars.

Schultz pinched his nose and got out of the bathroom as fast as he could, stumbling into the hallway. The smell was more than suspicious, it was a feeling: A body was near.

At the Byers' residence, Buddy helped set aside the newspapers for Kim. He knew the articles about Rob were important.

Perhaps someday a grandchild of his would be curious about what his daughter was going through. When Kim walked by the growing stacks of articles, she sometimes looked away. They made Rob's absence painfully real. Her father collected them all: *Chicago Tribune*, *Chicago-Sun Times*, *Des Plaines Times* and *Daily Herald*.

While the authorities continued to hunt for Rob, Kim tried to immerse herself in normalcy. This meant seeing Cory, going to school and swim and gymnastic meets, and on Thursday night, December 21, 1978, travelling with a big group of friends to see the movie *Halloween*. The plot centred on Michael Myers, a teen who killed his babysitter as a child and was out for more blood as a psychopathic adult. In one scene, a young boy proclaimed, "You can't kill the bogeyman".

Kim screamed on and off throughout the entire film. The bogeyman was horrifying and ominous, ever-present, and inescapable. She second-guessed her choice to come to the film as she sipped her orange Fanta over ice and munched on popcorn. No one else in the row of friends understood what she was living.

After the film, she found her car dead in the parking lot. The group of moviegoers slid on their gloves, helped jump it, and pushed it out of the snow. She thanked them and got in with the bogeyman, both real and imagined, whirling through her mind. She blinked and thought she saw Michael Myers's character dash in front of her, but then realised this was her fear, on high alert. Kim wondered about the trouble she'd find if she were to run into Gacy. She knew he took her friend. Would she be next?

She left downtown Des Plaines and made the 15-minute drive to Cory's house. He had written her a sweet card earlier that day to help brighten her spirits. She needed something, someone comfortable, safe. He met her at the door, and they cuddled on the couch.

Cory leaned in to kiss her and it was like she was seeing the scene – of her and Cory on the couch – from the window. Just as Michael Myers watched his victims from a distance. Her body didn't seem to have the energy needed to stay in the day-to-day.

She pulled away from Cory and tucked a strand of her straight, soft hair behind her ear.

"I'm so glad it's winter break," she said to distract him from her recoiling. Cory, too, straightened. He didn't know how to feel about his girlfriend wanting to escape his arms, but he didn't want to make the moment hold too much weight. She had come over, so clearly she wanted to see him. "We are going to have so much fun, Kim."

"I hope so," she said. He leaned in, hoping for a kiss again, but she turned her head, looking at the clock on the basement wall. "I think it's time for me to head home." Nausea overcame her as she pulled on her coat in Cory's home's bright entryway. Was it that Rob was still missing? Was it *Halloween*? Was it that Cory felt more like a close friend than a boyfriend? What was a boyfriend supposed to feel like anyhow?

———

PROSECUTOR TERRY SULLIVAN held out hope Rob was at Gacy's, still alive, maybe trapped somewhere. They needed to get inside again. Sullivan wrote another search warrant because Gacy was caught with marijuana while he was being followed by the officers, not long after the smell of decay was experienced by Schultz. This would hopefully give officers a chance to look closely, again. The receipt had proved Rob was there. The smell was worrisome.

When Sullivan was done writing the second search warrant,

he handed the document to the judge. The judge approved. "Get that SOB," he encouraged Sullivan. An arsenal of adrenaline powered the Des Plaines Police Department. Gacy was being held that day at the station over the possession. The officers trailing him saw him pass a bag of weed to a gas station attendant he knew. The act was enough for them to arrest Gacy for a short window. This was the perfect time for the second search to take place.

W. Summerdale Avenue was packed with cop cars, both marked and unmarked. Neighbours, wearing parkas and scarves and winter hats, exited their houses, wondering what was going on. They stood outside to watch. Many had noticed the odd and sporadic surveillance cars tracking Gacy, but they stopped feeling sorry for their neighbour when the first body bag was carried out of Gacy's front door.

Dan Genty, the evidence technician from Cook County sheriff's office, led the pursuit of finding Rob. Genty entered Gacy's house and immediately went for the crawl space. Meanwhile, a team began to tear down walls, then parts of the floor. Genty knew there weren't too many places to hide a body. He crouched down and crawled east, then south. A cool dampness in the air cut through the harsh smell of decay and cleaning chemicals. He spotted three small puddles, damp and muddy. He pointed his flashlight on the puddles and saw movement.

Thin red worms twirled in the mud. He gulped. It was by no means a normal occurrence, petite red noodles swarming in the thick muck. What were the worms eating? Genty shoved his entrenchment tool into the mud to explore, and to his surprise the metal hit something that felt like stones. He pulled up his stick and his eyes became wide with terror. Something had leached onto the rod. Soapy, almost translucent flesh. He dug some more, the flood light showing him what he did not want to see. Cobwebs wisped around him, and dust swarmed around his eyes with each of his movements. The footsteps of the men in Gacy's bedroom upstairs made creaking noises, as they searched for signs of Rob.

Genty dug and dug until he was six or seven inches down in the murky, swampy mud. He pulled up something so very recognisable: a shoulder bone with pinkish human flesh. Thick sweat poured over his furrowed brow. As in a magic act, the human limb turned from a cool pink to a glum grey once in the air. Genty looked around him to see if anything was casting a shadow, but it wasn't. The flesh turned colours when it exited the wet, chemical-fed trench into the muggy atmosphere. He locked eyes with other officers poking their heads through the trap door from the hallway above.

"Charge him!" Genty yelled up to the other officers, who were waiting for some sort of signal. "I've found a body."

"Is it Piest?"

Genty looked down. The body was so decomposed, it was unrecognisable. Bones with minimal tissue, no trace of the person this once was. "No, this body has been here way too long."

Two more men joined Genty. More floodlights invaded the crawl space, causing the tiny red worms to scurry. There was little room to manoeuvre, but it didn't matter. As the digging continued, they found a knee. In the southeast corner, two long leg bones.

During the exhuming of the skeletons, no one wore overalls

or face masks. No PPE. Diggers were in rugby shirts, flannel, and jeans, sawing and prodding. No one had handled anything like this before. Men were everywhere, searching and digging. Some bodies were face up, some face down; many side by side.

Genty left the crawl space to catch his breath. Above ground once again, he called the station from the phone in Gacy's kitchen. When the supervisor picked up, Genty didn't bother with pleasantries. "I think we have a basement full of kids here," he said.

Back at the station, Detective Mike Albrecht spoke to Gacy, who was being held in an interview room. Gacy asked if the search team had been in the crawl space.

Albrecht nodded.

Gacy said, "You know, Mike, I'm never going to spend a day in jail for this."

Gacy confessed the truth because he was already thinking about his insanity defence, noting multiple personalities in his confession.

On the evening before, Gacy had told his lawyer, Sam Amirante, about every victim. Amirante later said that when he took a shower that night, he felt like a victim at the Bates Motel. He expected someone to come through the shower curtain and stab him. He spent extra time using soap to cleanse his body, warm water pouring over him, as if washing off Gacy's truth was that simple. Amirante did not know the next day would turn up a graveyard under his client's suburban home. Amirante's first regret would be letting Gacy lead the charge in his own defence, trying to manipulate the officers by telling the truth to them.

At the grave site, investigators made the decision to recover the bodies as thoroughly as possible, in the manner of an archaeological dig. This meant that all surrounding earth was removed, exposing the human remains. After that, a careful process would excavate the skeletons and any other artefacts. The challenge with all of this was: How? How could the team perform this careful task without the press knowing, before Gacy was charged?

But the media was already there, swarming and hungry to share the truth with the neighbourhood and the nation. Channel 7's Jay Levine was the first to know, there on the scene with his head of thick black hair, tan trench coat, flared pants, and a microphone.

A month before, the world had learned the news of the Jonestown massacre, in which Jim Jones, the leader of a religious group called the Peoples Temple, ordered his followers to commit suicide by drinking poisoned Kool-Aid at their commune in Jonestown, Guyana. More than 900 people, dead. More than 900 bodies to recover. It would cost about $4 million and require great care to handle those bodies, and it whetted the world's interest in mass horrors.

Levine knew that the discoveries on W. Summerdale would attract similar attention, maybe more since this was in America's backyard and not halfway around the world. He put on a grim face, waited for his cameraman to point a finger, and began his report.

BACK AT THE station, investigators questioned Gacy more. Why did he do it? Whatever he said, could anyone really believe him?

All the truths about the bodies were direly one-sided. Everyone knew how these stories ended: The boy was dead. But how had each death begun? The dead were silenced, and Gacy was still talking. It was important to understand that Gacy lied, a lot. From the very beginning of the investigation, when first questioned about Rob's whereabouts. He told authorities whatever Kim Byers said about him was a lie.

And then, in that room, Gacy started narrating something that sounded like truth.

"Where is Robert Piest?" Albrecht repeated.

"The body is about an hour, hour and a half away from here," Gacy said.

Mike Albrecht pleaded with him. "Just tell me where it's at."

"Above ground," Gacy responded, firmly.

"How did he die, Gacy?"

"They were all strangled."

This would not prove to be the case for all of the victims, but certainly the majority.

Gacy went on to spell out the grisly acts he did with Robert Piest on the night of December 11, 1978. Gacy had tortured him, tried to commit sexual acts, and Rob denied him, horrified. This angered Gacy. He showed him his handcuff trick, making Rob place the handcuffs on himself, which gave Gacy access to Rob's neck. Rob's final minutes were gruesome.

Gacy's confession was against the advice of his legal team. But when the bodies were found, Gacy knew he had to pivot.

He believed the way he spoke, how he spoke, would all be in his favour.

The murders? They began in the early 1970s. The first murder was supposedly an accident. When Gacy had picked up his first victim, Timothy McCoy, at the Greyhound bus stop, the boy had been travelling home from Nebraska. Only 16, he was a free spirit. Gacy claimed to have woken up near dawn, when he saw McCoy with a butcher knife in his hand standing above him. There was no way of knowing if this was true. McCoy never got to share his side of the story.

Gacy claimed because he was woken up and saw the knife, he grabbed the knife in self-defence. The two struggled until Gacy overpowered the boy. McCoy was the first young man in the crawl space and set off a sick and disturbing addiction. He was the only victim stabbed. Gacy turned to strangulation, using his handcuff trick to lure his victims. Gacy enjoyed the feeling of trapping his victim and then making the choice of whether he would live or die.

At the Des Plaines Police Station Gacy confirmed he buried most of the victims in the crawl space and threw acid or lime on all of them. The other four who wouldn't fit under the house he left in the Des Plaines River, off the bridge on Interstate 55. He thought maybe one hit a barge when he dropped it, but the rest had splashed into the watery depths. His victims were mostly boys, some young men. Gacy told Mike Albrecht and the other officers that he was bisexual, not homosexual, and any relations he had with his victims were consensual. But who bought that?

Gacy's confession included an account of his arrival in Des Plaines. In August of 1971 he bought the house on W. Summerdale. The neighbourhood was lower middle class, blue collar. Most of the homes were built in the 40s or 50s. He slipped so well into and out of normal life. He had two ex-wives and two children. He wanted to look like someone who was socially adapted and involved in the community, as well as someone private, starting anew in Chicagoland suburbia.

Gacy recalled the beginning of the new year, being hungover, looking for someone to bring home. He named some victims. He shared that a former employee of his, John Butkovich, was by the barbecue grill, under the ground. When asked why he buried the bodies, Gacy said, "It was a secret place. Those were my bodies. No one could touch them."

He had an Oldsmobile with a big red spotlight on it, and he would use it to cruise. Posing as a cop, he would stop people in his car. He had around 50 police badges he had hoarded over the years. He also had a black leather jacket. He said he'd con kids by having them think he was a police officer, but he wasn't. Some of the victims weren't kidnapped. Some, like John Butkovich and Gregory Godzik, worked for him.

Gacy confessed his typical move to get boys to his house. First, something he called a magic trick. He would put a handcuff on himself, attempt to shake it off until eventually it slid off. He'd then look directly in his victims' eyes, and say, "Now it's your turn to do the trick. Put 'em on and I'll show you how to take them off without the key." The handcuffs became stuck. They'd ask how to do the trick, how to get them off. Gacy would say, "You don't. You need the key." Then the rope. He placed it around the victims' necks, turning it a few times, tightening it. A strangling.

He told the officers one of the last things he remembered Rob Piest saying was, "Why are you putting the rope around my neck?"

Likely at the same time, his mom's heart was in her throat at Nisson Pharmacy, or on the drive back to the Piest home.

Becoming unnerved, glimpsing her unlit birthday cake. One thing a mother can know, deeply, is the meaning of a birthday. Bringing a child into this world makes life a different realm. Life's markers were not the calendar year, but the time elapsed since birth. Police continued asking Gacy questions, while he rambled and went off on tangents, attempting to steer the conversation. His Miranda rights had been read to him. He was told everything he said could and would be held against him. He didn't care. He never shut up.

BACK AT GACY'S house, the excavators kept asking each other, "How many are there?"

White blankets covered the bodies as they were brought up from the crawl space and stacked in the kitchen. The men placed each exhumed body on boards and carried them away for loved ones and medical examiners to identify. Some still had a rope around their necks. Many were kids. Young boys, still in Scouts. Boys who enjoyed fishing and photography and science class.

Phil Tovar, of the police department, said he carried a coin in his pocket during the entire excavation. When he was at work, the coin stayed in his jeans pocket. When he got home, the coin went in a little dish. That was how he separated his walking self from the crouched version, as a gravedigger.

IT TOOK ONLY a day for everyone in town to hear about what was happening at Gacy's house. Kim first learnt the news from her mother. Barbara found her in her bed, still asleep. Kim's room was ethereal, not quite like that of a regular teen girl. Where other girls her age had posters of teenage heartthrobs, Kim wanted nothing of the sort. She had a Ringling Bros. and Barnum & Bailey Circus poster with its tiger's face, teeth as sharp as daggers. Her nightstand held her diary and love letters from Cory. She had some lotion her sister had given her that she hardly used. The room was small, but it was her private oasis, a place only she could know well. A room holds memories, and this one was pushing the bounds on its capacity.

Barbara quietly entered. Only the two women were at home. Barbara rarely left the house. She spent her time keeping up with the news, playing bridge, and smoking cigarettes. She ploughed through them, and the scent that lingered on her skin and hair and sweaters made Kim nauseous. Kim could smell her mom before she spoke. "Kim, wake up," Barbara said, softly. "There are bodies," she exhaled.

Barbara studied her daughter's face, which went from sleepy to alert. Her hair was in a braid, a little fuzzy from the bedhead. Kim's blue eyes grew round as she registered what her mother was saying.

"Where?" Kim asked. She threw the comforter off her and sat up. Was this all just a bad dream inspired by *Halloween*?

"At the man's house. The man that you saw leave with Rob," she said. "I'm so sorry, honey." Barbara sat next to her daughter, still so young. A little girl, but on the cliff of adulthood. She wrapped both her arms around Kim, tight.

Kim couldn't stop heaving under the weight of the news. "He's dead?"

"They don't know," Barbara said. "But the guess is, yes."

Barbara grabbed a tissue from Kim's dresser and wiped her

daughter's eyes. She wondered how she could have protected her from this feeling, this moment. In life, what was inevitable and what was fate? Was there even a difference between the two? She didn't know.

"How did they find the bodies?" Kim breathed, through crying coughs.

"Your receipt," she said. "You helped. You allowed them to get in that house."

Kim could feel her heartbeat in her left ear, in her palms. It was beating, racing, throughout her body. She took a sharp breath and then put her head down on her pillow. Barbara combed through her daughter's hair with her fingers, pulling tear-soaked tendrils out of her face. She kissed Kim on the side of her head.

"I'll let you get ready," Barbara said, and left. She felt hot and could hear her own heart thump in her neck. It was the kind of news you never wanted to break to your daughter. A ripple effect began spilling, out of the Byers residence, out of Rob's house across town, out of so many family homes of the people who knew or loved the bodies being pulled out and being placed under white sheets for observation, analysis, and identification.

As the door closed behind Barbara, Kim broke open her drawer and thumbed the pages of her journal, gently brushing her finger over the cherry blossoms sewn into the front turquoise cover.

22/12/78

Am about to go to practice after a very traumatic morning. Mom came in and told me they found lots of bodies in Gacy's house and he is now leading them on a search for Rob's. I hope Nathan comes home from Texas where he has started a new job. Will go to Rob's later. Well just about everything is out. Gacy has confessed to 20 murders. They have not yet found Rob's body. He said he dumped it into the Des Plaines River over the Kankakee Bridge, that's far and wide. What sent them back for the second search of the house was my film slip. They found it in Gacy's garbage can and did not realise that it came from Rob. Ken Piest called before work then he and Kerry came into the store. I went to their house. Mrs Piest is really upset and Mr Piest is showing strains. I called Nathan. He then called me at home. He wants to come home, but it is better that he is there. Power went out too.

Kim drove through the ice and snow to see the Piests. It was three days before Christmas, one of her favourite holidays all year. Except, it did not feel like Christmas. She parked her car on the sidewalk, in front of the Piest home. It had a single-car garage and a sidewalk out front.

"Who is it?" Mr Piest answered Kim's knock through the closed front door. He was trying to avoid the swarms of news folks parked on the front lawn. When he heard it was Kim he cracked the door to let her inside.

Kim slid off her gloves and parka. She looked around at the lived-in living room that looked so much like her own home. Newspapers were piled up. Old coffee cups lingered on the kitchen table. The house had a solemn, sad energy. There was no Christmas tree, which was different from Kim's home, which had one. She remembered how just last week the thought was that Rob was surprising his mom with a Christmas tree for her birthday.

"Can I get you a glass of water?" he asked.

"No, thank you." She gave him a big hug. They didn't need to talk about what had happened. They both knew. She felt him shake as he hugged her, then struggle to keep his composure.

"Is Mrs Piest here?" Kim asked.

"I'm afraid she is not," Mr Piest responded. He went to the kitchen to grab a hand towel to wipe his face.

There was talk of Mrs Piest's suffering, her loss of her little boy. Someone had said she could no longer take the news, and she had asked to be taken to the emergency room for help. Kim did not want to ask Mr Piest anything about it, so she asked if she could go say hi to Ken and Kerry. Kim's intention was to be present with the Piest family. Mourn with them. Share space. She had never been in a situation like this before, but her instincts kicked in and told her to go, be with Rob's family. Kim, Kerry, and Ken spent the afternoon together, listening to music, talking about movies. Thoughts and questions of Rob slipped into conversation intermittently, like dunking a tea bag in and out of a cup of lukewarm water.

BACK AT HOME, Kim saw that her dad had collected more newspapers. The local news about the digging at Gacy's house was quickly becoming national news. In the *New York Times*, the crimes began to be reported: "Three bodies found under home; Illinois suspect accused of murder."

The article, published on December 22, 1978, depicted the remains of three bodies that were found during the search in Gacy's crawl space. The article let readers know Gacy's age: 36. Police were tearing his house apart, trying to find more bodies.

On the front page of the *Chicago Tribune* on December 23, 1978: "Four slaying victims found; 28 more are feared dead." In the beginning of the unearthing, there was confusion about how many bodies authorities were looking for. Soon, the real number, 33, would surface. The front page had two sprawling images to accompany it – portraits of John Wayne Gacy and Robert Piest.

A multi-page spread displayed the unfolding dig: aerial images of the search at Gacy's house sprawled over the paper, with another image of Gacy with his head in his hands; officers carrying a body wrapped in a sheet.

The newspaper headlines and her time inside the Piest house left aftershocks on Kim. Her daily routine became sporadic, the organised life of a 17-year-old overshadowed by her new role as key witness.

<u>23/12/78</u>

Got up kind of late. Went to work at 9am. Ate a lot of junk. At about 4pm I felt real sick, nerves? Told Larry I was going home and slept 4.30-5.30pm. Gathered lots of articles about Rob.

Back at Gacy's house, uncovering the bodies grew increasingly difficult. On the second day of exhuming, the men digging and searching for the boys under Gacy's property were given a hand-sketched map of where Gacy claimed the bodies were. Because there were so many, exhumers measured the depths of the graves and placed piles of bones that were perceived to be of the same body into the white body bags. But errors occurred. One skeleton accidentally had two left arms, another two right arms.

When a detective stepped out of the crawl space for a breath of new air, walking through a house with so much floor torn up, he happened upon evidence of Rob – his blue parka – below the floorboards in the laundry room.

CHAPTER SEVEN

COMMUNITY

2022

David Nelson has spent a lot of time researching Rob Piest's disappearance. He waits for me outside a train stop about 20 minutes outside of Des Plaines, having commuted in from his apartment in Chicago.

Last year I interviewed him for a magazine piece about his book, *Boys Enter the House*, about the lives of the victims of John Wayne Gacy. We had bonded through our research. In our interview he opened up to me about how the case affected him and his own coming-out journey. He had imagined the same young men Gacy often picked up, walking around downtown Chicago. David shared that he was just like them, but their lives were cut short by Gacy.

He is wearing a navy ball cap, a white shirt, and grey shorts. I wave when I see him. Our plan is to visit some of the last places where Rob was alive.

David says he is excited to be here and closes the door to the passenger side of the 4Runner. Our first stop is Maine West High School, where Rob was a sophomore when he disappeared.

I pull up to the front of the building, passing the marquee advertising the homecoming game. It is just a bit after school was released. Students linger around the steps outside and the quad inside. Everything seems to revolve around the centre, and the school boasts three wings. I had known about the various wings at Maine West from my chats with Nathan. He and Rob spent a lot of time in the gym, practising gymnastics.

As we exit the car toward Maine West High School, I can't stop seeing the word homecoming in thick black letters on the marquee.

I take photos outside of Maine West, feeling a bit out of body. It is one thing to study a case from halfway across the country, but completely different to walk in the same space where these characters were people. The feeling is sacred, like the reaction one might get when visiting a sanctuary or an old church. I captured some video footage on my phone, too, because the campus has a certain sound, a cadence that is difficult to capture in a still image. The wind hums, lingering kids chatter, and cicadas buzz, with dusk approaching on the horizon. School is out for the day, but students sit on the steps. I picture Rob walking here, through the car park, into the main building.

The air has a curt, early fall breeze. It carries excitement for what was to come: homecoming, dances, fall carnival, Halloween. So much lies ahead for teenagers. High school is a petri dish of movement. Rob fit into this rhythm. From labs in biology, meeting friends in between classes at lockers, to the drive and grit he practised as a high school athlete, Rob very much fit in and, many would say, stood out.

"Nathan told me that we should check out the gym," I say to David. "He said it's in the A-wing." A couple of students leave the building and hold the door open for us to enter. We stride over to a balcony overlooking the indoor quad, where people eat lunch and mingle, telling secrets and making promises they couldn't know if they could keep. This building is like a nucleus, holding the most meaningful connections and encounters in the centre.

I see Rob in the atrium, flipping his hair back. I picture him everywhere. It is impossible not to. The school was originally built in 1959 over Des Plaines farmlands and remodelled this past summer. However, there are parts of the interior that appear original, like signs and a wooden "Good Will" awards wall.

After rounding a curve, David and I see the hallway that leads down to the gymnasium. The "A-wing" sign is original: black block letters over lime-green paint, and flaking.

As we make our way to the gym, I steal glances into classrooms through the large glass windows. I am on alert for lab spaces, hunting for the background of my favourite photo of Rob. In it he wears a Wrangler T-shirt, sitting, or at least appearing to sit, at a table with a small sink. In the background are large glass windows, similar to the ones I am peering through as I walk across the linoleum floor. He holds out his hand in the photo in an invitation, a gesture that says take my hand. His hair is in its usual curtain, but some strands hang in front of his eyes. He smiles, as though he just had his photo taken on a whim and was beckoning the person behind the camera to join him at the lab table. It shows an easy joy on a young man's face that would soon not smile ever again.

"Do you think this is the room?" I ask David. He looks in the direction I'm pointing. I take my phone from my purse and pull the image up to show him. His eyes squint. I'm sure he has seen this photo of Rob, too. "It could be," he says.

We continue walking. The gymnasium entrance is a large

double door. My instinct is to tug on the handles, to try to enter. "Locked," I say, stepping back. David points over my shoulder. To our right is an old wooden display case containing images of past gymnastics teams at Maine West. Rob was a member of the team for less than a year. It should not surprise me that he didn't make it into any of these photos, and yet my eyes refuse to give up searching for him.

I imagine the wooden bleachers and old tumbling mats piled next to the door. I wonder how he felt in his body, his mind when he practised. Roundoffs, forward rolls, handstands, handsprings off vaults; hip circles and fly-aways on the uneven bars. Chalk sliding between the grooves of his fingers, the dryness in his palms, the clang and dull clapping sound when he brushed his hands together, to level the chalk over the surface. Gymnastics required regimen; it required focus; it required care.

AFTER LEAVING THE school, I drive us to the old Nisson Pharmacy so David can have a look. In all his researching, he has never been here. I park and we stand outside the daycare together.

"This is the alley where he went to take out the trash," I say, pointing down the corridor on the side of the brick building. "Over there is the Iroquois Pool, where Rob and local teens would swim during the summer." It feels strange to be touring David through this landscape. I am protective toward this place even though these memories are not mine. Walking in the place of victims was like saying a prayer, a way to pay homage. But I know he gets it, too. He researched all the Gacy victims for years and holds a parallel vigilance.

"I believe this is also where the girl came out of the dance that night and threw a snowball at Rob," I tell David. "And there is the liquor store my mom and Rob would often go to for sodas before or during work."

"Let's go in and see if anyone remembers Nisson," David says. I don't try to dissuade him with the story of the last time I went in there and no one knew the old pharmacy. Since my first trip here with my mom, I had done my research on the businesses. Although the building remained an liquor store, it has changed ownership over the decades.

"Can I help you find anything?" a man asks, pausing his restocking to ask us as we poke around the aisles of bottles.

When we ask about the pharmacy, he leans against one of the endcaps. "Over there?" He points to where Nisson once was located. "Oh yeah, my best friend Rob used to work there, and that guy Gacy murdered him."

David and I glance at each other. "What's your name?" I ask. The man's eyes dart around the room, then back to the floor; he brushes his right hand through his short black and grey hair. I imagine Rob in his 60s, similar sprinkles of grey and the coarseness on the top of his hands that comes with ageing. "How did you two become friends?" I ask when the man refuses to tell us his name. I tell him a bit about the work David and I do in the hopes it will help him open up.

"Rob would come in here or I would go in there and buy things. We would get to talking. He was a nice guy," the man says. I can see them, two young boys, Rob sliding a couple of pops in glass bottles across the counter to ring up before a shift. My mom was the one to buy the pops that night, so this man, even if he was working, probably did not see Rob on the last evening of his life.

The man disappears into the back of the store before we can continue our conversation. The encounter feels a bit off to me. I'm not sure what to think except to wonder whether this person is telling the truth. Part of him reminds me of how Michael acted; this sort of nervousness, as though not wanting to say too much. David thinks it's because the two weren't really "best friends" and this person might have been an older kid, giving Rob the time of day. Rob made him feel special. Maybe he is right.

The more time I spend in Des Plaines, the more I feel the subtext of how Gacy's murders affected people's lives, jobs, and life trajectories. If you take time to talk with someone about the murders, they all have something to say.

A missing persons case has been unfolding for the past year-and-a-half in my hometown in Southern California. Maya Millete is a woman, a mother, who disappeared in a southern suburb in San Diego, about 15 minutes from where I live. No body has been found. No confession has been made. Left behind is a disgruntled husband who did not like that his wife wanted to leave him. News media report that he had hired a spellcaster to try to hex her, to steer her away from leaving him. He has given inconsistent accounts about what he did the day she went missing. Something like gunshots were heard, caught on neighbours' security systems, but unconfirmed.

Searchers combed the local mountains, the desert. Friends of the missing woman wondered what they could have done differently, if they could have prevented her disappearance. Her case reminded me of Rob's because it asked similar questions. How could this have happened in our town? How could people have known? Could they have stopped the disappearance? I think cases where women and children disappear into the night remind us that safety is never guaranteed. Maya's story reinforces my belief that so much pain stays after murder, after disappearance.

THE NEXT STOP we make is at the last place Rob was alive. David and I are following Rob's tracks. The gym at Maine West, eating dinner in the car and sipping warm milk from the thermos his mom packed for him, the ride over to Nisson Pharmacy. Then, of course, 8213 W. Summerdale.

We get into the car and I enter the route on my phone to put up directions. I turn on 70s rock. I think about what Gacy and Rob spoke of on the car ride over. Was Rob nervous? Did he have a feeling that something was not right? Did he feel safe and optimistic about this new job prospect? Did that hope, that feeling of being on the verge of something better, filter out any other signs?

I have given a lot of thought to that car ride. More thought than what happened when Gacy brought Rob into his house. That scene makes me want to look away. Gacy told authorities, in a stern voice, that he did not believe Rob Piest suffered on the night of his death. I never bought that. He literally took away his breath, his life force. That is suffering.

I pull into Norwood Park Township. I have been here before, but this time is different. I am not on the lookout for where the old lot was, I knew where it was, exactly, and the certainty makes my heart pummel in my chest.

"I'm going to park over here," I tell David, sliding against the curb a block over because I want to walk. I hope to run into someone on the street, walking their dog or running an errand. I've never spoken to someone who lives in this neighbourhood, only the mailman. Earlier, David conjectured that people would be out, gardening or enjoying their late summer afternoon. But the street is silent. No cars, no people. It is nearing dinnertime and I know in my neighbourhood in California, people are frequently out walking their dogs, driving home from rush hour traffic, readying to eat and unwind. But the street's only noise is a crow's caw.

I can feel my heartbeat in my ears. I look down at my tan boots, as I watch how the sidewalk crumbles and crunches beneath my feet, as though it is deteriorating. Then, it's smooth. A distinct line indicates where the old sidewalk ends and the new one begins. I rest my boots on the line between the original and the new concrete, poured after Gacy's house was torn down and a new one built.

Before this trip I looked online at the listing on Zillow. The house on Gacy's old lot recently changed hands. It has a blue room upstairs, a twin bed. A little boy's room, presumably. How strange that now a young boy slept on the same land where dozens of young boys were laid to an uneasy rest. I imagined this boy running down the stairs on a Christmas morning. The excavation had begun right around Christmas. Did anyone who lived here ever feel the victims' presence? Did they ever sense the evil that used to sleep under a different roof, on this same point of co-ordinates?

In an interview with the *Chicago Tribune* from the 1980s, a neighbour proclaimed that although they were glad something new was built, and that this parcel of land was not just a field of weeds, they had concerns over the lack of any monument honouring the victims. I wonder the same. How can the boys' lives be expunged with new drywall and a coat of paint?

After the bodies were excavated and the house was demolished, the plot was sold to Hoyne Savings and Loan Association in 1984, and then to Chicago resident Patricia Jendrycki. She bought the parcel of land for $30,544 to build a home for her ageing parents. According to reports, she knew the history of the boys and of Gacy. It is unclear to me if it bothered her to build a house on a grave site. The whole town watched her construction of this new house, which was at the time much grander than any others on the street. Patricia sold the home in 2004 for $300,000.

Some improvements were made, and the house went up for sale again in 2019, priced at $459,000. From 2019-2021, the Zillow listing took on an anxious drumming rhythm. Price change. Pending sale. Price change. Pending sale. Listed. Pending sale. Price change. According to the Illinois General Assembly, death or any other stigmatising factors do not legally need to be disclosed when selling a house.

The pattern seems clear. The house appears, from the outside, modern and new. A place to raise a family. Updated kitchen. A big backyard. My guess is that the buyers would find out about the murders before closing the deal. That is, until 2021. The house sold for a $100,000 under asking. Perhaps the new owners felt they were getting a good deal, regardless of the place's grim history.

David and I walk past the house. The ash tree out front is lush and full of green leaves, not the decrepit winter tree I met my first time here in the winter of 2017. As the current front door comes into view, my mind zips back to men carrying out flat boards laden with boyish bodies, placing them into vans, sending them off to be identified. Next door is the same single-story ranch house you can glimpse in certain photos. The front yard is xeriscaped, and a small trophy stands in the centre. It is the kind of award a youth might get after a season of playing Little League Baseball. Because of its age and the way the weather has worn down and tarnished the trophy's shine, it reminds me of the trinkets Gacy kept of the boys. I pull a flyer out of a box at the front of the neighbours' house, the chipping trophy nearby. The home is for sale. The flyer reads: "FOR SALE BY OWNER. Charming home in a great area is waiting for your ideas. Has loads of potential. Being sold 'as is', by appointment only." A telephone number is shown. Later, I call the number and speak to a woman, who is trying to sell the house for some family members. She says the neighbourhood was a nice area to grow up in. She says they hadn't owned the property in the 1970s or 1980s when the Gacy murders unfolded. I thought that must have been a relief for her family, to sidestep such a horror.

The street is without life. I hoped to talk to someone like Cory's wife, someone who remembered. But no one is outside gardening or walking their dog. No cars drive by. It's like walking onto a film set. It looks real, but I fumble trying to find proof of life.

The sun begins a swift set. My body feels achy, as if I have had too many sips of an energy drink. But I haven't had anything of the sort. This place, I realise, leaves me with low-grade body shakes, this full-body buzz of panic. Because my physical state feels uneven, I think it is best to leave. "Hungry?" I ask David.

Nathan had told me, before this trip back to Des Plaines,

that he and Rob used to grab pizza after practise or on Friday nights at a place by the school. He said it was still open and if I was going to be in the area, it was a must stop. Allegretti's is located on 933 E. Oakton Street in Des Plaines. The restaurant is small-town non-descript from the outside, sandwiched between a Mexican food restaurant and a liquor store.

Inside the small restaurant hangs bright market lighting. The walls are painted different colours: red, deep grey, orangish yellow. The tables are black and have black metal chairs with plastic-covered, cushioned seats. The floors are tiled black. A small TV hangs in the corner next to a sign that reads: "In Pizza We Crust." Each word in the sign sports its own colour. Another hand-drawn sign recommends the "Homemade Cannoli". An exposed blue Coca-Cola fridge sits near the dining area. The place does not have a traditional host stand, because it does not need one. You sit where you want and are handed paper menus. It's easy.

Only one other table in the restaurant is occupied when we sit down around 7pm, presumably the dinner rush. Perhaps the place is known more for takeout. Quite a few people enter and leave with pizza boxes and Styrofoam takeout containers. A woman greets us and asks what we would like to drink.

"Do you have any beer?" I ask.

It has been a long day, and my nerves are getting to me after being on W. Summerdale. I often underestimate the hold this case, these murders, the extinction of Rob's life have on me. Sometimes I assume the physical and emotional difficulty will ease up, but it seems impossible. I am not a big drinker, but I want a beer to scratch the back of my throat, to blur the feeling of leaving Gacy's old street.

"No beer," she says. David orders a regular Coke and I order a flavoured San Pellegrino. The bubbles tickling my throat will have to do.

We decide on a Caesar salad and a thin-crust pepperoni pizza. The food comes out in heaping piles. We're quiet as we eat. I think about what it means to be here, in Allegretti's, a family pizza joint, which locals and Maine West High School students frequented. I think about the power of immersing oneself in a place that used to mean a lot to someone you care about. I did not feel the need to chase a story, ask anyone questions in this joint. This is the story. The crisp of the pizza crust. The saltiness of the pepperoni. The metal chair pushing into my back. The quiet hum of the drink cooler.

"So strange to be here, right?" I ask David.

"I bet not a lot has changed," he says. I could not shake the feeling I got from being on Gacy's old street. "Let's grab a beer somewhere," I say.

I DRIVE US to Beacon Tap, a place now familiar to me, the oldest pub in Des Plaines, having opened in 1955. We sit at the bar. The inside is packed with people, busy and loud, much different from the small, quiet Allegretti's.

The wooden bar top loops around in an oval. TVs are strung around the bar like paper chains on a Christmas tree. We sit facing a baseball game, and I order us two Blue Moons.

A man sitting opposite me makes eye contact. "Cheers," he says. He raises his drink. His eyes are glassy. It's that time of the night when regulars welcome newcomers to their watering hole. We return the salutation.

"This is a great place, huh?" I ask the man.

"Come here every night," he says. I wonder if it's my all-black outfit with my camera bag or David's button-up shirt with Ray-Bans tucked into it that gives us away as out-of-towners. When I ask him if he has a story connected to the Gacy murders, he nods enthusiastically and sits up straighter on his barstool. He says that he had a cousin who had a run-in with Gacy at a different bar. But his cousin was huge, could bench-press 500 pounds. His cousin had this feeling that made him say something like "get the fuck away" to Gacy. Afterward, the cousin felt bad he didn't do anything about the weird guy. He said he carried a sense of guilt. Maybe if he had taken Gacy out, he could have stopped his murders.

The bar patron agrees with me: Everyone here has a Gacy story. Everyone knew someone. Maybe they had a run-in with Gacy. Maybe they were his neighbours. They could have been in law enforcement here in Des Plaines or had a relative or family friend who was. The murders were, in fact, the under current, a deep, lightless level of the ocean. Just because it was not visited frequently, did not mean the deep current did not exist.

Our companion offers to get us a drink, but David needs to make the train, and I need to call my boys back home. This is the first time I have been away from Cal for more than a night. He is 15 months now and Bennett is five. When I brought up the idea to take this trip for research, Nick encouraged me to go. He was planning to make it special for the boys: nights of making popcorn, putting on a movie, calling every night "Boys' Night". If I didn't have Nick, I don't think I would have been able to be here.

Although Nick's family history was not directly connected to a serial killer, there were rumours of a familial connection to Lizzie Borden, the woman who used an axe to kill her stepmother and then father, in Fall River, Massachusetts, in 1892. When I first told him about my mom's connection with Gacy, he was shocked. This kind of darkness wasn't supposed to have such a straight line to a family member. It was supposed to be a strange, spooky tale maybe, an anecdote to share at parties or when first dates needed a shot of adrenaline. When we were in our first year of dating, he shared Lizzie and I brought up Gacy.

Lizzie Borden is a shared childhood memory. On the playground jumping rope, we sang of her taking an axe and giving her mother 40 whacks, then giving her father 41. Retellings of Lizzie Borden's story began in 1933 with a play, *Nine Pine Street*, and she still serves as fodder for TV, film, and other media. The Borden house is currently a museum and a bed and breakfast. In the course of more than 100 years, Lizzie Borden has evolved from killer to mythical American plaything.

I wonder if the world will still know about Gacy in the 2100s. Perhaps they will, and perhaps this research I'm doing will limit the sort of reduction that happens with narrative over time. As decades pass, stories are watered down. It's dangerous to lose the voices of those who bore witness to atrocities.

The man at the bar ends our conversation by saying that a neighbour of his was an officer on Rob's case. He was there the day they found the receipt, and there again as the bodies were gently resurrected from the crawl space. He was also there when authorities began their search for Rob in the Des Plaines River.

CHAPTER EIGHT

WINTER

1978–1979

STILL IN HER COTTON PYJAMA set, Kim shuffled through the growing piles of newspapers, looking for an answer. Rob had not been found. Search teams were facing bone-chilling conditions on the Des Plaines River. Snow covered the banks, and sleet fell on the water's wind-driven surface. Divers wore thick bodysuits to protect them from below-freezing temperatures as they searched for Rob, following Gacy's suggestion. They looked under and around the I-55 bridge that crossed the Des Plaines River.

On Christmas Day in 1978, a light snow fell. It was like the smallest gift nature could bestow on the town. One of those picturesque snows. The ones that make you run outside and stick your tongue out to catch snowflakes or make a snow angel with neighbourhood friends. The snow that lingers lightly on the pines and paints a picture on sloped shingled roofs. It was so magical, Kim noted its beauty in her diary. Even with so much going on around them, you could see the smallest bit of wonder if you looked closely enough.

Buddy joined Kim at the kitchen table on Christmas morning. It was early enough that presents still sat under the tree untouched. He blew the steam from his fresh cup of black coffee. "This is too much," he said, picking up one of the newspapers. It had a sketch of Gacy's house that he had drawn, noting where he placed the bodies.

"I know," Kim said. Every morning since the bodies were found, she woke up with what felt like a tombstone in her stomach, unable to eat breakfast.

"Each day, more bodies," Buddy said. "That reminds me. I've been going to different stores to pick up more newspapers."

He handed her a blue pen he had been using to make a last-minute grocery list. "Write the date on anything you cut out.

When this goes to trial, you will need to know how this unfolded in the public eye," he said. She grabbed the blue BIC pen and wrote "25/12/78" on the top of an article titled, "Missing boy's family always feared Gacy".

The excavation was drawing a distinct line in the town's history. Time consisted of before the bodies, and after. Gacy would no longer be seen posing as a contractor, a clever Democrat, a backyard barbecue type of guy. He would never return to this house. He would sit in prison until his trial began in February 1980.

KIM SPENT CHRISTMAS Day with her family and later went to visit her sister, who had made a stocking for her. The morning was special. A break from the world of horrible truths. Kim was scheduled to work at Nisson Pharmacy that afternoon. She drove there and expected a slow day with extra pay for working a holiday. But the Nisson parking lot was filled with cars and news vans and reporters and photographers. She heard a clamour as her car pulled in. People knocked on the glass. "Kim, Kim!" She ran to the back office to find Larry. Although he was not at the store the night Rob went missing, she felt he had become protective over his employees.

"People are yelling my name," she said.

"I'll go see. You stay here," Larry said.

She crouched down under the back counter so no one would see her. She didn't know why they would want to speak to her, especially on Christmas Day. Larry opened the door. A chill jolted through the store as he heard their pleas. News had broken about her film receipt shortly after the first bodies were found. Although it had been common knowledge within the police department, the public space was just learning.

"Kim Byers. Film receipt," were the words echoing into the store. The reporters were hungry for a comment.

"She's not here," he said. "Best be on your way."

She raised her head, her fingers pressing into the counter's surface. The reporters and photographers eventually retreated into their cars.

Larry returned to the back of the store. She followed him into his office, staying out of sight. "Why don't you hang out back here for a bit? I'll work the front," he said.

Kim nodded. Her heart made an anxious spin. She didn't like the feeling of so many eyes. It felt strange to hear her name come out of so many mouths. She was still a kid. She lived with her parents, under their watch. She was not built for this kind of attention.

NO ONE CAME back to harass Kim for the rest of her shift.

Before leaving, she purchased some See's Candies to bring to the Piests.

Kim parked her car parallel to the house. She unbuckled her seat belt quickly, darting toward the front door before anyone caught sight of her. Her boots crunched across the fresh snow, and although it was cold, she didn't feel the normal frostbite eroding her skin when she was outside. Over the past two weeks, Kim had become less nervous when she was around the Piest family, especially now that Gacy was in custody. She and the Piests were of similar ilk.

"Kim!" Mrs Piest exclaimed, opening the door. Her frown lifted when she saw Kim holding a white box of chocolates. "Come inside, we were just going to have some hot cocoa and sit by the fire."

She came in and hugged each of them. The family's German shepherds ran up to her, licking her cheek. She laughed and gave them each a good scratch behind the ear.

"Merry Christmas, everyone," she said. Mrs Piest handed her a mug. "I brought you a little something," Kim said. She handed the box of chocolates to Rob's mother. Kim loved going to the Piests' because they lived in a single-family home and not in a row of apartments with shared walls. She hoped one day to have a home of her own, like this. Mrs Piest knew how much these chocolates cost Kim and pulled her into a grateful hug.

"Oh, Kim, you didn't!" Mr Piest said, from the couch.

Everyone seemed to be in good spirits for the first time since Rob's disappearance. A candle burned, filling the house with a peaceful aroma.

"I'm doing an interview about Rob tomorrow," Ken said, cluing Kim into what was causing the uplifted mood in the room. He had grown fond of her presence in the house during such a difficult time. "Not much we can do to bring him back," Ken said. "At least I can honour the life he had."

Kim looked over to Mrs Piest, who had turned her gaze out the window. It was as if she were waiting for her son to walk up the front walkway. Kim did not stay long at the Piests'. That night she went to bed, feeling full for the first time in days, maybe weeks. Even with the strange encounter at work, the day had been good.

But, just as the dig at Gacy's house would resume after the holiday, the case came barrelling back into Kim's life the next day.

ON DECEMBER 26, Jay Levine from Channel 7 and employees of the other local news stations camped outside Kim's front door. There seemed to be even more reporters than there had been at the pharmacy the day before.

"Kim, can we get a comment? What did you see the night Rob Piest left with John Wayne Gacy?" a reporter called from the walkway in front of her home.

"Kim, Kim, look this way," another begged.

She pulled her beanie over her head and waved away the news teams with their big white vans and bulky camera gear and bright white smiles. She jumped into the family's blue Buick Skylark and buckled her seat belt. The soft snow from the day before had hardened overnight.

Barbara watched her daughter to make sure she made it safely to the car, stepping down from the front door to yell at the news people to please leave. She was thinking that Kim didn't need this invasion of privacy at her own residence, her safe place. The authorities had pestered her enough, trying to poke holes in her testimony. Kim drove away and her breath became quick. Her eyes watered, warm on her rosy and chilled cheeks.

BACK AT GACY'S house, workers continued digging after the Christmas pause. One man working there told the *Chicago Tribune*, "If the devil's alive, he lived in this house." Each dig day began at 8am. The men arrived silent, grim. This was their job, but they wished that it wasn't. They drove shovels into the dirt deeper, deeper, until boom. A jolt would vibrate up their shovel to their hand. They hit pelvises, collarbones, skulls, legs. The kitchen floor that formed the ceiling of the crawl space was now completely gone. Authorities and those taking breaks stood above and helped by shining flashlights down into the damp earth.

Early in the morning, one technician yelled up, "I hit something." More members helped dig. They did not worry about fingers. Just the big bones, attempting to keep each body together to assemble at the end of the day. After the bodies were pulled, workers wearing firemen's hip boots sifted through the wet graves by hand. They used their sense of touch to find any rings or pendants, objects that would help identify the victims.

OVER AT THE Piest house, Ken went through with his interview with *The Journal*. It was a smaller press, but he felt it was what he could do to honour his brother. Todd Wessell was on assignment. The two sat at the kitchen table. Untouched coffees cooled in front of them. Ken folded his hands together, then nervously wiped them on his trousers. Wessell took out his notebook and pen.

"Within the family, we talked about Rob as being so mature," Ken began. "He always wanted to do something big with his life and to let people know who he was. He wanted to have a purpose in life. He would have never been satisfied with just a nine-to-five job."

Ken's eyes watered. Wessell noticed and rested his pen on the table to hand Ken a tissue. "I guess he did that one big thing," Ken said. "Because of Rob, this man was caught." He paused and swallowed. "Before Rob disappeared, nothing had been done. Hopefully this will not happen to anyone else!"

Ken could talk forever about his brother. "Something people don't often know is that we worked together. I taught him how to paint," Ken said.

"Did you have your own business?"

"The last two summers, we painted houses in the community for extra money." Ken looked away. Rob would no longer be painting, this summer or again." His nose twitched. "I think it was because of his painting experience that he went to check out that summer job."

Ken wiped his eyes on his sleeve. Everyone felt like Rob's disappearance was a little bit their fault. Everyone who loved Rob had their own version of how they could have saved him, protected him, altered the course of events on December 11, 1978.

If only. If only. If only.

Mrs Piest rested her hand on her son's shoulder. They shared a warm glance. She could see pieces of Rob in her only remaining son. But only pieces. Rob and Ken had shared similar eyes, but Ken's were larger in shape; Ken's facial features were more pronounced, and Rob's were softer. Elizabeth and Ken made sure the reporter knew that they appreciated everything the Des Plaines Police Department was doing to look for Rob.

"What has your experience been like, with the police department?" Wessell asked, in response to Mrs Piest's comment.

"They deserve a lot of credit," Ken said. "It looks like they have solved a crime that not a lot before seemed to pay attention to." Ken was grateful for the police, but he wanted to keep the conversation on his brother. "Rob's everywhere." He looked around the house, picturing his brother after a gymnastics tournament, watching a movie on the couch with his girlfriend, running over to his brother, excited to show him a new comic book.

"Seems like he looked up to you a lot."

"He looked up to me. My whole family. He loved us all and we loved spending time together. In Boy Scouts, my dad was his troop leader. Rob was only a few merit badges from becoming an Eagle Scout. I'm glad my dad and Rob got that experience of Boy Scouts together."

Ken's lips quivered. "No one will ever get used to Rob being gone. He made you feel special, you know? All I can do is try to accept that he is gone." Ken continued. "Maybe he didn't die in vain."

THE TIME BETWEEN the fall and spring semesters brought out a lot of feelings in seniors who had worlds with options. Kim's feet straddled: staying or going. Should she stay with her boyfriend or leave him? Where would she get into college, in Chicago or further from home? Would Rob's body be found? Would this cloud of loss be a part of her life forever? Would the snow ever stop? Would spring come, with the hope for something new?

So much lay ahead, yet so much remained undone here, in town. The reporters let up on her as more bodies were pulled from Gacy's house. Kim took a day off from Nisson Pharmacy to visit friends after the Christmas holiday. They weren't yet bogged down again by pulling books from lockers or staying up past midnight to complete homework assignments. That evening, Kim spent the time decompressing with her mom. Her dog, Jiffy, jumped onto the couch with Kim and her mom. She didn't want to eat her dinner. This worried Kim. The nightly news played in the background, the Gacy house always on the periphery of anything she did. That night in her diary she wrote:

27/12/78

Had a talk with mom about Cory. I don't feel as close to him anymore. It's too bad we didn't see each other today because absence from him makes me grow very independent and I won't see him tomorrow, Friday or Saturday and who knows about Sunday. Did homework. Officer Adams called. Will drop my pictures off at the store. Total of 16 bodies at Gacy's, a definite trial.

On December 28, the body count hit 21 at Gacy's house. Searchers still had more places to dig, more skeletons to find. That evening, Kim reconnected with Cory. She taught him sign language and decided he wasn't so bad. She loved languages, and sign language was engaging to her. She'd use it in her first career, many years later, as an occupational therapist.

She was desperate to stay connected to Cory. He was a good boyfriend, but she didn't feel capable of reciprocating his affection in the way she'd once wanted before Gacy. Kim was eager to find ways for them to stay connected, sign language being her newest idea. The following year the two would read V.C. Andrews's novel *Flowers in the Attic* together. Something about the otherworldly nature of the book's isolating attic, the gap between confinement and reality, would resonate with both of them.

ON DECEMBER 30, Kim drove to work. The temperature was a cold but manageable 32 degrees. She parked her car close to the pharmacy's front door, but not too close. Employees were not supposed to take the prime parking spots that faced the store, those were for customers. Her shoes made a clunk-clunk-clunk noise as they crunched into the snow on the pavement. A bell rang when she pulled open the door. She looked around for a co-worker to greet. But no one popped their head from behind one of the aisles or from behind the photo counter.

She yanked her scarf off her neck and removed her coat, thawing as she walked to the back of the store. The place had once been so lively, especially at the end of summer and in early fall. Kim loved connecting with her co-workers, making them laugh. The snap and fizz of pop bottles bought next door, to kick off the shifts. High school jobs were supposed to be opportunities to develop a work ethic and make friends. Everyone knew this wasn't Kim's career, but it was a chance to make some money and meet people. Kim thought the friendships she made at Nisson Pharmacy were meant to keep.

The heater buzzed above her in the back of the store. Larry was on the phone in the office. Not wanting to bother him, she smiled and walked past him to hang up her coat. The December 1978 schedule hung on the bulletin board in the back, out of sight from the patrons who entered to buy their pain medicine or candy or a belated Christmas gift. The edge of the schedule was curling from the moisture in the air. She brought her finger up to the date: December 30, 1978. Rob was scheduled. She traced his name in black ink with her finger. She closed her eyes and pictured the night of December 11, which popped across her mind like small explosions. Nineteen days? That it was. Many people cannot remember what they did the day before. She couldn't remember much from the morning of December 11, but she was surprised how clear the evening was. Memory, a devil. Rob's image was sharp, and she could smell the leftover sweat from gym practice, the dried snow from his parka. She could feel the warmth of the fleece inside his pockets. She could see the way his hair flipped in the wind as he walked out into the endless night.

After Kim's shift, she drove to the Piest house, where she had an open invitation at this point. She had felt Rob's presence so powerfully at the pharmacy and wanted to be with the people who understood his absence acutely. Parking on the street in front of their house, she left the car running. Her fingers fumbled with the keys, still in the ignition. The heater warmed her core. A cold tear plummeted onto her lap. She looked down, wiped it off her work pants with her thumb.

"I wish he was still here," she said aloud, alone in the car.

She looked to the Piests' front door. Over the past 19 days, she had felt safe walking through that front door. She knew Rob once had, too. Breath fogged the car. Her head tilted onto the chilled driver's side window. The warmth of her face cleared a halo in the glass. She remembered how, as a kid, she loved writing messages for her sister and her parents on cold car windows. She wrote ROB with a heart next to the B.

"What am I doing here?" she asked herself. She pulled down the mirror. Pressing her palms into her eyes, she attempted to stop. Stop feeling. She saw her reflection, no longer that of a little girl. Not even a young adult whose largest ambition was getting into college. Disappearance and death dissipated grades and boyfriends and futures. What did her choices matter, she thought. What would she do with this singular life of hers if anyone could choose to take it from her?

Kim realised that she probably liked visiting the Piests because they felt it, too. The shattering. The way the world kept turning, yet theirs was mired in December 11. She remembered how sad a classmate had been during junior year of high school when his parents divorced. Rob's disappearance, of course, was nothing like that. But she now understood what it meant to feel as if the path had been pulled out from under one's feet. She didn't know what the next day would hold, but she decided where she would go next.

Her hand turned off the ignition and she opened her car door and walked inside the Piest home, for company, for conversation, for memory.

On New Year's Eve, it snowed over 8.9 inches. The winter of

1978–1979 broke records, totaling 89.7 inches of snow. Dive teams continued to search for Rob. Other victims had been found in the river: Frank "Dale" Landingin, James Mazzara, and one who would be identified later in January, Tim O'Rourke. But Rob was still missing. Gacy had been charged with the murder of Robert Piest. Terry Sullivan remained confident about prosecuting Gacy, even without Rob's body. Sullivan was named the chief prosecutor in the case, to be assisted by Robert Egan and William Kunkle. Sam Amirante and Robert Motta were the defence.

In the first week of 1979, news reports announced that Gacy would undergo psychiatric evaluation. The judge also gave conditional permission for Amirante to bring in his own psychiatrists, as long as they would be identified to the court in advance.

By the new year, 27 bodies had been pulled from under Gacy's home. Lt. Ron Fox of the Will County Sheriff's Office, whose jurisdiction included the area where Rob's body was presumed to be, just south of Joliet, halted the search for his remains. It was just too cold. Operations would resume once the weather warmed. Boaters and divers would again be sent out. Meanwhile, barge and river lock operators had been alerted to look out for a body. Fox told *The Journal* that if there was a body, it would be found.

Neighbours and onlookers had crowded W. Summerdale for almost two weeks. Those working at the dig said they would not give up until they were certain there was not another body to be found. During Gacy's indictment and arraignment, searching and digging continued. Later, in March, a 28th body would be found under Gacy's driveway, and the 29th body would be found under the dining room. Cook County medical examiner

Dr Robert J. Stein had been shocked and perplexed about what was coming across his desk. And then he found clarity.

He shared his insights in a taping of Chicago News Conference, a WMAQ radio program. The wind whipped outside the radio show's building, and the headlights of cars lit up the streets.

"Can you give us an update on the bodies coming out of Gacy's house?" the radio host asked. The men sat across from each other, each with a microphone and headphones. They recapped the bodies being pulled from underneath Gacy's house. They discussed the chatter in the media about Gacy being insane. The prevailing view across the nation was that one had to be crazy to do what Gacy had done. But Dr Stein had a different opinion. He wanted Chicago and anyone who would listen to understand.

"A sane person could have done all of this. And a sane person can go all the way to the electric chair."

"Is that what's going through your head?"

"Absolutely. Look, the placement of the bodies was orderly, well thought-out."

"This perception, this debate between sanity and insanity, will influence the upcoming trial."

"Absolutely. I stand by my belief that this man was sane when he buried these young men. Most of the bodies were laid in long rows, lining three outside walls of the house. Other bodies were intricately placed diagonally inside that pattern. The bodies inside that pattern were pointed toward the centre of the crawl space like spokes on a wheel."

The radio host mouthed, W-O-W. "This is nothing we have read or heard yet in all the press on these murders.

"It's upsetting. They are all boys, too. All strangled, but one was stabbed to death."

"How many have been identified?"

"We are working hard on this. It's not easy, given the state and decomposition of many of the bodies. An anthropologist is helping us out this Thursday, in an effort to determine the ages of the victims, as well as understand how long they have been buried. So far six out of 29 bodies linked to Gacy have been identified."

"How are you identifying them?"

"Dental records. Authorities have obtained dental records from families of missing youths."

"Any word on a trial?"

"A grand jury is scheduled to begin investigating the Gacy murders this week. So far Gacy has only been charged with one murder, that of 15-year-old Robert Piest, whose body has not been found."

"Thank you, Dr Stein, for coming on the show. This is Chicago News Conference On WMAQ. Have a good night."

Outside, the winter clouds hung low in the sky and the moon, a waning gibbous, illuminated the night.

RADIO STATIONS DELVE deep into this case. The angles one could take to discuss it remained limitless. Kim began listening to the radio when she could, although it was easier to clip the newspapers when she had a spare moment. If her name appeared in the paper, she always underlined it in pen, not because of pride, but out of concern. She was worried someone would come for her, like the monster who had taken her friend.

Ken Piest called Kim that Sunday night, after the radio show interviewed Dr Stein. He told her Father O'Shansey of St Eugene's Church was holding a memorial service for all of Gacy's victims on Thursday at 8pm, and he asked if she would go.

"I'll go," she said. "Will you?"

"I'm going," Ken said. "But my mom is not."

By January 7, 1979, 10 bodies had been identified: James Mazzara, 20; Frank Landingin, 19; Rick Johnston, 17; John Szyc, 19; Gregory Godzik, 17; Michael Bonnin, 17; Robert Gilroy, 18; Jon Prestidge, 20; Russell Nelson, 21. Eight of the young men were retrieved from under Gacy's house. Landingin and Mazzara were pulled from the Des Plaines River in Will County. The same river Rob was said to be adrift in, somewhere out there.

On Monday, January 8, Gacy was indicted in the murders of seven young men. Everyone knew there were more bodies, but this was the number able to be presented to the jury at the time.

ELIZABETH PIEST SAT on the far side of the courtroom in the Criminal Courts Building. Under her short, permed hair, her lips were thin; her eyes looked bruised from lack of sleep. She felt on display, her grief far too visible. The room seemed too full, too packed.

Gacy was brought in, secured by handcuffs. His dusty hair was parted to the left, and he wore an ill-fitting chocolate-brown blazer, white dress shirt, and black tie. He looked more like a job applicant than a man accused of murder. Half a dozen guards surrounded him, seeming more apprehensive than Gacy was as they entered the building. Gacy towered over his lawyer. He was obscured from Mrs Piest's view, but she could make out an outline of him in the room, behind bullet-proof glass.

Judge Richard Fitzgerald read Gacy's indictments. Elizabeth's lips quivered when Judge Fitzgerald said, "For the murder of Robert Piest…for the deviate sexual assault of Robert Piest…for the aggravated kidnapping of Robert Piest… for taking indecent liberties with a child, Robert Piest."

On Thursday, January 11, the *Chicago Tribune* ran a story entitled, "A mother weeps as Gacy is indicted." During the hearing, defence attorney Amirante expressed concern. "Nowhere in the annals of history has there been such pre-trial publicity," he shouted through the court building. "I don't think it's possible for my client to ever get a fair trial. That grand jury had to be tainted." Amirante also sought to halt the search for bodies, on grounds that the financial ruin for his client would be immense.

Chief Deputy State's Attorney William Kunkle responded, "The search will stop when we are sure to a scientific degree of certainty that there isn't another body in that house."

Gacy pleaded not guilty. He would be held without bond. Friends and acquaintances of Kim called her house all evening. She was talked about on WGN Radio and Channel 7. She wrote in her journal that her phone did not stop ringing.

As WINTER WORE on Kim found herself at a crossroads, with her boyfriend, with her mother, with herself. At one point, her mom asked her not to date Cory anymore. Her daughter had changed and Barbara wanted her little girl back. Her mother felt Kim was losing herself in the business of school, sports, friends, dating. Something was always keeping Kim busy: King of Hearts Dance, five to nine at Nisson Pharmacy, checking in on the Piests, sneaking off with her boyfriend. Barbara was realising, swiftly, how hard it would be to protect her daughter if something went wrong. But Kim's preoccupation with the bustle of a teenage life was meant to distract her from what was really causing a change. The damage had begun when Rob went missing.

WINTER SNOW MELTED in April. Perfect Virginia bluebells, blood-roots, tulips, and black-eyed Susans blossomed throughout Illinois. The Des Plaines River unfroze. It flowed into the Illinois River south of Joliet. On Monday, April 9, 1979, a crane operator spotted a body floating near Dresden Lock. Dan Callahan, a lockmaster, called Lt Ron Fox. The body was pulled from the river and quickly transported to a funeral home. Des Plaines authorities met the body at the funeral home in New Lenox, Illinois. From there, they travelled with it by car to a hospital in Joliet. By early afternoon, a positive identification was made using dental records. The body was that of Robert Jerome Piest.

A call was made to Mr and Mrs Piest that afternoon. Their son had been found.

9/4/79

They found Rob today, in Morris where the Des Plaines River meets the Illinois. I was at work when Nathan's dad called me. I then went to the Piests' until 11.30. Talked to Nathan. He will be coming home. I'm glad, we need each other. Terry Sullivan called while I was there. Autopsy will be tomorrow (Tues). Dental something will be Thursday. Funeral is not planned yet but will be soon. I will stay home part of the day tomorrow. I need some time for myself.

The medical examiner reported later that week that death was determined to have been caused by suffocation. Kim was called into the high school counsellor's office at Maine North, to speak with her counsellor, Mr Tanner. She'd spoken to him before, when Rob first disappeared. But this was different. Any imaginative fragment that Rob was alive, that none of this happened to her friend, dissipated when Rob's body was found, bloated and pale in the frigid river. In the counsellor's office, she broke down. Sitting in the wooden chair across from him, she said, "I don't know who I am or what to do."

Mr Tanner told her that her feelings were valid. She had experienced something that many people would never understand. With the trial looming, and with her being the prime witness, the ordeal was not over now that they had found Rob's body. "You can either be a victim to all this, or you can find purpose, find meaning."

At the time, she didn't know what he meant. Maybe he was saying she could do good by Rob, for Rob. His words stayed with her as she went about her busy life. She would come to understand that she could reframe how she saw the events. If she had not saved the receipt, how many other boys would Gacy have murdered? She began, then, to view herself and Rob as Hansel and Gretel, and the receipt as a little breadcrumb Rob left behind in Gacy's house, to do his part in stopping Gacy.

She told the counsellor, "Maybe Rob dropped the receipt, as a sign for us to find him. To prove he was there. Maybe he knew the worst was coming, but that receipt would help us find him."

She visualised the two of them as a team, stopping a goliath monster.

On April 23, Gacy was charged with the murder of 26 more young men and boys. The grand jury returned within two hours of being presented the evidence. A formal announcement was released: Prosecutors would seek the death penalty.

CHAPTER NINE

ALL SAINTS

2022

In Des Plaines, the end of summer carries a feeling of wanting to hang on, like eating the last slice of cut watermelon. There is a sweetness to enjoying the last of something. Out the window of the hotel room, I watch the planes fly overhead. Every few minutes, a new one caresses the sky, off to new endings, fresh beginnings.

I sip my now-cold coffee from the free breakfast downstairs. My laptop is perched on the desk in front of me. Because I am going to visit Rob today, I need to check something. I open an older email David had sent me when we first started discussing the case. Six months ago, he sent me Rob's toxicology report and autopsy. Although he hesitated to share the documents with me, knowing it would be difficult for me emotionally, he thought it was important for me to see Rob's ending. It took me many attempts to open the report and read the medical findings of Rob's body.

I open the zip drive. The scanned pages are yellowed and worn. I recognise Dr Stein's name, his commentary. It is difficult to connect the boy in my mom's early diary entries with the body in Dr Stein's records. I envisioned him kayaking, stocking over-the-counter vitamins and medicine, snapping photos out in the woods. Sneaking off with his then-girlfriend during lunch. Sticking the landing on the thick mat on the gym mat, wiping chalk off his hands and watching it fall to the floor. Even in his disappearance, his post-mortem body had remained figurative to me. The post-mortem made Rob's death real. Here, on the page, my mind could not escape what had happened to him. A body was both a relief and an anchor of truth.

Rob's system contained no opiates or barbiturates. Nothing but a small dose of alcohol. Gacy had that Tiki bar just off the kitchen, near where he claimed Rob was murdered. I wondered what Gacy served him. Was it a shot? A mixed drink? A beer? The report, like most of the typed documents from 1978–1979, had been prepared on a typewriter. This elongated typeface makes the document feel as if it is from a different world.

The pathology report and protocol, conducted by Dr Stein and the Institute of Forensic Medicine, is lengthier, three pages. The top of the report has Dr Stein's physical observations of Rob. He says the deceased appeared to be 17 (he was 15 at death), 68 inches, and 120 pounds. In two columns Dr Stein describes the external evaluation.

MUSCULATURE:	**SKELETON:**
Pigmentation	Slender
Edema	Medium
Decubitus	Powerful
	Deformed
	Amputations

THE NEXT SECTION on the document is "SIGNS OF DEATH". Dr Stein reported Rob's corneas to be cloudy-turbid, dry, and shrunken. This state of his body is unfortunately on par for being underwater this long. For the decomposition, he listed: skin-slip, tissue gas, discoloration, dehydration, putrefaction. After that, many paragraphs detailed the full picture of Rob's death.

HISTORY OF DEATH:

Hair, eyes, soft tissue of nose, 80% of the scalp missing due to skeletonisation of the skull.

Subject was found in Illinois River near Morris, Ill. For further history refer to chart number 231 of April, 1979. Subject pronounced dead at the scene by Chief Deputy Coroner of Grundy County, April 9, 1979 at 1.05pm. Subject brought to the Institute of Forensic Medicine by police officer number 101 district number 664.

The head consists of skeletonised remains which is attached by means of cervical vertebra. Only fleshy decomposed tissue present are the right left masseter muscles as well as some musculature over the face.

Scalp in the frontal parietal region is absent, some scalp is present on the left occipital region. Remnants of the right and left eyes are present. A number of teeth are missing, these have been documented by the dentist. The lower jaw is exposed and devoid of any tissue. The neck structures exposed, some of the musculature is evident. Mummification and adipose formation of the skin is present. The upper extremities show the absence of terminal phalanges of both the right and left hands, these are clearly disarticulated, the genitalia are those of a male.

> Two brown coloured knitted socks are worn by the
> subject. Examination of the back shows preservation of the skin. Examination of both the anterior
> and posterior aspects show no evidence of any
> incised wounds or any bullet wounds.

DR STEIN FINISHED the autopsy report by stating that, in his opinion, the cause of death of Robert J. Piest was suffocation due to foreign bodies (paper-like) in throat. There is further commentary in the report: foreign body impaction of the mouth, throat, and larynx; fractured hyoid bone, a bone shaped like a horseshoe in the centre of the throat; post-mortem decomposition; absence of skin, muscle, and segments of bones or extremities, probably due to crustaceans and fish. The final evaluation from Dr Stein:

> Based on gross anatomic findings, the cause of
> death is suffocation with asphyxia due to foreign
> body impaction, throat and larynx. Manner of
> death: homicide.

THE BROWN SOCKS and the broken hyoid bone catch in my throat when I read the report. Gacy's nasty rope trick spins in my head. Gacy had shown the rope trick widely. It was all too easy to picture. Then there are Rob's socks, still on his feet. I feel motherly when I imagine the socks covering his ankles, the crushing weight of a body disposed of with only this part covered. There is an intimacy when it comes to putting socks on a child's feet. The simple act is the result of a complex care routine: not losing them in the washing machine, checking for holes, slipping them over a toddler's feet before they take their first steps.

Each morning when my children were little, I helped them

through the ritual. Sometimes a sock creased the wrong way, causing the little one to holler for a re-adjustment. In winter, they enjoyed sleeping in socks. Socks offered warmth. They offered protection. But they also offered a habitual form of love.

I imagined Elizabeth Piest taking the laundry in a basket, finding matching brown socks for her son, slipping them in his drawer.

It is nearing dusk when I make it to All Saints Catholic Cemetery and Mausoleum. Also nearing is closing time. The facility is almost 100 years old, having been established in 1923, and located at 700 North River Road. The setting sun slices in through the car window with a heavenly intensity. The clouds are minimal, but present enough to leave a bright light in the sky. I park outside the mausoleum where Rob rests. Nathan warned me the crypt was difficult to find, but gave directions. We were supposed to be here together, but he decided he could not do it. It would have been too difficult. When he visited Rob, he usually did so alone.

Inside, the mausoleum feels endless, like a maze. Beautiful stained glass climbs from floor to ceiling at the ends of hallways and corridors. The air is chilly because of the stone floors and walls. The last time I had been in a place like this was when my mom took me on an unforgettable trip to Italy. So many popes and dignitaries buried among each other in St Peter's Basilica. I had a similar feeling halfway around the world as I did in this mausoleum off the main road. A stillness, a quieting of my breath. "Better hurry," a security guard says, coming from around the corner. "We are closing soon."

But I struggle to find the crypt in the vastness of this building. I pull up my phone to confirm I am close. Even then, I had only about 10 minutes to visit Rob's burial site. I had thought closing time was an hour later than it actually was. I turn left, then right, and I see the tomb in the corner, by a window.

Before coming here, I had seen a photo of Rob's crypt online. His family is buried around him. Only his sister, Kerry, is still alive today. Elizabeth Piest is the most recent person laid to rest here. She died less than a year ago, peacefully, at age 89, in December of 2021.

I bend my knees and place my hands over Rob's name etched in stone. I had wondered for many years about the significance of this mausoleum. It offered a different kind of security and protection than a burial plot outside would. Part of me always wonders if Mr and Mrs Piest made the choice to keep their son at a distance from people, from the elements. Rob was lost in the river for nearly four months. Beyond the terror of Gacy, the water and the fish defiled his body, too. In the mausoleum, nothing could touch him, ever again. No one can stand on him from above. No one can dig him up in the night. A security guard patrols, watching the guests. It feels secure in here. Safe.

Robert J. Piest
1963-1978

Between his birth and death years, a red heart is peeling. Only a sliver of red film remains. Above his name is a brass-like figurine attached to the crypt, Jesus nailed to the cross. Next to him lay his mother, and next to her his father. An empty tomb rested above Mr and Mrs Piest. Above it is another double tomb spot, presumably for Kerry and then for Kenneth, born in 1954 and deceased in 2007. He passed a year after his father. It is said over the years that the Piest men took losing Rob unbearably hard. Mr and Mrs Piest divorced after losing Rob, but still found their way back to be close to one another in their deaths.

It was strange and beautiful to view the final resting places of a family that I had come to love through the eyes of my mother. How can we love someone we've never met? Perhaps it is easier than we think.

THE PIEST FAMILY set up a foundation in Rob's memory, The Robert J. Piest Memorial Foundation. On Saturday, April 14, 1979, the Piest family, their lawyer, and members of the Des Plaines Police Department made a public announcement about the award. During the press conference, Elizabeth Piest and Kerry stood together with their hands interlocked to give strength to one another. Elizabeth Piest could not speak. A statement released by the family read, "The purpose of the foundation is to recognise and support those individuals and organisations or activities committed to helping reduce crime against children."

Someone from the press asked how they would decide who received the award. Harold Piest responded that the family felt unqualified to decide who should receive the yearly grants. A board would be selected, from diverse areas of work: journalism, medicine, law enforcement, child welfare. "There's always more room for people to help out in the field of crimes against children," Harold Piest said.

A benefit for The Robert J. Piest Memorial Foundation was held in the community at The Name Is Games and McGreevy's in Talisman Village. Everyone was welcome to come, enjoy themselves, and help raise money in memory of Rob. Although the foundation had hopeful intentions, somewhere along the way the foundation fizzled out. I was saddened to hear it was not running anymore, but I also understood. Grief and the nature of life after loss accelerate incongruities. The fizzling of the foundation also represented a larger metaphor for the victims. As time waned on, people talked less about them, but never stopped talking about Gacy.

After leaving the mausoleum, I drive to the location of Rob's funeral, which was held on April 18, 1979, in Our Lady of Hope Church. The church is not far from All Saints Cemetery, and when I park, my mind, in its typical fashion, imagines what this space looked like before all the high-rises went up around it. The church and some fields alone in their peaceful solitude. Three hundred people flooding the walkway into the sanctuary. I pictured my mom walking in with the Piests. She wore a blue dress with white flowers on it. The dress was her one nice one, and she would wear it to her sister's baby shower three years later.

During the service, someone in the Piest family presented my mom with a plaque to thank her for her help in discovering what happened to Rob. The plaque was about a foot long, wood with a bronze-coloured plate and a poem engraved on its front. It meant a lot to my mom that Rob's family recognised her as someone who was integral to stopping Gacy from harming more boys. The poem called on Rob, now with the Lord, asking him to protect the rest of us down here, on Earth. Like the good friend, son, and brother he was.

The plaque had been tucked away in my parents' garage for decades. It was something I passed by on my way to get my bike or procure a boogie board for summer beach days. I didn't realise that it was in a cardboard box on the shelves for all those years. I expected maybe an etched photo of Rob with a memorial quote, something one would find on a tomb. But I didn't expect a poem. There is shelter in poetry. The words didn't have to be perfect, they only had to be from the heart, and they were. It was a nice touch to a ceremony to honour Rob. No one needed to give my mom a plaque. But someone did.

Reporters attended the memorial service. My mom saw herself on the news that night. "It was surreal," she tells me, later, on the phone. "It was weird to see myself on TV. I was shown walking behind the Piests." I imagine she looked like a second daughter, the same withdrawn expression on her face as the Piest family wore. My mom didn't feel she was meant for the bright lights of television. Although she was quite social as a girl, she was also shy. She loved staying busy, but it took a lot out of her, which sometimes resulted in headaches, sick days, long baths, and sleeping in. Nowadays she would be called an extroverted introvert.

On Friday, April 20, 1979, Maine West High School's newspaper, *The Westerner*, released an article following the funeral. A faculty member in attendance, Mr Coburn, was interviewed for the article, "Rob Piest's Funeral Held". Mr Coburn reflected on the service. "The service was very comforting to me, and I hope it was to family and friends. Rob's death was a real loss to us all."

The sun swiftly sets over Our Lady of Hope. I take photos of the gorgeous vincas hugging a tree near the pathway inside the church. The grass surrounding Our Lady of Hope is gorgeously green and thick. I snap a few photos of the chrysanthemums in pots surrounding a statue of Mary near the front entrance. Her head is bowed down and her hands held up, as though she is mid-prayer. Her eyes are shut to maintain focus at the task at hand, and a rosary adorns her neck.

Knowing Rob's memorial service was held here gives me a feeling of peace. If Gacy's house made me inextricably unnerved, this place made me feel weightless, like floating in a pool at night while watching the stars.

BACK IN THE CAR, on my way to find a drive-thru for dinner, I consider my instinct to pick up the camera. I first started taking photography classes in high school. I found the dark room mysterious and a little sexy, the pools of cold water, the strings with clips to hang damp paper on. I used to imagine how it would feel to kiss a crush in the dark room, both eyes meeting in the dimness after choosing which negative to develop. Rob and my mom had to feel the same sensation of creation, relishing the complexity of art, the eye of precision, the promise of something on the verge of developing.

Photography opens questions that don't always have answers. Why were the small white flowers circling the tree at the church so quietly precise? Who had dropped off the plastic pots of early fall mums? How did it feel to get one's photo taken coming and going from this place, for Rob's funeral? Photographs offered a way to survive history, to approach a murder.

DURING THE SAME week Rob's body was found, the demolition of Gacy's house began. The roof was pulled off, the foundation was drilled and broken into smaller pieces. The walls were struck down. The driveway was torn up, debris hauled away. Even some of the earth below the property was removed. Within two weeks, there was no sign of what had once existed on the property. New dirt was brought in to lift the lot up to a proper height, so it didn't look like a torn-up graveyard. Although it was spring, nothing beautiful or green grew from that space. Birds flying overhead dropped seeds, but nothing of substance took root.

By spring of 1979, Des Plaines authorities were exhausted. Many of them had been running on survival mode and adrenaline to get the job done: charge Gacy; find bodies. Then in May they were faced with another one of the country's worst moments in history. They'd just finished working on the grave site, now well known as the country's worst murder site in history, when they were called to O'Hare Airport.

On May 25, 1979, an American Airlines flight headed for Los Angeles fell from the sunny sky shortly after take-off. It was Memorial Day weekend. People were headed to the beaches and the star-filled countryside of Los Angeles for a good time. Flight 191 was outbound and midair when its left engine detached. The plane made it less than a mile off the runway before crashing in an open field next to a trailer park. The crash site rested just north east of O'Hare, at the intersection of Touhy Avenue, the same street as Nisson Pharmacy.

Before my trip, I spoke to a man named Joe who worked as part of the surveillance team while the Des Plaines Police were trying to make sure Gacy did not disappear before authorities charged him. Joe told me that after all these years, he never forgot the scent of dead bodies. He could not erase the odours of the bodies buried under Gacy's house, and then the fresh scent of death from the ones that burned on American Airlines Flight 191.

"I couldn't believe it," he said to me. "We had just finished this horrible thing at one place, then right away we were called to another."

The crash site fell within the Des Plaines Police Department's area of responsibility. Joe's team was called for recovery and rescue. On board the DC-10, 258 passengers and 13 crew members all died on impact, causing a bright and billowy black explosion. Two people who worked at a nearby repair shop were also killed when the plane crashed. The total of 273 fatalities made it the deadliest plane crash in United States history.

"How could we have just left this massive, history-breaking body retrieval at Gacy's, then attend another history-breaking tragedy less than half a year later?" he asked me.

It's a question with no answer. A ripple effect of that crash connected with the one already radiating from W. Summerdale Avenue. All the families and friends who loved and lost someone due to a faulty engine. The people who witnessed the tragedy or had to recover the bodies and identify them. The same sheriff and medical examiner teams were tasked with both jobs. When American Flight 191 combusted, Terry Sullivan was eating lunch a mile away and preparing for the trial against Gacy. He set his napkin on the table and pushed his chair back as he heard and witnessed the plane roll in the air, fall, then explode. Black smoke, a screeching boom. He found his way as quickly as he could to the crash site. Everyone ran in and out of Nisson Pharmacy to purchase film from Kim. She was ready to get out of this town with death everywhere she turned.

In early January of 1980, my mom, a freshman at Winona State University, received a knock on her dorm room. A strange man handed her an envelope. It had been about six months since she left Des Plaines. She pressed her fingertips into the parcel. She could run from her hometown, but she couldn't hide.

Back in the hotel room, I pull a blanket and my mom's old diary onto the couch. I turn the page to a new decade, out of the 1970s and into the 1980s. The decade of determining.

CHAPTER TEN

WITNESS

1980

Kim sat on her freshman dorm bed, debating whether she should head down to the dining hall for dinner with friends or open this very serious-looking piece of mail. Her hair was still frozen from the walk home from swim practice. At Winona State, she was on both the swim and dive teams. Kim pulled the folded piece of thick white paper from the pristine envelope. The weight of the document in her hands sets off nerves.

> THE PEOPLE OF THE STATE OF ILLINOIS V. John Wayne Gacy. WE COMMAND THAT YOU SUMMON: Kimberly Byers to appear before the honourable Louis Garippo on February 18, 1980, in room 600. Circuit Court, 26th Street and California Avenue, Chicago, Illinois, at 9am. YOU ARE COMMANDED ALSO to bring the following: This subpoena will be of a continuing nature until your testimony is completed. YOUR FAILURE TO APPEAR IN RESPONSE TO THIS SUBPOENA WILL SUBJECT YOU TO PUNISHMENT FOR CONTEMPT OF THIS COURT.

Terry Sullivan's name was on the bottom of the document.

He had called her in advance, so she knew this document would be coming. She just didn't know when. At college, she was trying to create distance between herself and Gacy. As far as she knew, no one on campus knew about the receipt or Rob, which allowed her a freedom she'd forgotten, one that was hers before this nightmare began. Returning, she worried, would tear the stitching out. She'd be vulnerable on the stand. She'd look into the eyes of the same men who had tried to silence her – the defence attorneys and Gacy himself – who had accused her of lying. She steadied herself to take the stand and tell the truth.

AFTER ROB'S BODY was found in the river, Kim stopped writing in her diary. During his disappearance, its pages had offered a space to turn to, as someone lost in the wilderness turns to a compass. She decided to pull out her diary in early January of 1980, right around the time she would receive this subpoena in the mail.

6/1/80 (2.30am)

My god. Haven't wrote in this for a long time. I'm in school now (Winona State) and tonite is my last night home. I'm still seeing Cory (believe it or not) and we are on a high right now. He gave me a black agate ring for Christmas. During these past months we've had our lows also. My hair is short now (as of 2/1/80) and I've grown up some.

The trial was set to begin on February 6, 1980. It would take place almost 14 months after authorities pulled the remains of 29 bodies from under the house, and another four from the river. Sullivan and the prosecution team decided to begin with family, those who loved the victims. For proof of murder, there must, too, be proof of life.

SULLIVAN CALLED KIM and decided to move her testimony up nine days. Besides Elizabeth Piest and co-workers who worked in Nisson Pharmacy on December 11, 1978, Kim Byers was one person who could provide Rob's proof of life. She could also detail his disappearance, the proof of death.

When Sullivan called Kim a final time before the trial, he said, "Be on the lookout for your plane tickets in the mail. You will be flying Mississippi Valley Airlines, Flight number 304. It will be a Thursday. We want to make sure no weather stops you from arriving on time to the trial. You will fly back to school on Sunday, depart from O'Hare at 4pm and arrive in La Crosse, Flight number 305." La Crosse was a small public airport on the Wisconsin-Minneapolis border. Mississippi Valley Airlines was a popular way to travel in the upper Midwest. The airline however, would exist only between 1968 and 1985. Kim scribbled down her flight number and arrival and departure times. She'd make sure to pack that piece of paper and bring it with her to Chicago. She'd hang on to it for decades to come.

She pulled open her dorm room's desk drawer and rummaged for a pen. On her calendar, tacked onto a bulletin board on her wall, she wrote: 'go home' on February 7, 'trial' for February 8 and 9.

The underlining matched the intensity she felt stewing

inside her. Her hometown had seared in her a trauma that she wouldn't learn to process, fully, for decades. Des Plaines would never be the place of safety it was when she was a kid. It held danger, especially for women and children.

Kim stared at the calendar page for February 1980. The artist Václav Vaca had adorned it with mystical paintings of unicorns.

This month, the primary image showed a maiden with hair the colour of an orange sunset. Her mouth was closed. Her gaze was direct, projecting strong eye contact. Around her shoulders was a baby lamb, or was it a baby unicorn? The maiden secures the baby animal with both of her hands, gripping its legs, just above the hooves. The creature's fur is clumpy and white. Its gaze is turned upward, toward the sky. The maiden is barefoot, exiting a forest green bush. Behind her, the sun sets behind snow-capped mountains. Close to her, on her right side, is a unicorn. The unicorn appears to be adolescent. Its shy, sleepy eyes avoid the onlooker.

She would not know it at the time, but 43 years later her future daughter would reach out to Václav Vaca, who would tell her about the meaning behind this painting. He posed the question: What is the real meaning of something beautiful? He said the maiden and the unicorn were an ancient theme. A virtue of the unicorn horn was supposedly its healing power. And he said that perhaps this is also the meaning of art: healing and saving the world through beauty.

Kim tried to imagine herself as the woman in the image, carrying the baby lamb. In folklore, the lamb holds many narratives: the sacrificial lamb; the lamb as offering. But in the image, the woman does not look like she is taking the animal to slaughter. She appears to be a mother to the animal, trying to protect it from harm. The unicorn materialises as her faithful friend to walk the path with her.

Kim envisioned herself and Rob walking a path together back to Des Plaines. She kept reminding herself of this, or she wouldn't have been able to make sense of how to proceed. It was too tragic, too much. She needed to find a purpose, find meaning in his death. She saw the maiden in herself. She knew she could take the stand and look Gacy in the eye. She knew she could do it because she loved Rob, just as the goddess loved her animals.

Kim flew from La Crosse, Wisconsin, to Chicago, Illinois, on the second day of Gacy's trial, as the people at home, from around the country turned on their TVs and turned up their radios to follow the story that both horrified and fascinated them. The trial was not televised, but a constant chatter erupted on the nightly news to discuss the updates. On the day of her flight, she was grateful there was no delay. Winters were so very unpredictable. She sipped a 7 Up in a window seat, to help settle her stomach. Turbulence rumbled, and she felt a hotness sweltering across her face. She sucked an ice cube to cool herself down.

On the plane she felt like everyone was watching her, but of course they weren't. She felt as if she was carrying a secret, something no one knew. Perhaps they would come to know her later if she did her job at the trial. As she stared out the window, down to the flat earth of suburbia below, Kim untucked her hair from behind her ear, letting her newly-styled, short hair fall in front of her face. Her long hair had carried with it so much sadness. She hoped cutting it would help purge unwanted memories.

THE CLICKING SHUTTERS of cameras and buzzing of voices speaking into microphones echoed in the grim limestone Criminal Courts Building at 26th and California in downtown Chicago. The marble corridors were packed with onlookers. The courtroom had been expanded to hold a herd of press. Extra pews were provided for the men and women with microphones and cameras; 50 spots were slated to be taken by the news outlets. Additional seating was provided for the families of the victims who wanted to be there, hoping their boys would get their justice. The jury box was expanded, too, to accommodate the 12 jury members and four alternates.

The prosecution team sat at a table in the centre, right in front of the judge. From an onlooker's perspective, staring at the judge from the pews, the jury sat to the left of the judge. Opposite the jury, Gacy sat at a table with his defence attorneys. Behind the defence waited the prosecution's exhibits. The main one was a four-foot by eight-foot board. Huge. It would eventually display photos of each of the victims and become known as the Gallery of Grief. Next to it, a 4ft x 12ft map showcased the plots where 29 bodies were uncovered. As the trial went on, these two larger-than-life pillars would be difficult to unsee.

The goal of the prosecution was to share enough evidence, enough testimonies that proved Gacy was sane enough to commit the acts he did. The team knew that the defence would lead with the only angle they could: Gacy was insane and out of control at the time of the killings.

Bob Egan locked eyes with the jury and others in the courtroom to deliver the opening statement for The People of the State of Illinois v. John Wayne Gacy.

MR EGAN: I want you to picture, if you will, a young boy, he is 15 years old, he is a sophomore in high school, he is a gymnast at the high school and in the evening he works at the pharmacy. He works at the pharmacy because he wants to buy a car, so he is saving his money. His name is Robert Piest.

Egan relayed the narrative of the evening of December 11, 1978. How Gacy convinced Rob to get in his car. The promise of a better-paying job. Gacy did not know that Rob had told women in the store that night where he was heading or who he was joining. Gacy assumed Rob silently departed into the cold night. Egan told the members of the jury about the handcuffs, the rope, the tourniquet.

He moved through the timeline of what Gacy did with Rob's body. At 6am the next morning, Gacy brought Rob up to his attic, to store his cold corpse. On the next night, Gacy dragged Rob into the trunk of his vehicle. To bring him to the Des Plaines River, the I-55 bridge, to discard of him. Egan informed the jury this was not the worst part of this story. The worst part was that Rob was the final victim on the string of 33 young men and boys. All who Gacy killed.

Egan explained how Gacy tripped up the first time authorities spoke with him. Gacy didn't know a young girl named Kim Byers had witnessed him speak with Robert Piest. He didn't know that young girl was watching him so closely. So Gacy did what he always did. He pivoted, he lied, said he didn't know what she was talking about. Authorities asked him to come in for a statement, and he said he had more important things to do, and he'd get there when he gets there.

When Gacy finally arrived at the Des Plaines Police Department, it was in the middle of the night on December 13, and he was covered with thick mud. A sloggy mess. When police questioned Gacy about his physical appearance, of wet dirt blanketed over him, he said he had just pushed his car out of the mud on Summerdale and Cumberland Avenue in Chicago. This was an area impossible to get stuck in. Egan shared with the jury the truth. Gacy had been stuck in the thick muck down by the Des Plaines River, where he was dumping the very body of Robert Piest.

The opening statement moved the jury. The choice to focus on Rob created an immediate emotional connection to the story. Rob was the jury's entrance into the case. Over the next two days, Thursday and Friday, mothers, fathers, friends, a girlfriend, an uncle, and a sister were called to testify. On February 7, 1980, Bessie Stapleton took the stand. She was a mother of one of the victims: Samuel Stapleton. Her heels clicked the floor as she approached the stand. Halfway through her testimony she collapsed when she was shown Samuel's bracelet. Her body made a thump as it buckled to the floor. The press captured the moment. Later, she was recalled.

At the end of the first full day of witness testimonies, Harold Piest felt on edge. He approached Terry Sullivan.

"You need to get a paramedic and ambulance here on duty," Harold Piest insisted. "What if what happened to Bessie Stapleton happens to my wife tomorrow?"

Sullivan responded, "We will take care of it. A team will be here."

The next day, Harold noticed a local fire department rescue crew in the presence of the court. As each witness identified the victim they had loved, the photo and name were placed on the large evidence board. The prosecution had been ordered not to leave all the photos on the board for the jury to look at during the weeks that would unfold. This was a request of the defence. However, where each photo had been, a name and a frame stayed on the board. The empty frame, with the name situated next to it, looked like an empty grave.

The last mother to be called to the stand on Friday, February 8, 1980 was Elizabeth Piest. Terry Sullivan would do the questioning.

MR SULLIVAN: State your name please.
THE WITNESS: Elizabeth Piest.
Q: Is that Mrs Piest?
A: Yes.
Q: How many children do you have?
A: I have three.
Q: You have three children now?
A: No, I have two.

Mrs Piest recounted Kenneth's and Kerry's names and ages.

Q: Did you have another son?
A: Yes, Robert.
Q: What did your family call him?
A: Rob.
Q: How old was Rob at the time he disappeared, Mrs Piest?
A: He was 15 years old.
Q: Would you tell the ladies and gentlemen of the jury what type of education Rob had?

A: He was a sophomore at Maine West High School. He was on the gymnastic team in his first and second year. He was on the honour roll in his freshman year. And he was in Scouts, and he was about to make Eagle Scout. He was two merit badges away and a community service project of cleaning the Des Plaines River, and then he would have been an Eagle, which he wanted very badly.

Q: Did Rob have any employment, Mrs Piest?

A: Yes, he was working at Nisson Pharmacy.

Q: How did Rob get the job at Nisson?

A: I had driven to the store to get some milk and Rob went in to get it, and Kim Byers, who was working at the drugstore, asked if he wanted a job and to put his name and telephone number down, they were looking for help.

Q: Did you yourself know how much Rob was making at this job?

A: He was making $2.85 an hour.

Q: Do you know if he was happy with what he was making?

A: No, he wanted to earn more.

Q: Had he discussed this with you?

A: Yes. He wanted to ask one of the co-owners, Phil Torf, for a raise.

Elizabeth Piest shared more about Rob's routine, in both work and school, and how she would pick him up to take him to where he needed to be.

Q: Calling your attention to December 11, 1978, which was a Monday, did you pick Rob up at Maine West High School?
A: Yes, he got off early that day.
Q: Where, if anywhere, did you go with Rob at that time?
A: He wanted to stop at K-mart on the way home, so we stopped there and he ran in to see about something there and then we drove home. It was getting close to about 5.30. And our daughter Kerry had fixed him a hot ham and cheese sandwich with milk to eat before he went to work.
Q: Was there anything special about that day, December 11, Mrs Piest?
A: Yes, that was my birthday. And my husband had bought me a cake, birthday cake, and we were going to celebrate my birthday when Rob came home that night.

Mrs Piest recounted how she dropped her son off for work at 6pm and then returned for him at 9pm.

Q: Did you in fact go inside the store that night?
A: Yes, I went in. I knew I was early.
Q: Did you see anybody in the store that you recognised there at that time?
A: Yes. There was Kim Byers, who was there, and Phil Torf.
Q: Did you also see your son in the drug store?
A: Yes.

And here Sullivan set her up to deliver the distinct proof of life of Robert Piest on the evening of December 11, 1978, that was necessary for the case.

> **Q:** Can you describe the jacket he was wearing to the jury?
> **A:** It was light blue and it was a down jacket, had snaps down the front.
> **Q:** Do you remember the brand of it?
> **A:** Yes, it was Pacific Trails.
> **Q:** Did your son approach you at the store on that Monday night?
> **A:** Yes. I walked—
> **Q:** Go ahead.
> **A:** I walked toward the cash register. Rob was standing next to Kim. When I came in the store, he came around to the aisle where I was. He said it would be a few minutes. He says, "I want to talk to this contractor about a job, a summer job," and it paid about $5 an hour minimum.
> **Q:** Did he leave at that time, Mrs Piest?
> **A:** Well, I told him, I said, there would be no problem, I said I'll browse around the store and I'll wait for you.
> **Q:** And did he leave then?
> **A:** I didn't see him after that.
> **Q:** What did you do after that?
> **A:** I started walking down the aisles just looking around, waiting.
> **Q:** Did you hear anything at that time?
> **A:** When I came up on the aisles, I was approaching the

cash register, where there was Phil Torf and Kim Byers, and I heard, I don't know what Kim said, but I heard Phil say he's—
MR AMIRANTE: Objection.
THE COURT: Objection sustained.
THE WITNESS: He talked
MR SULLIVAN: Did you have a conversation with Kim Byers that evening, Mrs Piest?
A: Yes.
Q: And did you leave the store a little later?
A: Yes.
Q: And did you say anything to Kim Byers at that time?
A: Yes, I had told her that I was going to go home.
Q: Where did you go, Mrs Piest?
A: I went home. I went home and I told my husband and daughter and son, I said something was wrong, we can't find Rob.

Mrs Piest detailed her phone calls back to the store, checking on Rob. She first spoke to Kim Byers, and then to Phil Torf. She was worried, as the store would be closing soon. She asked Mr Torf for a night number she could have, to keep in contact with him. She also inquired about the man doing contractor work at the store that evening.

Q: Did he give you a name at that time?
A: Yes, he said his name was—
MR AMIRANTE: Objection.
THE WITNESS: (Continuing) John Gacy.
THE COURT: Objection sustained.

MR AMIRANTE: I ask that be stricken.
THE COURT: It will be stricken and the jury is instructed to disregard the last answer.

The objections came frequently during the trial, as a way to stall, as a way to not get too close to the truth. Mrs Piest kept her composure and detailed the plight of her and her family, and how she told Mr Torf she was going to the Des Plaines Police Department.

> **Q:** Did you give them all the information that you had up to then?
> **A:** Yes, I gave them a description of Rob. I gave them the name of John Gacy. I gave them the number of Phil Torf, his night number, his home number.
> **MR MOTTA:** Objection to this, Judge—
> **THE COURT:** The answer will stand now.

Sullivan continued asking Mrs Piest about the details of what she did the night Rob disappeared. The defence objected to Mrs Piest's narrative, and the judge, the defence, and Mr Sullivan argued for the next few minutes. The men approached the bench. The following proceedings occurred outside the presence and hearing of the jury. Mr Motta called Mr Sullivan's question about where Mrs Piest went "stupid". The main fight was over the question of whether the Piests tried to go to Gacy's house before the investigation truly unfolded. The truth was that Mrs Piest wanted to go there, instinctively thinking Gacy was suspect, but couldn't find an address. However, it was ruled at the bench that this narrative was hearsay and Elizabeth Piest was not allowed to say any of her plans, as they might inaccurately influence the jury. All she could do now was identify the evidence. Two pieces of evidence were presented to her once the trial resumed. The first, the blue parka.

> **MR SULLIVAN:** Let the record reflect I am opening a covering of a jacket marked No. 78-35203, affixing to that label People's Exhibit No. 38 for identification.
> **Q:** Do you recognise this parka?
> **A:** Yes, it was Rob's.
> **Q:** And on the inside is it marked Pacific Trails Sportswear?
> **A:** Yes, it is.
> **MR SULLIVAN:** Thank you.
> **Q:** Mrs Piest, were you advised on April 9 of 1979 that your son's body had been retrieved from the Des Plaines River?
> **A:** Yes.
> **Q:** I show you at this time what has been marked as People's Exhibit No. 39 for identification, a photograph, and ask you to look at that and tell me whether or not you can recognise that?
> **A:** Yes, it's Rob.

The defence had no questions. During her time on the stand, Elizabeth Piest had done what she said she would do: provide proof that her son once existed. Even with Gacy sitting in the same room, staring her down, she did it.

The court adjourned for the day. Elizabeth went home with the image of Rob as he was in the photograph stuck in her head. She had already had to identify him before, after he was pulled from the river. Today, she was brave enough to do it again. She hoped the jury, after hearing what she had to say, would think: How could Gacy not be guilty?

THAT NIGHT, KIM tossed and turned in her bed at home. Her mother hardly slept either. Nerves overtook them both, and her mother smoked more than she typically did as the hours ticked toward dawn. Barbara never wanted her daughter, now a freshman in college, to testify in a murder trial, far less, one the whole country watched.

On the morning that Kim Byers would open the trial with her testimony, Buddy, Barbara, and Kim made sure to look their best. Kim wore her nice dress, the same one she wore to Rob's funeral. They drove to the courthouse together. The courtroom was filled with media by the time she arrived. From their seats in the middle they could see Gacy. He kept his head down, not wanting to make much eye contact.

Kim was ushered away to wait in the evidence room. It was dimly lit, cold, and quiet. The light seemed old and flickered a bit. The chair waiting for her was hard, metal. A familiar nausea made her feel like she might faint. Her eyes couldn't look away from two pieces of evidence, just sitting out in the open next to her.

The first one was the blue coat. Her skin knew the inside of the jacket, the puffiness, the warmth. The garment was now a bridge that connected Rob's life and her own. The second piece of evidence was the entrance to the crawl space, which had been carved out of Gacy's floor to serve as a piece of evidence.

It was square and haunting in its devilish chipped wood. She shuddered, sitting next to the portal through which a man carried a congregation of bodies. The moments in the small space made her claustrophobic. It seemed like hours passed before a court officer called her to testify.

Thus began the fourth day of the trial, February 9, 1980.

Taking the stand, Kim combed the crowded courtroom with her eyes. She saw her parents in their seats. Despite the distance, she felt their support. She saw Mr and Mrs Piest, along with Ken and Kerry. Terry Sullivan began his case.

DIRECT EXAMINATION
BY MR SULLIVAN:

THE SHERIFF: Just have a seat here. Hold the microphone in your hand. Talk loud and clear.

MR SULLIVAN: Hold the mic about this far.

A: Right here.

Q: State your name, please.

A: Kimberly Byers.

THE COURT: I don't think the microphone is on.

MR SULLIVAN: Try that again.

A: Kimberly Byers.

Q: Spell your last name, please.

A: B-y-e-r-s.

Q: How old are you, Kimberly?

A: 18.

Q: Are you employed?

A: No.

Q: What are you doing at the present time?

A: I am a student.

Q: Where are you a student?

A: Winona State University in Minnesota.

Q: What year are you in at Winona State?

A: A freshman.

Q: Prior to going to college, did you reside with your parents?

A: Yes, I did.

Q: What address did your parents reside?

A: 8704 Gregory Lane.

Q: What city is that?

A: Des Plaines.

Q: How long have you lived there, Kim?

A: 18 years.

Q: From what school did you graduate?

A: Maine North High School.

Q: During the time that you were in Maine North, were you employed, Kim?

A: Yes, I was.

Q: Tell the ladies and gentlemen of the jury where you were employed.

A: Nisson Pharmacy.

Q: During the time that you worked at Nisson's, did you have an occasion to meet an individual by the name of Rob Piest?

A: Yes, I did.

Q: I show you what has previously been marked as People's Exhibit No. 39, for identification, a photograph, now in evidence, and ask you if you recognise this photograph?

A: Yes, I do.
Q: Tell the ladies and gentlemen of the jury who this photograph depicts?
A: Rob.
Q: How did you meet him, Kim?
A: I kind of introduced myself. He came into the store. I asked him if he wanted a job.

Kim continued sharing her schedule as well as Rob's schedule at the store, working for Phil and Larry Torf. She was then asked to recall the night of December 11.

Q: Do you know approximately what time you arrived at work on December 11?
A: About 20 past 5pm.
Q: Did you have various conversations with Rob during the night?
A: Yes, I did.
Q: At any time during the evening, did you see in that store an individual identified as John Wayne Gacy?
A: Yes.
Q: Tell the ladies and gentlemen of the jury where you saw him within the confines of Nisson Pharmacy.
A: In between the aisle. He was taking measurements.
Q: Measurements for what?
A: They wanted to remodel the store.
Q: Was he introduced to you?
A: No.
Q: Were you advised that, in fact, he was a contractor who was remodelling the store?

MR MOTTA: Objection.
THE COURT: Overruled.
THE WITNESS: What's the question?
MR SULLIVAN: Were you advised that he was a contractor who was remodelling the store?
A: Yes.
Q: Other than being in the aisle, Kim, had you seen Mr Gacy at any other places in the store?
A: Yes, I saw him talking to Phil near the pharmacy counter.
Q: Can you describe very briefly where the checkout till would be at Nisson in relation to the front door?
A: It's right near the front door.
Q: If I were to walk in the front door, where would the till be?
A: On the left.
Q: And in relation to the front door, where is the pharmacy counter?
A: In the back of the store.
Q: Far back?
A: Far back, left.
Q: Left as you would come in?
A: Yeah.
Q: I ask you at this time, Miss Byers, to look around this courtroom; tell the jury whether or not you see John Gacy in the courtroom today?
A: Yes, I do.

She saw him, all right. Hunched over the defence table, he was large, but she was larger up on the witness stand. She was no longer afraid of him. Kim was so angry at the way he sat there, scribbling on a legal pad as if he was building something against her while she testified against him. The jury took mental notes.

> **Q:** Please stand up and point him out.

Kim stood up and pointed. Instead of looking at her, Gacy glanced over to the wall. It was a moment she would never forget. She had been waiting for this confrontation since the night Rob went missing, since her first dreams of Rob's body in the trunk of a car, trapped, with no way out. Kim thought he was a coward for not looking.

> **A:** Sitting right there.
> **Q:** Thank you. You may sit down. At any time during the evening on Monday, December 11, did you see Rob back by the pharmacy counter?
> **A:** Standing near the pharmacy counter?
> **Q:** Sitting or standing?
> **A:** He was sitting in front of the counter checking in items.
> **Q:** When you say checking in items, explain what you mean.
> **A:** Certain nights of the week we would get supplies and articles for the store and he would have to put the price tags on them.
> **Q:** During the time that he was checking in items, did you see where Mr Gacy was?
> **A:** No, well, at that certain time he was talking to Phillip when I walked in.

Q: Do you recall what you were wearing on the night of December 11, Kim?
A: Yeah, I was wearing black pants and a short sleeved shirt.
Q: Do you know any of the clothes that Rob Piest was wearing on that evening?
A: Yes, he was wearing brown pants, a beige shirt, and a blue down jacket.
Q: Now, did he have any duties that would require him to put on and off that jacket during the course of the evening?
A: Yes, he had to take the rubbish out.
Q: At any stage during the evening, Miss Byers, did you see that down jacket in the checkout counter?
A: Yeah, it was sitting next to the counter.
Q: Would you tell the ladies and gentlemen of the jury whether or not you, in fact, used that jacket?
A: Yeah, I was cold because the people were coming in and out of the store. So I put it on.

The same blue coat that had shared space with her in the evidence room was on display. Kim was asked to answer: Did she recognise the jacket?

A: Yes, I do. It's Rob's jacket.
Q: Is this the same jacket you put on that evening?
A: Yes.
Q: Now, during the time that you were wearing this jacket, did you do anything in relation to any photography?

> **A:** Yes, about 7.30pm that night, the store was kind of slow and I had some pictures I wanted to be reprinted and I filled out some envelopes and I made a few mistakes and finally completed the one envelope and I tore off the receipt and usually just throw the receipt in the bin. I hesitated. Then I stuck it in Rob's jacket.
> **Q:** You were wearing the jacket at this time?
> **A:** Yes, I was.
> **Q:** Now is this a receipt that you tear off the top of the film package?
> **A:** Yes.

Sullivan asked Kim Byers to identify the envelope she filled out, People's Exhibit No. 40. He asked her to tell the jury whether she did or did not recognise it.

> **A:** Yes, I wrote this envelope out myself.
> **Q:** What number is on the receipt?
> **A:** 36119.
> **Q:** 36119?
> **A:** Yes.

He asked her to examine every inch of the envelope and the matching receipt. It was her handwriting. She explained the photos she was developing. They were reprints of homecoming pictures of her and Cory. She had wanted to give them to her sister, Karylee, for Christmas. She and her date had gotten dressed up for the festive evening.

Her skin was still tan from the summer. Her hair was straight with natural blonde highlights. The dress was pink, spaghetti strapped. A corsage of white and pink flowers for her; a matching boutonniere for him.

The images weren't just photos. They were a time capsule, recording that place between summer and winter, childhood and adulthood. The state of becoming everything she was so curious to be. She grew tired of proving something as simple as filling out the envelope, but the questions about the receipt continued.

> **Q:** The customer receipt, Miss Byers, would you read what is in the upper right-hand corner under the number?
> **A:** Nisson Pharmacy Company, 1920 Touhy Avenue, Des Plaines, Illinois.
> **Q:** Please keep your voice up.
> **A:** Okay.

And then the final descent began, back into the night.

> **Q:** Miss Byers, did you see Mr Gacy enter the pharmacy that evening?
> **A:** No, I didn't.
> **Q:** Did you ever have any physical contact with him while he was in the store?
> **A:** We accidentally bumped into each other.

She could still feel the uncomfortable brush of his arm. Her eyes peeked over at him, to see if he, too, remembered how clumsy he had been, unaware of the contact. Did he remember how he didn't scare her? Could he see it now? She wanted him to know she wasn't afraid.

Q: Calling your attention to approximately 8.50pm, did anyone enter that store that you recognised at that time?
A: Yes, Rob's mother, Mrs Piest.
Q: And had you known Mrs Piest before then?
A: Yes.
Q: Did you see Rob at any time between 8.50 and 9pm that evening?
A: Yes.
Q: Where did you see Rob?
A: He asked me to come watch the register and he walked outside.
Q: Did he take anything with him when he left?
A: Yes, he grabbed his coat.
Q: The same coat you have identified?
A: Yes.
Q: Did he say anything to you at that time?
A: Yes.
Q: What, if anything, did he say?
A: He said that—
MR MOTTA: Objection.
THE COURT: Overruled.
THE WITNESS: He said he was going to talk to the constructor guy about a job, he would be right back.
MR SULLIVAN: Did you ever see Rob Piest after that?
A: No, I did not.
Q: Did you have any conversation with him about the adequacy or inadequacy of the money that he was making?
MR MOTTA: Objection.

MR AMIRANTE: Objection.
THE COURT: Sustained.

If a question could be interpreted as leading or unfair, in terms of the portrayal of the defendant, the defence often objected. Sometimes the answers stood, sometimes the objections were sustained. The bickering continued while Sullivan attempted to craft his question, seeking Kim's knowledge of Rob's shared thoughts over his salary. Of course, Rob had told her. Just as he had told his mother. Kim didn't care for the defence lawyer's aggressive shouting.

MR SULLIVAN: What time did you leave Nisson Pharmacy that night, Miss Byers?
A: 10pm.
Q: The next day did you go to school?
A: Yes, I did.
Q: Did you later that morning have a conversation with other members of the Piest family?
A: Yes, Kerry and Ken came to see me at school.
MR AMIRANTE: Objection.
THE COURT: The answer will stand.

The final section of Kim Byers's testimony circled back to the subject of photographs. She was asked to identify the log from Nisson Pharmacy. She pointed to her handwriting on the log, the second line from the bottom. Date: 11/12. Envelope number: 36119. The same number she had captured in her diary. She had tapped into her intuition, as if knowing deep inside that she was about to be up against something big. That same intuition held her here, on the stand. In front of Channel 7; mothers of murdered sons; her own bewildered parents; Rob's remaining siblings; a room full of grief, of tears. She sensed the energy of this space, a current that told the ladies and gentlemen in the room they were all taking part in something bigger than themselves.

That seemingly ordinary scrap of paper was treasure, sacred. She didn't know the magnitude of this choice until she saw its consequences today, in this room, blown up on bulletin boards. The receipt did what the trial had set out to do: show a proof of life and a proof of death.

Kim Byers left the stand, asking if she was done. Amirante chose not to cross-examine her.

She met her parents outside the courtroom for an extra-long embrace. Barbara tried to squeeze the pain out of her daughter. Kim was so good at showing she was brave, but a mother always knew the truest feelings of her daughter's heart.

WHILE THE PROSECUTION carried on, Amirante and Motta requested several motions for mistrial. None were granted. Dan Callahan, a lockmaster on the river, would testify and identify Rob. He was the one who found him. He testified, yes, to finding his body in the place Gacy had dumped him and the others.

When considering what the prosecution knew about the defence, they had to pivot and move from the family and the victims to the psychology of the case. Terry Sullivan knew the defence was going to try to prove Gacy to be insane. Too insane to knowingly comprehend the murders he was causing.

The medical examiner, Dr Stein, continued to exert his

expertise on the saneness of Gacy's murders. Kunkle questioned him for trial. He finished his questioning by asking Dr Stein about all the bodies that had been found and so far identified in the crawl space at W. Summerdale Avenue.

> **MR KUNKLE:** In your capacity as medical examiner of Cook County, were you responsible for the ultimate identification of the various bodies?
> **THE WITNESS:** I was.
> **Q:** Based on the information given to you by the Forensic Odontologist, the Anthropologist, and the Radiologist, did you in fact issue death certificates or official announcements regarding the identity of 22 of the individuals?
> **A:** I have.
> **Q:** Doctor, in relying on the work of the forensic odontologist, what means did the separate dentists use to arrive at identification?
> **A:** I have a correction, sir, 19 identified bodies.
> **Q:** Right, I am sorry. The other three were in the river. So you specifically engaged in the identification of 19?
> **A:** Yes, sir.
> **Q:** Please answer.
> **A:** The methodology used by the forensic odontologist was one, charting of the teeth and the skulls of the decedents of all the 30 cases that we had, then, comparing those with any dental X-rays which were sent to us by the nearest of kin. These were compared, and if there was a 100 percent match, an identification was made.

However, it must be stated that we had four dentists involved in the identification. All four, each and every one of these dentists went through each and every one of those cases, and unless all four agreed, there was no identification. There had to be identification among all of the four.

> **Q:** Relying on your own determinations and the reports back to you, did you in fact issue death certificates listing the name of what we refer to as Body No. 1. as Jon Prestidge?
> **A:** I did.
> **Q:** Body No. 2, John Butkovich?
> **A:** I did.
> **Q:** Body No. 3, John Szyc?
> **A:** I did.
> **Q:** Body No. 4, Gregory Godzik?
> **A:** I did.
> **Q:** Body No. 6 is Samuel Stapleton?
> **A:** I did.
> **Q:** Body No. 7 as Randall Reffett?
> **A:** I did.
> **Q:** Body No. 8, Matthew Bowman?
> **A:** I did.
> **Q:** Body No. 11, Robert Winch?
> **A:** I did.
> **Q:** Body No. 12, Tommy Boling?
> **A:** I did.
> **Q:** Body No. 16, Russell Nelson?
> **A:** I did.
> **Q:** Body No. 17, David Talsma?

A: I did.
Q: Body No. 23, Rick Johnston?
A: I did.
Q: Body No. 25, Robert Gilroy?
A: I did.
Q: Body No. 27, William Kindred?
A: I did.
Q: Body No. 29, Darrell Samson?
A: I did.
Q: Medical Examiner's No. 31 for April 1979, Robert Piest?
A: I did.
MR KUNKLE: Nothing further. Thank you.

Over the course of the day, when Amirante cross-examined Dr Stein, he and Kunkle approached the bench to speak to the judge. Amirante disclosed that he had concerns for the family, for the people in the room. He wanted to ask them on various occasions to leave, this being one. There were possibly a couple of intentions for this choice. One, the details of the deaths were gruesome and Amirante felt he should offer a forewarning as a form of basic decency. Two, a family's reaction, their palpable emotions in the courtroom, had a real chance to sway a jury.

MR AMIRANTE: Judge, before I go on to the next thing, I am talking about stuffing things in the mouth and everything; do you want the family here?
THE COURT: They have heard a lot worse so far.
MR KUNKLE: They know what is coming. They are

here because they want to be here. We can't order them in and out.

As the cross-examination continued, Amirante went down a strange path. Could these victims have accidentally killed themselves? A case of autoerotic asphyxia? Sure, it could happen. Did it happen here? That was the question Mr Kunkle asked during his redirect examination.

Q: If somebody used a ligature, a piece of rope on an individual and strangled them to unconsciousness and not to death, and then in fact killed them by stuffing a wad of cloth or paper in their mouth, would that make it any less a homicide than if they had accomplished it on the first try?
A: It is a homicide.
Q: If somebody used an appliance like this on a 15-year-old boy and then stuffed paper in his throat and he was not even dead yet, and then dumped him in the river and he drowned in the river, would that make it any less a homicide?
A: No, it would not.
Q: If a person used an appliance like this on a teenage boy or young adult and strangles him to unconsciousness and then buried him in his basement and he dies of asphyxia from his own grave, would that be any less of a homicide?
A: It is a homicide.
MR KUNKLE: Nothing further.

Poetry flowed through Bill Kunkle during the entire trial. He had a gift, a way of catching a rhythm, let it sing, develop a pattern. A pattern the jury could track, could feel. There was innate power in naming the bodies. He'd do it now, and he'd do it later, in his closing. The linguistic patterns elicited strong emotions and ties to the victims.

Amirante and Motta brought up friends and family of Gacy's to the stand. Gacy's mother shared with the court the abuse Gacy experienced as a young boy. Gacy's sister disclosed how her brother was verbally abused by their father. A neighbour of Gacy's, Lillie Grexa, expressed how wonderful and neighbourly he was. On the stand, Grexa called Gacy a very brilliant man, refusing to label him as crazy. This conflicted with the defence's story.

When the defence brought up their psych team, it was almost too easy to poke holes in their testimonies. A major thread used throughout the defence was the metaphor of Dr Jekyll and Mr Hyde. But what else could they do?

The man had murdered at least 33 boys and young men.

The question continuously pushed forward by the defence was whether Gacy was sane enough to commit a crime. Their answer was no. And to produce that evidence they formed a team that would attempt to show the jury this. However, who is to say that the crying mothers, the careful placement of bodies, the prosecution's witnesses had not already made the bed? The whole room, the whole country, knew the defence had to move a mountain to win the case for insanity.

Dr Helen Morrison completed her time on the stand a month after Kim Byers, on March 8, 1980. Morrison was a forensic psychiatrist. Twenty years later, she would go on to write about her experiences in a book, *My Life Among the Serial Killers: Inside the Minds of the World's Most Notorious Murderers.*

Motta was the one to question Helen Morrison.

> **Q:** Now, based on everything that you reviewed and your clinical examination of Mr Gacy, did you reach a diagnosis?
> **A:** Yes, I did.
> **Q:** What is the diagnosis stated in psychiatric terms?
> **A:** In psychiatric terms, the diagnosis is mixed psychosis or atypical psychosis.

However, the diagnosis was never named in Morrison's report. Throughout her examination she focused on a type of splitting she claimed Gacy experienced. This was on theme for the Jekyll and Hyde argument. Gacy had suppressed rage from childhood due to his brutal and abusive father. He did not know how to properly handle or channel this rage. He committed acts of murder. This diagnosis, of course, did not always mean murder. But it meant, Morrison attested, Gacy was unable to "appreciate and conform his conduct during each of the acts [murders]". Motta then ended his questioning, leaving the final line out of Morrison's mouth vague at best.

CROSS EXAMINATION BY MR EGAN:

> **Q:** Dr Morrison, you indicated it is your expectation to be paid for your testimony today? Is that correct?
> **A:** That's correct.
> **Q:** And as a result of your consultation and what you

have done in this case, you have submitted a bill for in excess of $9,000 to the court, correct?
A: Yes.
Q: Now, I believe you testified on your direct examination that John Gacy is suffering from a mixed psychotic or atypical psychosis, is that correct?
A: That's correct.
Q: And that is your diagnosis based on your examination and your examination report, correct?
A: That's correct.
Q: Now, do you recall whether or not you used the words "atypical psychosis" in your report?
A: No, I did not.
THE COURT: Will you hold the microphone up?

A common theme occurred with women on the stand, a certain demand of speaking voice from the court. This request was disproportionately directed at women. This gender dynamic could be traced back to Kim Byers's first conversation with authorities, about Gacy's word versus hers. The power of maleness was a favoured subtext.

MR EGAN: I believe in your report you indicated as follows: "At best he may be said to be suffering from a psychosis with paranoia, intermittent delusional thought processes, that is layered by a borderline syndrome of extremely low levels of functioning." I believe those are the words you used in your report, correct?
A: That's correct.

Q: You did not use the words "Atypical psychosis"?

A: That's correct.

Q: Are you aware that the definition is as follows: "Atypical psychosis: This is a residual category for individuals who have psychotic symptoms, delusions, hallucinations, incoherence, repeated derailment, marked poverty of content of thought, marked illogical thinking, and behaviour that is grossly disorganised or catatonic who do not meet the criteria for any specific mental disorders." Are you aware that is how the American Psychiatric Association views atypical psychosis?

A: Now, yes.

Q: I assume you would not agree with this definition.

A: I would not disagree.

Q: You would not disagree?

THE COURT: Would you hold up the microphone up?

MR EGAN: You would not disagree with this definition, is that correct?

A: Not in total, correct.

Q: I would assume you would disagree with the aspect and definition which indicates that a person suffering from atypical psychosis suffers from hallucinations?

A: I would agree with that.

Q: You would agree with that?

A: Yes.

Q: What hallucinations was John Gacy suffering from?

A: It's a hallucination, if you are discussing it only in the context of whether he hears voices or sees things, it would be more in the context of seeing something.

Q: What evidence do you have that John Gacy saw things that weren't there?

A: That at the time that the crimes were occurring, he felt that he saw parts of him that were split off, that were disposable parts, he saw the parts of his father that he felt were destructive, terrifying parts.

Q: What did they look like to him?

MR MOTTA: Objection.

THE WITNESS: They did not…

THE COURT: She may answer if she can.

MR EGAN: What did they look like to him?

A: Because of the disorganisation, they did not have form. They were psychological hallucinations.

Q: What facts can you point to surrounding the killing of Robert Piest that indicate to you that he was operating under a psychosis?

A: The same type of pattern that had existed in the other murders, the seeming ability to separate himself from the actual occurrence from things that were going on in the external world, they were split for him. He was psychotic at the time that he killed Robert Piest.

Q: I see. So the fact that he drove Robert Piest to his home would not change your opinion as to the psychosis at the time, correct?

A: No, it would not.

Q: The fact that he coerced Robert Piest into being handcuffed would not change your opinion, correct?

A: That's correct.

Q: And the fact that he answered the telephone and spoke with a business associate immediately after

murdering Robert Piest would not change our opinion, is that right?
A: It would not.
Q: And the fact that he stored Robert Piest's body in the attic and at a later time took it from the attic and put it in the trunk of his car in the dead of night and threw it in the Des Plaines River would also not change your opinion as to whether or not John Gacy was suffering from a psychosis at the time?
A: It would not change my opinion.

Egan began catching Dr Morrison's foot in her mouth. His questions began, of course, with how she was paid, how she pursued the police reports and drew some conclusion that Gacy could operate in society but was not sane enough to understand the criminality of his operations. Egan asked her if she thought Gacy would have murdered Rob Piest if a police officer had been present. She thought he would. It became clear at the end that Dr Morrison had chosen a diagnosis and tried to make Gacy fit, with little evidence to back it up, beginning with the lack of written evidence on her part, the atypical psychosis diagnosis.

The trial demonstrated that psychologists on many counts testified to their belief that John Wayne Gacy was a master deceiver. In their interviews with him, the professionals often doubted his words, his so-called truth. This was made clear when Gacy was called to testify directly after Dr Morrison.

Mr Amirante stood to make an announcement to the court.

MR AMIRANTE: Mr Gacy wants to make a short statement to the court.

THE COURT: All right.

MR AMIRANTE: In as much as we have rested in sub-rebuttal.

THE COURT: All right.

THE DEFENDANT: Your honour, I don't feel that...

THE COURT: I can't hear you.

THE DEFENDANT: Your honour, I don't feel that I can add anything to what is going on since I am not fully aware of myself—

THE COURT: Well, the question—

THE DEFENDANT: —in regard to testifying.

THE COURT: Well, the question is, do you wish to testify in this case or not?

THE DEFENDANT: I don't feel that I could add anything to something that I don't understand myself.

THE COURT: You realise you have the opportunity?

THE DEFENDANT: Yes, I do.

THE COURT: And by this you waive your right to testify before this jury, is that correct?

THE DEFENDANT: That's correct.

THE COURT: Ladies and gentlemen, this concludes the evidence that you will hear today. I would just like to point out the case is winding down and we are projecting that this case will be argued to you by Tuesday. This concludes the evidence you will hear this week. Tomorrow you will be with your friends and family again. And, again, enjoy your families. Resist the temptation now, really as the case goes on it becomes more and more tempting to begin to discuss it among yourselves, or with anyone who might legitimately come into contact with you. Resist the temptation because you have come a long way and no use spoiling it at this stage. Have a good weekend. We will see you Monday morning at 10am.

The courthouse emptied; the jury lined up like soldiers on active duty. Their hearts and brains swirled with information. What else could make them change their minds? Were their minds made up? On March 13, 1980, the closing statements were made. Terry Sullivan went first, followed by Robert Motta, Robert Egan, Sam Amirante, then William Kunkle. Sullivan was the opener and Kunkle was the closer for a reason.

MR SULLIVAN: On Sunday, March 16, Robert Piest would have celebrated his 17th birthday. Instead, his body was recovered from the Des Plaines River, the very river that he had volunteered to clean to become an Eagle Scout.

On Monday, March 17, John Gacy will celebrate his 38th birthday. Before that, you will decide whether or not he is allowed to tell a friend, on the telephone, "Didn't I tell you I'd be out? I beat the system again." Or you will be the ones to tell John Gacy, in a loud and clear tone, a message that says, "John Gacy, your cruising days are over. Young boys need not fear you any more."

There have been other mass murders, but seldom, if ever, has anyone been so cold, so cunning, so calculated over such a long period of time as John Gacy has. Gacy was like a spider caught in his own web as the Piest investigation progressed.

Thirty-three boys were dead and the lives of parents, brothers, sisters, fiancées, grandmothers, friends, were left shattered. John Gacy has accounted for more human devastation than many earthly catastrophes, but one must tremble – tremble – when thinking just how close he came to getting away with it all.

John Gacy, you are the worst of all murderers, for your victims were the young, the unassuming, the naïve. You truly are a predator.

Gacy responded with a laugh that the whole courtroom could hear. Sullivan pivoted and turned toward the jury.

MR SULLIVAN: You saw him laugh at me. You are the only ones who can tell him – loud and clear – "We refuse to be used or manipulated by you, John Gacy." If you find him not guilty, then do so, remembering that 11 unidentified male bodies are still in Cook County morgue.

Sullivan told the jury that if they were to find Gacy not guilty, they were doing so in spite of each victim. Mr Sullivan, one by one, placed the photos of the victims on the Gallery of Grief for viewing. Family and friends left in tears during this part of the closing. It was one thing to have the board full of empty frames, with just names, as ordered by Judge Garippo. But now the names all had faces.

MR SULLIVAN: And, ladies and gentlemen, if you find him not guilty, do so over Body No. 30. Paperlike material in the throat. Male, white, five foot eight inches

tall, one hundred forty pounds. Last seen alive on
December 11, 1978, in Des Plaines, Illinois, identified
April 9, 1979, as Robert Piest.

The defence tried to make the point that the prosecution had not done their job, had not provided enough evidence to prove Gacy was sane enough to commit these murders. The issue was this was no isolated murder. This was not a one-time psychotic break or hallucination. Graves were dug, bodies hidden and decomposed, drives taken down to the I-55 bridge in the bleak of night. It was a difficult defence to make. Kunkle closed, and the courtroom welled with emotion as he concluded the prosecution's argument.

> **MR KUNKLE:** John Gacy has always sought power. He sought the ultimate power, the power over life and death. The power of playing God.

Kunkle turned to the jury to remind them this case was not a plea for sympathy. No matter what would be decided in this court, nothing could bring the lives back. He asked the jury to not show sympathy but show justice.

He grabbed the photos that Sullivan had used to decorate the Gallery of Grief and threw them through the crawl space entrance, exposed in the courtroom for the jury. The object that Kim Byers had sat next to before her testimony. The wooden square through which Gacy hauled bodies, young men and boys he had chosen to kill. The emotion in the courtroom climaxed, and a silence remained after the photos Kunkle hurled settled on the courtroom floor.

Kunkle concluded his closing statement by advising the jury that although they did not have the power to change the past, they had the power to control the future of John Wayne Gacy. They could do justice for the whole state of Illinois, and not allow Gacy to walk this earth. They could allow this evil man to stop his path of terror. If they allowed him to continue walking this path, he advised: God help us all.

WHILE THE JURY deliberated, the defence and prosecution teams waited at Jean's, the little saloon not far from the courthouse. It was packed with reporters, spectators, people waiting for any news. How long would the jury deliberate? Sullivan sat at the bar with his father, who had joined him on this last day of the trial. Sullivan had not yet finished his first beer when the bartender got a call. He hung up and faced the prosecutor. "The jury's back."

Sullivan's stomach sank. It was too soon. He could not help thinking something had gone terribly wrong. He worried the jury would agree with what Gacy's defenders said from the beginning, long before the trial even began: This guy is nuts. Judge Garippo asked the jury to read their verdicts. It was simple.

The jury found John Wayne Gacy guilty on all counts. The room roared. But the ordeal wasn't over.

On a new day the jury would have to decide, after counsel and clarity of what this decision meant from the judge, whether John Wayne Gacy deserved to walk this earth, even behind bars. When that day arrived, the jury disclosed that they unanimously concluded that the court shall sentence the defendant, John Wayne Gacy, to death. Gacy would sit on death row for the next 14 years.

CHAPTER ELEVEN

POST-TRIAL

2022

I MESSAGED TERRY SULLIVAN ON FACEBOOK when I first booked my flight for Chicago. I figured he would be difficult to get a hold of. He had kind of been difficult to get in touch with in 2017, when I began to immerse myself in the case. We chatted briefly, and he remembered my mom. He asked if he could send me a copy of *Killer Clown*, his book about the trial and conviction of Gacy, and I said of course. I received the mass paperback edition, with his signature inside. He and his co-author had chosen my mom's name, Kim Byers, as the words to open his book.

To my surprise he wrote me back immediately this time. We agreed to meet at a restaurant in downtown Chicago, not far from the courtroom where he led The People of the State of Illinois v. John Wayne Gacy.

Terry still has an office in downtown Chicago, as well as a few others throughout the area. We were meeting at an Irish pub called Corcoran's. On my walk from the parking garage, I notice a sign: "Athletico Physical Therapy." It makes me think of Nick. He is a physical therapist and whenever I see any physical therapy establishments, I snap a photo and text it to him because I am thinking of him. I relished morning pictures of the boys eating breakfast and FaceTime calls when we could sneak them in, before and after school.

As a mother, it is not often I get to trek anywhere by myself. In my teens and twenties, I often found myself moseying around places, just existing and taking the world in, road tripping around the country or once booking a highly discounted last-minute flight to Australia. But life looks different now with two kids. A beautiful different. But different nonetheless. Being in Chicago, I feel an echo of my old self reemerging. Someone who felt a flush of adrenaline walking down an unknown street.

On the other side of the street is Corcoran's. The restaurant is loud and teeming with people, as if everyone left work and came here. The few tables out front on the patio are filled. I see a man I thought could be Terry Sullivan. He is squeezed in close with about five other men and women, some around his age, some younger. Lots of silver hair and pints of beers. This man has a water in front of him. I hope he notices me standing near the steps up to the patio, unsure of where to go. I had told him I would be in a pink top.

"Courtney!" Terry waves from his table. My hands shake with nerves. I hadn't mentally prepared to sit with a group of strangers. They all smile at me and wave me over, but I feel out of my element.

"Welcome to the city," Terry says. He is in his late 70s, and in a checked button-up shirt, more relaxed than the courtroom suits. "These are some of my friends." The people sitting around him wave and he introduces them each in turn. There is no chair for me, so I stand, smiling and sweating.

To my relief, Terry says, "It's too loud here, let's walk and find somewhere we can sit and chat."

We say our goodbyes and return to the outside world, walking side by side, south on Wells Street, a part of Chicago I learn from Terry, is called Old Town. The street is lined with Victorian-era buildings and pubs, boutiques, gyms, and restaurants. A great fire in 1871 devastated this area of the city for days, killing hundreds of people and burning 17,500 buildings and 73 miles of street. A Catholic church was one of the few buildings to survive the conflagration. Walking around today, 150 years later, it is impossible to know this part of the place's history just by looking. The city could survive the unthinkable. Perhaps that kind of resilience, that belief system, is carried in its residents.

We stop in front of a Japanese restaurant, Kamehachi. I later look the restaurant up and learn it has been around since the 1960s. We take seats at a corner table with metal chairs and a matching metal table. Terry orders a Diet Coke, and I order a water and tuna poke for the table. Terry asks me how I ended up here in Chicago. He wants to know about my work and my family. I ask him the question I had been wondering about for years.

"Why did you choose my mom's name as the first two words in your book?"

Before an answer, a friend of his walks by. Terry shakes his hand, and he acts so excited to see him. This is a common phenomenon, Terry has friends everywhere. Being with him is akin to sitting with the mayor. Everyone knows him, and everyone has something to say to him.

After his friend says goodbye, Terry returns to my question as if there's been no interruption. "The whole initial investigation centred around your mom because of the jacket and the photo slip. I can see her in the drugstore. I remember her as a teenager. The role she played was immense for getting rid of this guy."

"Do you remember her coming in for the trial? Or how you prepared her?"

"I do. She was absolutely fine. A little recalcitrant. But that is normal for anybody. As you could imagine, back in this time, nobody ever imagined somebody killing 33 boys could ever happen. It was a big shock. Witnesses did not want to come forward. With all the crime we have today, I'm not sure it would be as big."

I agree and disagree. I didn't want to consider I was raising sons in a world where a serial killer murdering 33 boys would not be shocking and front page newsworthy.

"I can tell you it was such a thing back then," Terry continues.

"Shortly after we arrested Gacy in December, I was with some of my friends in a car out to have Christmas or New Year's dinner and we stopped to pick up some beer. I will always remember there was this newspaper box there that had Gacy's face of all things as I'm going into the 7-Eleven. By the time I got back to the car my friends said to me, 'The guy must be crazy.' I took that with me throughout all the preparation and education for the trial. It was something that scared me because at that time, nobody thought somebody sane could do what he did."

"Was that the moment that framed everything for you?" I ask. Terry's phone quacks to announce an incoming text. He picks the phone up to look, then sets it back down, undeterred.

"When your close friends know you are a prosecutor, and the media is saying the same thing, then our burden was not only to prove he was guilty but prove he was sane. That weighed heavily on me."

I wondered how Terry felt by the end of the trial.

"It was kind of a non-event for me by the time it was over," Terry admits. "We had worked so hard for so long. We had certainly expected the jury to be out a bit longer. The remnants of what we had been through were yet to set in. The remnants not necessarily that I would have nightmares, I haven't."

"You never had any nightmares?" I ask. "I haven't," he says. "Mostly, it was about the victims. I had dealt with so many of them. A mother who collapsed on the stand. We had to take three or four recesses for her. I can still see her. A girlfriend of one of the victims who I drove by when she was walking the long distance from Western Avenue to the courthouse, in the snow, in the dirt. She didn't speak very much, but she was someone who just made it even more important to me to remember all of the people that were affected by one person."

Sitting in front of me, Terry Sullivan is talking about the same cultural, personal, and social patterns I have been hunting down. The mass orbits one man made, altering so many lives by his choice to murder.

"I don't think it's been talked about a lot," Terry says. "When you think about it, thousands of people have been affected. Not only the mom and dad and brother and sister. I thought a lot about the friends. I thought about my friends on my baseball teams growing up." Terry tells me that he is certain that if one of his baseball friends had disappeared, it would have had a deep impact on him, his teammates, the teammates' families. "It's just amazing how many lives one criminal can hurt. I still don't think that has set in completely the way I want to express it."

"I know what you mean," I say. It felt like coming home, to speak with someone so deeply involved in the case who could feel the tremors I felt from the periphery. "That's part of my work. Now I am understanding how this has affected my mom. It has impacted her mothering. This case has been a part of my fear-building. You know, my mom always had to have so many locks on the door at night. She taught me to not walk alone in the dark."

Curiously, Terry interjects, "Is that how your mom has been affected?"

"Yes."

"Still?"

"Still. It's in our family history, in our DNA. It happens in my own mothering. I won't let my son talk to a neighbour we don't know for too long while on a walk or bike ride."

The server drops off the poke garnished with avocado and wonton crisps. We talk a bit about parents. I ask Terry about his parents and what they thought about his role in the case, if they were alive during the trial.

"I come from a lower-middle-class family," Terry says. "We lived in Roselle, the country part of it. That's why I played so much baseball and ran like a coyote everywhere I went. My parents were wonderful. There were four of us kids. My older brother was a national merit scholar, and then we got dumber as you went on down the line. He became a lawyer and I kind of followed in his footsteps. He went into tax and corporate, whereas I ended up in the DA's office. I've been doing criminal and trial work since then. My parents were proud. My mom never came to the trial, but my dad did several times."

"What do you remember about your dad at the trial?"

"I remember, after the trial was finished, we all went, as we always did – prosecutors, public defenders, cops – over to this little bar called Jean's. About a block from the courthouse. It was a wild place. A shot and a beer joint. We all rehashed with each other. Fights broke out sometimes. After the trial, my dad was there. I was going to get him to stay the night at my house. I thought, at least, we would be back the next day. But then Jean gets a call. This happens with all our jury trials. And my dad was so disappointed when I told him, 'Dad, we gotta go back.' I think it had been an hour and fifty minutes or something like that. And he had just started enjoying his martini."

Terry laughs, remembering his dad next to him, at Jean's. They thought they had the whole night ahead of them for drinks, then dinner later. Maybe a call would wake them up after the sun had set and rose again.

"I'll never forget what he said to me: 'What's up, Charlie? It can't be, it's only been two hours.' I told him, 'Dad, that's the way it works. Let's go back.' He was so disappointed by that. We did go back to the place after the judge read the verdict."

He told me both his parents had been supportive of his profession; his dad, like an Irish politician, got to know the cops and everyone during the trial by first name. His mom, the quiet support on the home front. His voice lowers as he says, "They are both gone now."

"I'm sorry," I say. I had assumed as much, but it's clear from the shadow that crosses Terry's face that the loss is ever present. The cycle of life moves incredibly quickly; sometimes it feels like I am scratching my way back into time, time to listen, time to learn, time to love. I can't imagine the woman I'll be by the time I also say, they are both gone now. And I never want to, just as I can see Terry doesn't want to, either. It makes me want to go home and give both my mom and dad a big bear hug.

"Did you have any moment you can't forget about that trial?"

Terry takes a sip of his soda. "Just the fear that the jury would find him insane. When we were called back, I had fears we had not shown he was sane. But I did have a bit of a panic attack when giving the closing argument."

I think about their choice to have Rob frame much of the opening and the closing. They had painted Gacy to be of sound mind when working at Nisson Pharmacy, including his interactions with my mom, with the owner. In hindsight it clearly worked, but I can see a younger Terry stewing as he walked over to Jean's, concerned about their understanding of what would persuade a jury, that maybe they'd retraumatised people on the stand for nothing.

"Do you remember Elizabeth Piest?" I ask.

"Certainly."

"She passed," I say.

"Yeah, I heard," he responds. "She was a sweetheart. Her husband was extremely nice. I got to know Kerry very well. Lost track of her, too. Got to know her brother well, too, at that time. Very nice family. They were the first ones that I talked to other than the first detective that came to see me. He convinced me without much effort that he had met a couple who had a son who would never run away. That was the start of everything. That was before your mom. But not much."

"And when did you first talk to her?"

"I have no idea."

We both laugh. "It was a long time ago."

"Anything you remember Elizabeth Piest saying?"

"I don't want to sound old because I'm not. But it was a time they didn't investigate missing kids. It was one of the phoniest things in the world. I was amazed. This was also before computers were used. They had little card catalogues, and that is where they would keep the names. You have Cook County, which has all these little police departments that typically work the same. If we hadn't done something about Rob Piest, then supposedly in a month, or two months, or six months, the detective would go through, pull out the card, ask around to see if anyone had heard from him. Then put the card back in the catalogue. I was shocked."

I ask if this laissez-faire attitude was because of the sheer number of missing kids, and Terry says, no, it was just the way they practised. All missing people were labelled as runaways. Always. It's different today, even with cold cases. Now, at least, when someone takes an interest in a case, then you have a unit and that's all they do, focus on one case. Whether that is in the Cook County Sheriff's Office or different police departments. They will start digging again when everyone has given up on it.

"Do you know Jason Moran?" I ask, wondering if he kept in touch with the person assigned to the case now. Some of Gacy's victims remain unidentified to this day.

"No," Terry says. Still living in the world of the case, he speaks about the equipment and surveillance cars for the search and lookout for Gacy. One time on the road, Terry remembers a car broke down while following Gacy and the engine started smoking. Gacy got out of his car to see if the officers were okay. Terry said the equipment he dealt with at the time was not good, and that when people hear the term "surveillance", they certainly didn't imagine shoddy, half-broken cars.

I ask Terry about the receipt.

"When we found the coat and the receipt at Gacy's, the receipt wasn't torn exactly on the perforation. I don't know if your mom knows that. But that was good. It had some jagged edges. Once we got the film back, it fit perfectly."

We spoke about the harm that comes from those desperate to change the narratives of famous cases like Gacy's. Conspiracies have arisen about the case. Some people theorise about Gacy having accomplices. Others questioned the validity of Gacy's arrest and the initial probable cause. Terry acknowledges, but says it happens with other high-profile cases, too, such as the Kennedy assassination.

We talk about the way Gacy's story can never go away, both on personal and cultural levels.

"I have thought about that many times. I have told many of my friends that if and when I die, I don't want his name on my tombstone." He says this to show how close his whole life has felt in conjunction with Gacy's name.

I chuckle. I didn't expect him to say that, but I understand the sentiment. "Exactly. You don't want him to follow you to the end."

"No! But he has for a lot of time. I have had mixed feelings about it. You know, I have done a couple of the shows. But it's hard to keep it in front of me. I'm entranced with why the younger generation makes such a big deal. Well, one thing I have learned from walking through a book store is that they have whole sections for true crime. You know that."

I nod. I know. True crime has evolved, too, though. We are in a new wave of true crime: more literary, more nuanced, offering new angles and insights. Storytellers working hard to defy the over-simplification and sensationalism that has long characterised the genre. But, of course, the genre also has the foundational texts that never slipped into this category, like Truman Capote's *In Cold Blood*. There has always been space for this kind of work, but the space had widened a bit, allowing for more voices.

I circle back. "How has Gacy followed you for your career?"

"Good question. I can't really quantify how the case has helped. Sometimes it has hurt. I still am doing legal analysis for WGN. I was introduced to that probably from this case. And probably from the book [*Killer Clown*]. I have seen copies in the station when I have been there. But it works two ways. Once I left the prosecutor's office, I started my own firm. I did a lot of criminal law, but I tried to get away from it to some extent because I didn't just want to be just a criminal attorney. I felt I was competent in so many other things in the practice of the law. I did some things for some corporations out in the suburbs. But they were so conservative, they didn't want to hire someone who had a reputation. I'm proud of the work we did, but it stuck with me."

"What do people see as bad about your reputation? You did well."

"Big corporations don't want publicity. They want lawyers who are quiet, mundane."

"Boring?"

"Boring."

I laugh. "Probably for the best, no? You have too much personality."

"Maybe," Terry says.

"And Gacy never haunted you in any way?"

"No," he says. "By the time he was set for execution, they were giving out tickets. I was given a ticket out of maybe, like, 10. I refused it. People thought I was crazy for turning it down. I just didn't need to see any more death. I don't think as a person, a Catholic, a farm boy, I have ever really been a death penalty sort of person. And certainly, my team had enough people on it who were in favour of it. They could take my place. The only thing I regretted after giving up my ticket was that one too-good politician ended up with it."

"Where were you on the execution date?"

"I believe I was in Philadelphia at the time."

"What were you doing there?"

"Some legal matter. I can't remember what it was. But I remember people calling me."

"You didn't feel anything when it was done?"

"I didn't have any other axes to grind. The execution wasn't anything I had a say in."

I ask him what he is up to now, what kind of law he practises. He says he does general practice, DUIs, adoptions, wills, personal injury cases.

"Did you ever take a murder case again?"

"I think deep down I probably stayed away."

Although he says Gacy didn't affect him, I wonder if there was a ghostly, invisible haunting that occurred for Terry. The choice to avoid murder, death. He had seen too much because of Gacy.

He asks me what made me dive into the case. "The diary," I say. I tell him about my mom's choice to chronicle her life in 1978, during the time of Rob's disappearance. I also tell him about my belief that we are all connected to national events, whether we were touched by them, like my mom or Terry, or if we were merely witnesses. If we pay attention, we are affected.

"At least once a year someone comes up to me and says they knew Gacy or lived near him or had a best friend work for him."

"What do you do when that happens?" I ask.

"I listen to them."

I can see that Terry Sullivan has a good heart. The act of listening is intimate. "People carry so much. The number of people who survive and carry this case with them is unending."

He comments on the guilt people carried, the "what-ifs" that tormented people who wished they could have altered the outcomes.

I tell him about my unease that the victim could have been my mom that night if someone like Ted Bundy, instead of Gacy, had walked into the pharmacy. "If the killer who crossed paths with her focused on young women," I say, "I wouldn't be sitting here, sipping lemon water in downtown Chicago."

The subject moves on to his memory of William Kunkle, whom he called Bill. He says Bill went on to be a judge, and that he was very pro-death penalty. It is intriguing that two men who helped make closing arguments at the end of the Gacy trial held opposing beliefs, the case spinning their lives in wildly different directions. Terry tells me Bill still has a connection to the crawl space doorway used in trial. Because he had thrown the pictures through the object in the final remarks. Terry tells me he thinks Kunkle might have had the crawl space in his garage at some point in time.

"Did he plan on doing that, or was it on a whim?"

"Part of his plan, but I didn't know," Terry says. "I put the pictures up on the board during my argument, and he took the pictures down as he was making his argument. Very powerful. Excellent lawyer."

A shade settles over our table. A fluffy cloud blocks the late-evening sun. I should get back to my hotel before evening. I thank Terry for meeting me.

"Can I take your picture?" I ask.

"No, no," he says. "You don't want a picture of me."

"How about a selfie?" He smiles and agrees. I take the photo on my phone, then send it to my mom. "Wow!" she texts back.

Terry walks me in the direction of my rental car. It turns out that he lives near the physiotherapy practice, Athletico. Before parting, we promise to keep in touch.

Instead of walking back to the car, I stop by Lincoln Park. People are just getting off work and are on runs. Young parents push their babies in prams, while their dogs walk on leads close by. The air is about ten degrees cooler than it is in Des Plaines. Lake Michigan beckons hello, peeking over the rolling hills of healthy grass. The body of water is vast, like the horizon of the ocean.

I am beginning to see the whole picture.

CHAPTER TWELVE

CALIFORNIA

1994

Bacon crackled in the pan. Kim flipped the meat with tongs. In a glass bowl on the counter next to the stove, she beat eggs with a fork. The metal tines made music on the bowl.

Since Gacy's sentencing, Kim had created a new life for herself in California. In the living room of her home, her two daughters watched Sesame Street before school. Elmo made Kim's toddler, Danika, giggle. Her six-year-old daughter, Courtney, took out wooden blocks while watching the show with her sister. Sam, her husband, was in the kitchen with her, in charge of the pancakes. The two enjoyed cooking together. To anyone on the outside it appeared to be a regular, busy Tuesday morning on May 10, 1994. But Kim knew what today would bring and she didn't want to think about it. Not yet. She remained close to the stove, listened to the eggs hiss as they hit the melted butter in the pan, and allowed the chaos to tune out the thoughts in her mind.

In the past 14 years, she yearned to both leave the past and hold on to it. The one person who represented both was her high school boyfriend, Cory. Although she slowed her diary entries after the trial ended, and John Wayne Gacy was found guilty, she did make updates occasionally.

3 or 4/1/81 – 1.10am

Talk about a long time. One year has passed. And gosh how much has happened. To begin with, I completed my 1st year of college at Winona State with a 3.3 average. I swam competitively (and dove) and made a lot of close friends. Spent spring break (Feb-Mar 1980) with Nathan, caused a lot of wakes with Cory. Yes, I am still seeing Cory. We have seen each other on and off but have never stopped caring for each other. He went to Germany in May 1980, I was a little mixed up this summer, not sure where I was going or what I wanted to do. Finally decided on Western Michigan University because it had so many programmes to offer. I decided to follow the career of occupational therapy. I finished my first semester there with a 3.4. Physiology (B/C), Psych/Child (A), General Ed (B/A), Mysticism (B/A), Diving (A). No intercollegiate activities for me. Lots of Intramurals. I am working as a lifeguard (work study) and doing volunteer work at a local state hospital. I am still seeing Cory and that is my main reason for this writing. After all these years of caring for the boy and surviving all the ups and downs, I have discovered how much I love him. But I always had a feeling something wasn't quite right.

27/5/81

Finally a chance to sit down and write. Right now I am in a fraternity house in Michigan (Ann Arbor) called Chi Phi. The plans were to stay here in A2 for the summer and work to get in-state residency. Cory is here also do-

ing the same thing. However it did not work that way. The job market is empty and I couldn't find a job. I had a temporary one but it's over. So I took a camp job in Decatur, Michigan. It's called Lake of the Woods Camp for girls. That begins June 1. So before that Aunt Martha from California is flying me out to San Jose for two weeks. That should be nice. I'm going to relax and get lighter + darker.

My second semester at Western went quite well. Finished with a 3.55 (made the Dean's list). Took a few road trips this year. Went to Key West. Met a guy down there. He is a nice friend, isn't that a funny word? It can come in so many degrees. I've been having a lot of problems lately with socially adjusting. I went through this brief spell where I was a social butterfly and I couldn't miss out on anything. I had too many irons in the fire. But those days are coming to a close. I can't wait to get away from people my age, especially the males.

I went and am still going through a lot of emotional turmoil. I love Cory very much, he is my best friend – and I never want to lose him – but right now he doesn't fulfil any other type of role. I think it is because he represents home to me. And I can always remember how things used to be, and I won't let go.

Kim had transferred out of Winona State both for a change and to be closer to Cory. Once she graduated from Western Michigan, she headed west as fast as she could. She had spent summers during her youth at the beaches and by the pools of California with her mother's family. She could not picture herself happy, whole, in any other place. She needed a new start again. In San Diego, she landed an occupational therapy job. She would meet lifelong friends. No one at her new job or in her apartment complex knew her as the girl on the witness stand or the one running to California. She was simply "Kim".

Cory tried to join her in San Diego. But by some bad stroke of luck, he never found a job, at least not one he liked. So he moved back to the Midwest, started a master's, and began a new life without her. It was the best thing that could have happened for both of them. But it wasn't easy to let go. It never is.

In 1984, Kim agreed to go on a blind date. She was still in touch with Cory by phone, and he took the occasional trip out to the west coast. She had gone on dates before this, when Cory had become more like a brother than a romantic interest. Kim was excited to be set up but didn't want this blind date to think much of her; she didn't know if she could actually ever leave Cory.

Her date phoned to ask if she would meet him in Seaport Village, a quaint sea area on the border of downtown San Diego. The village was known for its boutiques, like an odd hat shop and overpriced seafood. "I'll be wearing pink shorts," she told him.

He arrived early and waited on the boardwalk. He was tall, but not too tall, and had thick hair. He saw someone he thought might be her approaching, but just a bit late, in light pink shorts. Her skin was tanned, and her hair was the colour of deep vanilla and sunshine.

"I'd recognise those pink shorts anywhere," he said. "You must be Kim."

"You must be Sam," she replied.

At the bar, he had a Heineken, and she had a white wine spritzer. They talked all night. The talking rolled into the next day. She found his little quirks charming. Like how he laughed when he was nervous. How he liked to keep homemade chicken and egg salad in the fridge. She enjoyed opening the Saran Wrap from the bowl whenever she visited his little apartment in Hillcrest. He was also driven, like her. He was a competitive swimmer, and Kim loved his strong shoulders. He had his own catering company, which he founded with his sister, called Oui Cater. Sam lived with his sister, so dating was not ideal at his place, but Kim didn't care. She liked the company of his sister.

Sam was from the Midwest too, Minnesota. He, too, had come to California to leave the past. His mom died from unknown causes when he was 11, probably cancer, but no one talked about it. Losing his mother broke Sam in a way that made it impossible to stay in the town where everything reminded him of her. He still loved his dad, his siblings, his hometown, and his friends, but he wasn't faring well. The west coast offered a spotless slate, a sparkling new chapter.

After Kim and Sam dated long enough, he was bothered to realise she had two boyfriends: him and another person named Cory.

Late one afternoon, the sky was painted orange and marbled with pink, and the two sat on the front porch to discuss the matter. They had been having a lot of these conversations out on the porch. Sam began to label these types of conversations as the Porch Series. A space to talk about what was difficult, what was bothering Kim. A patient and gentle man, Sam also felt like he had waited enough for her to pick Cory or pick him.

"You will have to make a choice," he said. "Him or me."

Kim picked at the peeling white paint of the porch step. She looked out at the people throwing Frisbees in Balboa Park across the street. Children laughed while swinging on the monkey bars and doves soared overhead.

"I choose you," Kim said, finally certain with her choice. Early into their dating life Kim shared with Sam about what had happened back in Des Plaines, about Gacy, about how Cory was there for her through it all. Sam understood her need for him and wasn't asking her to cut off contact. He wanted clarity on who she wanted to exclusively date. Sam was really the only other person she had seriously dated, and from dating him she had recognised that Cory had become more like a sibling to her.

Kim flew back to Illinois to break the news to Cory. He was living with his grandmother in Chicago. They sat together in the living room. Both couldn't believe this chapter was closing.

They cried, honouring the couple they had been, and the new paths ahead of them.

Within a year, Sam and Kim were married. The year after that she had her first child, a daughter named Courtney. When the child was six weeks old, Kim flew back to Illinois for her mom to meet her baby girl. A dismal shadow prevented this from being a perfect trip: Her mom was dying of bone cancer. These were the final days, Kim knew.

"Here she is," Kim said, handing her newborn to her mother. Barbara's soulful, watching eyes matched those of her first granddaughter. "She's everything and everything more," Barbara said.

Kim held back her tears. Just nine years ago she had been a high school senior with her mom helping her navigate the disappearance of her friend. How could Kim have known – how could Barbara – that they had less than a decade left with each other? They could never return to all that had once mattered in the small apartment on Gregory Lane. That life was over. Kim couldn't bear to think of a future without her mother.

The baby lay face down on her grandmother's chest. A handmade Winnie the Pooh blanket rested between them. Kim snapped a photo. It would be the only one of her child and her mother.

A few nights later, Barbara passed while Kim and her baby slept upstairs at her childhood home, in the room she used to return to after late nights of work at the pharmacy.

The baby's scream woke Kim. Her body jolted into motherly action, hurtling straight out of bed to the open drawer, a makeshift bassinet, where her child slept. She had once kept her pyjamas in that drawer. Seeing the baby had fallen back asleep, Kim kissed her head. Maybe it was a nightmare she thought. Seconds later, the phone rang. She answered it and found out her mother was gone. Later, Kim reflected and thought that her mom's spirit passed through the room the night she died. And she travelled right through her daughter.

In the hospital room where her mother had died, her father, Buddy, sat with his wife long after she passed. He held her hand, brushed his fingers through her hair. Love didn't retreat when someone stopped breathing.

Kim left Illinois for California, sad and solemn with puffy eyes, a soft post-partum body, and extreme fatigue, along with a raw ache that would never go away. A yearning for her mother. A new mother needed her mother perhaps more than anyone in the world.

When Kim was about to head to the airport, Buddy handed her a book. "Take this," he said. His glasses fogged. "Your mom was so proud of you." He was a man of many words when it came to everyday chit-chat, but few words when it came to the deep stuff. He knew how much his daughter would miss her mother. He took the baby, rocking and singing to her as Kim opened the book. It was the one she had heard about. *Killer Clown*.

Inside the flap was a handwritten note from her mother. Kim moved her shoulder up to her face to avoid letting any wetness fall on to her mother's handwriting.

> *Kim Byers (22-8-1961) was a senior at Maine North High School, Des Plaines, Illinois on December 11, 1978, when this ordeal began!*
>
> *She was a freshman at Winona State College, Winona, Minnesota when she was flown in to testify February 9, 1980. The whole thing was a trauma!!! We were very proud of her poise, recall and ability to be the #1 witness for the prosecution.*
>
> *Our love and support are hers, Mom and dad, Barbara S. + Howard P. Byers.*

Kim looked at her sleeping baby with the orange hair and blue eyes and wondered if she would one day read this note.

Kim still had not processed what she had been through. She would now need to compound Rob's murder into her mother's early death. She sensed a hallway in her head. The long, dark, arduous corridor got darker as it spewed into the ocean of her mind. She had always shut the doors on events that made her feel like she was crawling out of her skin. She tried to frame it positively. She told herself how lucky she was: able to bring her new baby, the daughter with the name that her mom chose, to say hello and goodbye.

Kim boarded the plane. The flight attendant asked what she would like to drink. "A 7 Up." The lady with the wings on her black suit dropped off the fizzing lemon-lime soda in a plastic cup of ice. It was the same drink she'd ordered when she'd flown in 1980. But this time, she was really going to leave the past as she continued to build her new life in California.

The years crept by. Gacy was not only still living, but in the news. It seemed he was always filing an appeal. He claimed his lawyers did not do their due diligence in representing him. National conversations surrounding the death penalty were divided. Since Gacy had been charged, many of the prisoners who were sentenced to death no longer ended their lives in the electric chair, but, rather, died by lethal injection. Serial killer Ted Bundy, whose name came up in cultural conversations as much as Gacy's did, was executed in the electric chair. The two killed masses of young people, and culture often put them in similar tiers of terribleness.

During Gacy's imprisonment, he attracted followers who were curious to hear from him, know him, stare at his odd art featuring clowns and celebrities like Elvis Presley. Being a murderer who painted, for some reason, gave him a sense of intrigue. He received more mail than any other inmate at the prison facility. People called into his phone line he had set up and paid $23.88 to listen to a recording of him denying the crimes.

On the morning of May 9, 1994, Gacy was flown by helicopter from Menard Correctional Center, where he had been for the past 14 years, to Stateville Correctional Center north of Joliet in Illinois. The penitentiary, which opened in 1925, was massive, with walls that reached toward the heavens, keeping anyone and everyone out. Crowds formed that evening, awaiting his final breath. Many victims' families were angered that they were not allowed to sit in the observation room and watch Gacy die.

The prison grounds were a war zone, filled with groups who were in favour of capital punishment, and those against it. College students were said to have thrown barbecues in celebration. Bill Kunkle made sure he got a seat in the front row. Sam Amirante stayed far away, hoping the finality of death would bring some closure for the victims' families.

Gacy was the most hated man in the country. Yet no one could look away. All over America, people threw Gacy's Day Parades – echoing the name of the Macy's Day Parade in New York City – in celebration of Gacy's death. It was a big deal. And a long time coming. In fact, Gacy's execution was the first in years for the state. From 1962-1990, Illinois had executed no prisoners. From 1990-1999, 12 would be executed, while over 100 others awaited the death penalty. Eventually death row would be emptied, and at the early turn of the next century, it would be halted. If Gacy had not been caught in 1978 – if he had been apprehended just five years later – he might still be alive today. He might even have talked his way out of death.

On the night of Gacy's execution on that May day, Sam Amirante was not celebrating. He visited a bar near Gacy's house and chatted with people he knew there. He left the bar to pick up his son from a school event. Although he had planned to go back to the bar later that night, once home, he changed his mind. Instead, the family went to Plush Pop, a hot dog joint.

The man working behind the counter asked Amirante, "How are you celebrating the Gacy execution?"

Amirante laughed. "I am not celebrating," he said. "I was his lawyer."

The cook behind the counter nearly dropped his spatula full of sweet caramelised onions.

Back home, Amirante turned on the news. He saw Bill Kunkle on TV arguing with another man about whether or not Gacy had been given drugs before his execution, to ease the tension in Gacy's body, before being pulled on a gurney into the execution chamber. One of the men Kunkle was talking to mentioned he saw a "flutter" in Gacy's eye. Amirante was said to have recounted that flutter many times while representing Gacy, it was not drug-induced, but rather a part of who Gacy was.

At Stateville Correctional Center, the night of May 9, 1994, was mostly clear. The air was coldish and cunning. The victims' families held their breaths for too long, awaiting Gacy's demise. Gacy, now in his 50s, and no longer the 30-something-year-old murderer posing as an ambitious businessman, was set to be executed after midnight. In the penitentiary, he spent his final hours in a seven-by nine-foot cell in a single-story structure named Building X. It had been completely cleared of other inmates. In his final hours he didn't seem worried; he still proclaimed his innocence; and he also talked about the Chicago Cubs to the guards. His last meal was fried shrimp, fried chicken, French fries, and strawberries.

Right before the clock buzzed at midnight, Gacy was put on the gurney and rolled into the execution chamber. The noise of the groups outside of the prison walls could be heard from inside. Kunkle took his seat in the front row, humming along to the tune from the outer walls as demonstrators sang, "Na Na Na, Hey Hey Hey, Kiss Him Goodbye!" Other chants were "Strap down the clown!" and "Stick the prick!" Kunkle smiled at the enthusiasm. Because the families of the victims were not allowed into the observation room, Kunkle felt a responsibility to see the execution through on their behalf. Just as he had stood up for them in court, he would do so in the hour of Gacy's death.

The lethal injection was supposed to be a more humane method of execution than the electric chair. The first means of capital punishment, beginning in the 1800s, had been death by hanging; then came the electric chair; then lethal injection. Gacy was first injected with sodium thiopental, which put him to sleep. But an error occurred: a clog in the IV line delayed the second injection. Gacy lay there, about to enter the in-between, while technicians prepared his execution.

About 10-20 minutes later, the clog was cleared and the second drug, pancuronium bromide, entered Gacy's bloodstream. The third and final drug, potassium chloride, stopped the beating of Gacy's heart. In the first hour of May 10, 1994, at 12.58am, the monster was dead.

Eugenia Godzik, a sister of victim Gregory Godzik, was in the crowd outside. When asked by a reporter what she thought about the execution, she said, "I'm glad it's over. I just wish there could have been more suffering, so to speak."

Tim Nieder, a sibling of victim John Mowrey, spoke to a reporter, with his voice trembling. "I'm just glad a little justice was done in this matter." Note the choice to use "a little". It was not enough that Gacy was gone, it would never be enough. The death penalty was supposed to bring justice, closure. And to some extent, it did. But it could never bring a full measure of closure to anyone's lives.

Bill Kunkle spoke to the press after exiting the small viewing chamber. He wore a black suit with a black and white striped tie and a white collared shirt. Audibly, he let the demonstrators, on-lookers, families, and press know, "He got an easier death than any of his victims. In my opinion, he got an easier death than he deserved."

The group roared, "Kill the clown! Kill the clown! Kill the clown!"

Women and men alike chanted, and many wore shirts that read: "No Tears for the Clown." A handful of people, who were against the death penalty, held candles and stood vigil. A woman named Debbie Hope-Hast said to a reporter, as a death penalty opponent, "He [Gacy] did horrible things. The things he did were truly evil. But that does not give us the right to take his life."

This sentiment grew culturally through the country, even as Gacy was thought to be a poster boy for the death penalty. The criminal justice system contained undeniable flaws. Not everyone on death row had done what Gacy did, and over the years the state of Illinois abandoned capital punishment altogether.

But it was undeniable: Gacy was dead. During Gacy's execution, Helen Morrison, psychologist and witness for the defence, waited at the Holiday Inn in Joliet to begin the examination of his brain.

Kim hadn't turned on the news or picked up the newspaper

on the Tuesday morning following Gacy's execution. She woke up early to walk the neighbourhood as the sun rose over the streets of southern San Diego. She tossed the dogs a tennis ball before slipping off her shoes and walking in through the back door to find Sam at the kitchen and the girls in the living room. As Sam finished the pancakes and the girls played with wooden blocks, the phone rang. It was about 7.30 in the morning. Sam answered. "Kim, it's for you. Your dad."

He handed her the receiver, and she placed it to her ear.

"He's gone. Gacy's dead," Buddy said to his daughter.

Kim turned her back to the living room, facing the back door into the kitchen so her daughters wouldn't see her. Like a ragdoll, she melted to the floor. She sat on the linoleum floor, moving the cord of the phone between her fingers. "He's gone," she repeated back to him.

Kim heard the sound of a book whacking shut. The thick cover pushing the fine pages together. That's what it felt like to hear the news, both a relief and an intensity. Finally, that guy is dead.

Courtney crawled into her lap and asked, "Why are you crying, Mommy?"

Kim told her daughter that a long time ago a bad man had taken her friend and hurt him. His name was Rob. She said that finally something bad happened to the man.

"I miss my friend," she told her daughter. "In life, always be careful. There are bad men out there. If a man pulls up in a van and offers you a ride or a popsicle or to see his puppies, you do not go. Never go. If he takes you anyway, you fight. You scream. You never give up. If he says he will kill your parents if you scream out, scream."

Kim was surprised about how easy the instructions slipped from her mouth. Was it pre-determined for all mothers? Or was it different, more complicated, more real because the loss had happened? She didn't remember her mother ever giving these kinds of directions, implanting a fear of strangers in her young, impressionable mind. Kim was part of a growing generation of parents who felt fear over losing their children to a world with ill intent. But this fear was not hypothetical to Kim.

Courtney wiped the tears dripping down her mother's cheeks with the palm of her small hand. "Okay, Mommy," she said. "I'll always be careful."

At such a young age, Courtney could not know the complexity and vastness of her mother's emotions. But she knew this was serious in the way nothing in her life had been before. Courtney recognised a danger she didn't have language or imagery for. Courtney knew she would obey.

AFTER GACY'S EXECUTION, families and spectators and people of the community in and around Des Plaines were invited to an auction to be held in Naperville, Illinois. Gacy's art was being offered for sale, set up by his lawyers. Some of the Piest family attended and were pleased with how the event unfolded.

Businessman Joe Roth spent thousands of dollars to buy dozens of Gacy's paintings during a May 14 auction. Joe Roth owned a shop that sold truck parts. In a press interview, Roth stated that he had been fed up with the media coverage of Gacy's conviction, his too-long wait on death row, citing that the message had been all wrong. The media was focusing too much on Gacy and not enough on the damage his crimes caused victims and their families. During the auction, Roth said, "We're going to burn all the pictures and try to get the attention of parents to watch their kids so this never happens again," he said. "Young people have to be watched, so there's never another Gacy."

Roth couldn't buy all of them. Of the 40 pieces sent to be auctioned, he secured 25. Others went to Gacy's sister. Gacy had mailed out many pieces of art in the time leading up to his execution. He wanted the art to be a part of his story, his legacy. Although only 40 were auctioned off, many more remained in private hands.

At the bonfire, huge planks of wood were pushed into each other, creating a four-foot-tall steeple with the auction art at the centre. Gatherers circled around the bonfire, standing in dirt. Harold Piest was at the forefront, tossing Gacy's work into the billowing fire. He wore a blue polo shirt and white khakis. His brown hair was slicked back, sweaty from standing so close to the flames.

He was infuriated, still and forever, at what happened to his youngest son. He was eager to throw the killer's art into the flames and watch his handiwork disintegrate and dissipate into the sky. The last thing he wanted was for people to collect Gacy's art, create value around it. None of the victims' families wanted that.

Still, interest in Gacy's art grew. It became a focus for niche museums around the country. Every year people travelled to view the paintings of the notorious serial killer, curious to see what John Wayne Gacy left behind. In the same way an artist survives because of their art, Gacy lived on in the culture. Just a mention of his name in the streets of Des Plaines, or in San

Diego, or in New York, and chances were good that someone knew him. Or they knew of him.

Occasionally, people confused Gacy with Jeffrey Dahmer or Ted Bundy or Ed Gein, but they knew he killed. Sometimes people just knew "that clown". What most didn't know was the aftershocks. Just as an earthquake destroys a town or city or small country, murder has an epicentre, where and when the devastation took place, and its aftershocks reverberate. With murder, the aftershocks don't ever go away.

Over the next decade, American media – tabloids, YouTubers, streaming services, sensational cable television, literature, film, documentaries – would aid in making Gacy a cult killer. The years Gacy lived in the public eye, showing up in people's living rooms on the evening news, while on death row, piqued public curiosity. There was a fascination around the details of the murders; the myth of him dressing as a clown; his denial of accomplices; the friendly neighbour act.

The victims' stories surfaced rarely; those whose lives were forever altered by the murders; the mothers and fathers who mourned; the ones who loved the young men Gacy killed for his pleasure. For decades, these "other" stories became buried by the buzz and loudness of Gacy, still so very alive, even after his final breath.

CHAPTER THIRTEEN

THE RIVER

2022

On my final day in Illinois, I drive south. I'm taking the route to where Gacy pushed Rob's body over the bridge, into the river, and ending my trip at the prison where Gacy was executed. There is a certain finality in these visits. Both stops represented an ending.

I want to experience these spaces I've only read about. What does it feel like to drive to the I-55 bridge? Was the Stateville Correctional Center as fortress-like as it looks in the photos?

The drive from the Hyatt Place to the bridge takes over 45 minutes. For Gacy, it would have been closer to an hour, over 60 miles from his home. This is no quick and easy drive. It was long. However, Gacy went in the middle of the night, and I'm already parting with his methodology, travelling in the late morning when semi trucks pack the highway. A "Welcome to Bensenville: Gateway to Opportunity" sign pops up on the side of the road. I wondered if that same sign was up when Gacy made the drive in the murk of night.

I stop for gas on the way to the bridge. While the tank fills, I run in to get a cold Smart water. The air is hot, but a small wind belts through the flat lands. My pump at the gas station clicks, and I hang the nozzle in its slot and pull away. As I approach the bridge, I take out my phone to film. I press record as the 4Runner rolls beneath the metal crossties that crown the bridge's entry. The bridge is split in two lanes for each direction. Greenery covers the banks of the river on either side.

After crossing, I loop around and pause on a gravel road with a barbed wire fence between me and the water. Thin, wild sunflowers wave in the wind. The bridge is visible from a distance, but I wonder if it would have been the night he disposed of Rob's body. Was the barbed wire here to keep people away from the bank, thick with frozen grass, during December 1978? Did Gacy really throw him over the bridge, unnoticed by anyone driving past? Or did he merely push Rob and the others over the bank, under the bridge? So many verbs had been used to describe Gacy's act: throw; dump; discard; push.

I am equally guilty of repeating these words to record what happened. But here now, looking at the bridge, I am sure that with a man and a car covered in mud, on a narrow, two lanes in, two lanes out, split bridge, no throwing could have happened in plain sight.

Perhaps there was heaving and huffing and shoving or dragging. Gacy must have struggled, hence the mud, everywhere. On him, on his car. It was even spoken about at trial. The mud became a point of fascination. When Gacy confessed to having disposed of Rob in the river, the narrative built was that Gacy "threw" bodies into the river. To throw a body off a bridge alluded to a God-like super strength, a will bigger than that of the average man. He would have had to be superhuman to accomplish this, the first brushstroke in painting him as something other than just a man you couldn't trust.

It seemed impossible now, but so possible before I came to this spot to really look.

I take more photos and decide to follow the river. Just past the bridge, the Des Plaines River, moving southwest, meets with the Kankakee River and turns into the Illinois River. As I follow the water, I feel a convergence in my own understanding of the story. The history of this place, of Rob, and of my mom, is my story, too. The Illinois River was where Rob's body was discovered. I search for where Rob might have been found.

I make a lot of wrong turns, attempting to parallel the river. I end up in a sanctuary-like fishing town with a private restaurant overlooking the river and another small body of water, Heidecke Lake. Spotting two men, I ask them if they know about any bodies being found over the years. They point north. They know of Rob, and they knew of others pulled from the river through the passing of seasons. I come to terms that it's wishful thinking to believe we live in a world free from bodies showing up, floating at the water's surface. In 2022 alone, there has been a stark number of bodies being found in Chicago waterways. Cultural conversation surrounding these Chicago-area deaths prompt serial killer theories.

I make my way back from the fishing pond to the river and finally, I think I find what I've been looking for. I enter a space full of trimmed, finely cut grass and manicured trees, with tall, healthy geese waddling freely. This is Dresden Island Lock and Dam. I park my car and dash across the lawn to look out over the swift-moving water. The bank is covered with rocks, marsh, plants, old fishing lines. An easy place to trap a body.

I peer through a chain-link fence at the riverside and say something like a prayer. A plea for peace, for love, for gratitude, for solace, for relief of pain, for guidance on how to move forward, for staying and leaving, and to understand all the in-between ways the ending of Rob's life had shaped my own. Here I am, thousands of miles away from home, staring at a river in the middle of Illinois, while my one-year-old is at daycare, my five-year-old is in kindergarten and my husband is at work.

A quiet meditation feels like the only way to process and accept all that has happened and all that is to come. Even after leaving this place, the story never leaves: a marsh, a river, a road, a town, a heart.

When you spend so much time thinking about the past, it's important to be able to re-enter the present. I needed a lively space, with the bustling sound of footsteps and voices of people talking on cell phones and in communion with each other. So I did what any traveller would do: I went to one of those ginormous gas stations that sells shirts and stuffed animals and houses a bevy of food establishments inside. This one has a Charleys, a beacon of cheesesteaks, and honestly, it sounds delicious.

The place is packed. Customers are lined up to order sandwiches and fill big plastic cups with Dr Pepper, while meats make sizzling sounds on the griddle behind a counter. I order and enjoy the swaying movement of the people around me, also waiting for their lunches. I watch them take calls on their phones, here on a stop from a regular workday or family road trip. My shoulders settle and my chest lightens.

Back in my car, I pull up directions to Gacy's place of

execution. The Stateville Correctional Center is kind of on my way back to the hotel. Before the sun sets, I want to get in and out. I do not want to be anywhere near that place after dark.

THE RIGHT TURN signal clicks as I enter the maximum security prison. A looming wall greets me on my right. Thirty-two feet high, built to keep in what has been cast inside. This correctional centre is rated level one out of eight, maximum security. In layman's terms, it requires the most security because it often, but not always, houses the worst offenders – murderers and paedophiles and mobsters and kidnappers.

There is an open parking lot. The only security seems to be for physically entering the building. I park and pull my car door ajar, and the wind sweeps it open, almost aggressive. There are no signs of life on the outside, no voices or sight of prisoners. In a small car that drove in after me, two people exit and make their way toward the front of the facility. They knew where to park, where to walk. They were in civilian clothes, no uniforms, so I imagined they were visiting with someone on the inside.

A navy-blue truck pulls up next to my 4Runner. A man eyes me from the driver's seat. At no time on this trip had I felt unsafe as a woman. But when that man pulled up, my neck muscles tightened.

"Can I help you?" he calls out his window. "You know you can't be taking pictures."

"I'm sorry," I say, clipping on the lens cap of my camera. I was taking photos of the wall, the nearly empty parking lot, the original red brick on the facility, which was eerily beautiful. "I am just here to look around."

"They saw you on the security cam and told me to come talk to you," he says. "I'm so bored. So ask me anything."

"Okay," I say, making eye contact with one of the faraway security cameras. "Do you know where John Wayne Gacy was executed?"

"Back there," he points. "Behind that wall."

This man knows what happens behind that wall. After my meeting with him, I scribble down notes I wouldn't be able to read because of how badly my hands were shaking. The Stateville staff used to live across this parking lot, in on-premises dorms, where they would lose their marriages and lives by staying up late drinking and getting it on with each other, then roll out of bed and walk to work at the prison. He talks about a young female psychologist who used to visit the inmates, and how they would be disgusting toward her, pulling out their junk, attempting to get off while she was doing her job. The way he laughs about it makes me feel uneasy. He talks about his job, which is to patrol, looking out for the men who were at high risk of escaping. He shows me a crumpled printer paper full of coloured mugshots of men in jumpsuits he's on the lookout for. One man on the page has eyes that dart in opposite directions and his hair is box-dyed bright orange.

"I should go." I point to my car, anxious to extricate myself. Faced with the stories of what this place is really like makes me second-guess how prepared I was to visit a place abominable enough to hold Gacy. "Thanks for sharing."

"No problem," he says. He stares at me, the wind violently twists around me, like a slow dance I didn't agree to. "You know your skirt is blowing," he says.

"I have shorts on," I shoot back. I walk to my car.

"Hey, you got Instagram?"

"No," I shout back.

"Snapchat?"

"No."

"Well, how can I find you?" he asks.

"You can Google me and can read my work." I shut the door, my heart racing. I don't think I gave him my name, or if I did, he didn't retain it. He never found me.

I drive away and don't look back.

Even in my discomfort, there is a security in the trepidation gripping me. It is a carefully crafted sense of danger passed down to both my sisters and me from our mother. Both my sisters shared a fear of being taken. Danika, the sister between Sydney and I, almost was.

Danika, like my mom, carries a worry of someone taking her during her sleep. My mom will not sleep on the first floor of a house if there is a second floor available. In fact, she refused to live in a single-story house again after the intruder entered her backyard when I was a young child. A couple years later, we packed it up and moved to a new town, for a new start. When I asked Danika why she cared about the second-story bedroom so much, she said, "It gives me more time to fight back."

During her final year of dental school in San Francisco, a man broke into Danika's townhome at 2am. He opened her fridge, peering around for something to eat. No one knows what else he did. In the middle of her sleep, she was awoken by a man's voice yelling, "intruder! intruder!"

The man who lived in the building across from her was awake and saw the intruder hop their six-foot-tall fence that housed a small patio and pry open the sliding glass door to the first-floor living room. The neighbour immediately called the complex's security, and they rushed over. They were not able to catch the man, as he ran back into the city.

She couldn't sleep well again for months and installed three cameras and sensors for the glass. My mom has a multitude of security cameras in her house and around the property, too, for the fear of an unwanted presence on her property. But cameras are everywhere now. We are not alone in our desire for a feeling of protection. When I take walks in my neighbourhood, a security camera shouts at me every few houses: "Hi, you are currently being recorded."

Danika says she now sometimes sleeps with a crowbar next to her and pepper spray on her nightstand. One can never be too safe.

Danika claims she has what our mother has, that knowing something will happen without knowing why, the strong intuition and keen awareness. She says she knows the difference between anxiety and this feeling. She describes anxiety as low volume, constant. The seeing into the future feeling she says is loud, strong, and takes over her whole body. Before the intruder came, she had a vision weeks prior of someone breaking in. She didn't know when it would happen, but she had a feeling telling her it would.

I feel it, too, that seeing into the future, although mine doesn't seem to be as finely tuned as Danika's or my mom's. My other sister, Sydney, is probably more like me. She gets strange feelings and is highly in-tune to people's energy and non-verbal cues.

When I was younger, I had visions. A vision of our desert turtle sinking to the bottom of the pool. My grandpa losing his hat in the ocean's waves. My friend getting in a car accident in her blue truck after taking a right turn. Maybe as I got older, I tuned them out.

Sometimes I wonder if not only fear was passed down to my sisters and me, but this gift.

As a mother, I worry less about being taken myself and more about my children.

———

AFTER I AM far enough away, I peer into my driver's side mirror. The Stateville Correctional Center seems smaller and smaller as I create more space between us. I catch the sun setting out the driver's side window, an honest display of Mother Nature's breadth: swirls of blood and peach dripping in daylight. Back at the prison, my inner broadcaster voice had signalled for me to trust my instincts. To leave.

In the final moments of each young man's life that Gacy took, his victims must have had a desire to flee. At first, I feel disappointed by my time at Stateville Correctional Center and my own impulse to flee. But then I consider the proof that this is the kind of place where danger communes, unfettered by human decency. The type of place suitable for Gacy in his final moments.

CHAPTER FOURTEEN

A FIGHT FOR GOOD

2011

THE BONES OF BOYS WITHOUT names were scattered across cemeteries in Chicago with simple headstones that read: "We Remembered."

Grass grew thick next to the tombstones. The boys waited underground for someone to finally, hopefully, find them, know them, call them by name. By 2011, the eight remaining unidentified bodies, buried underground, were Victim No. 5, Victim No. 10, Victim No. 13, Victim No. 19, Victim No. 21, Victim No. 24, Victim No. 26, and Victim No. 28.

In that year, the Cook County Sheriff, Tom Dart, and Detective Lt Jason Moran had a serious talk. Moran wanted to move the Gacy case from cold and closed to open. He believed it was worthwhile to re-evaluate all the evidence using new technologies like DNA sampling to find positive identifications. Much of the evidence associated with the Gacy case – from murder weapons to victims' belongings – is stored in a warehouse in Cicero, southwest of the heart of Chicago and operated by the Cook County Sheriff's Office. It's 260,000 square feet and keeps home to much of the trial evidence, including Gacy's crawl space entrance.

Moran and Dart agreed they would reopen the case. Even if they might not be able to positively identify any of the unidentified victims they would try. Their attempt would mean a lot to the families who lost so much.

As a busy working mom, Kim watched the news sporadically. Her father kept watch for her. He had remarried, another Barbara, and relocated from Des Plaines to nearby Deerfield, Illinois. Although Gacy was not in the news nearly as much as before, sometimes he popped up. These days, it was because the Cook County Sheriff's Office was working to solve the case of the eight unidentified victims. People can come and go from a police department, but the evidence remains timeless. This is how history holds on to truth.

On November 29, 2011, the first victim was given a name.

Camera shutters clicked, video cameras rolled, and the nation watched online and from work and at home. Tom Dart spoke at the press conference.

"Victim number 19 is never going to be known by a number anymore. Victim 19 was William George Bundy."

Bundy was a diver and a gymnast from Chicago. He disappeared in late October of 1976, at 19. When the bodies rose from the graves, under Gacy's property, Bundy's parents had a feeling. Could that be their son? He was last seen on his way to a party, having left his wallet at home. Bundy had dropped out of high school as a junior and picked up construction jobs infrequently. Bundy's family thought because Gacy often lured his victims with promises of construction and remodelling jobs, Bundy could have been a victim to his trick. Bundy was labelled as body number 19 when his 5ft 4inch tall body was found deceased in the crawl space at Gacy's house on December 28, 1978.

Although the family sensed he had been one of Gacy's victims, there was a problem: the dental records. When the medical examiner asked Bundy's mother for the records, she said the dentist who had seen her son had retired. When she reached out to the dentist, requesting those records, he said they had been destroyed.

"Back then, as many of you know, dental records were the primary and somewhat exclusive way of identifying remains," Dart continued. That meant even if the family believed their son was under the crawl space, there was no way to identify him.

The Cook County team was able to use DNA as a positive measure of identification. Bundy's family chose not to exhume his body, and rather leave him in his burial plot in Justice, Illinois. Coincidentally, Bundy had family members already buried at the same cemetery. The family did, however, choose to update Bundy's plaque to something more personal. Moran and Dart's findings brought closure to the family. But this did not erase the span of decades left waiting.

Over the years to come, Moran and Dart would carry on their work with the goal of naming all the victims, continuing into the next decade. No matter how long a victim was deceased, the team believed they deserved to be named.

KIM'S FATHER CALLED to tell her about the November 29, 2011, identification of William George Bundy. She was happy to hear her father's voice, to hear good news. Her life, in recent years, had almost broken her. More than Rob's disappearance, more than the loss of her mother.

In 1997, she received a cancer diagnosis. It came shortly after she completed medical school, which included spending a month in a coroner's office, examining bodies, post-mortem.

The melanoma was between two of her toes, a small, oddly shaped mole. She sometimes forgot to put sunscreen on her feet when she lifeguarded at the neighbouring apartment complex pool as a teenager. To remove the melanoma, she'd need to have two toes removed. During this time, she returned to the same diary she had kept when she was 17. Now, she was a grown woman, a physician, a wife, a mother. The diary was about halfway filled.

On the night before the surgery in 1997, Kim took a bath and examined the two toes she was about to excise. They had helped her kick in swim meets, clutch the diving board, and push off the balance beam. She wiggled them and felt saddened and uncertain about the rest of her life, if she was promised much life after this. After draining the bath, she grabbed a white towel and a pink robe. She drew her hair into the towel and put on flannel pyjamas.

Back in the living room, her family had gathered: Sam and the three girls, Courtney, 10, Danika, five, and Sydney, an infant. They painted her toenails bright apple red. A goodbye. Kim prayed. All she wanted was to see her girls' lives unfold. She wanted to be there for them when the world felt too heavy; she wanted to celebrate the small and mundane and the brilliant and big. She wanted to live.

The surgery was successful, and Kim remained cancer free. However, in 2007, she would be challenged again, this time with a surprise pregnancy. Courtney was a freshman in college, newly dropped-off at her university dorm. Kim wore an ear-to-ear smile when she told Courtney about the new baby at parents' weekend. Kim, surprised by her own news, thought she was menopausal. Courtney was happy, but also worried about a potential disconnection from her mom, her family, as she was no longer living at home with them through this next chapter. She also had a strange feeling, as if the news invited in a cataclysmic cloud.

Gavin was born in the summer of 2007 and looked like Kim's daughters, with thick hair and ocean-blue eyes. But six weeks after birth, he began regressing. He stopped being able to breastfeed. He started having 104-degree fevers every Wednesday. Doctors thought it was meningitis. Kim knew it was bad.

After three months of testing, Gavin was diagnosed with a leukodystrophy called Aicardi-Goutières syndrome, also known as AGS. The disease was caused by genes Kim and Sam both carried. It had nothing to do with maternal age. The result was nothing Kim did, which was a relief. In the early days of Gavin's testing, medical professionals had hypothesised Kim had exposed her baby to something dire, perhaps mouse faeces in the backyard feed shed.

Doctors told Kim and Sam to prepare to lose their bundle of blond love, now just over four months old. Kim had wanted to name him Gavin, because it meant "Battle Hawk". This name was chosen while her son was healthy, in utero. She chose it because of her love of hawks, and not because she knew what her son would be up against.

Gavin was placed in the care of in-home hospice, to try to keep him comfortable as he approached the end. When the brain calcifications took place during his high fevers, seizures stormed, rolling his eyes out back and vibrating his tiny body. He was in danger of aspirating on his own vomit.

When the bad times came, Kim was reminded of what she had already gone up against. If Kim's life began to crack from all the things that had shaped her, the original fissure began with Rob. And even before that, her wicked neighbour who had imprinted on her the danger of merely being a young woman. Back at 17, she began writing her own bible on how to live in crisis. When Rob disappeared, she was presented with a choice: be a victim or fight. Fighting, of course, looked different for each major event. Sometimes fighting looked like a quiet journal entry, a way to remember who she was.

"Battle Hawk" as a metaphor for her only son seemed appropriate, a premonition even. When Gavin turned one, he did not die as the doctors had predicted. His life would look different from those of her other children. The brain damage that occurred in those early months caused irreversible harm to his body. She called these sessions, when his body did not seem to belong to him, "visits from the monster". The illness was the monster.

As Gavin aged, he was able to process the world around him. He laughed at fart jokes and enjoyed long car rides, with the windows down. But he had weak physical and motor control and spoke only in nods of yes and no, small word sounds sneaking out when they could. His only mode of travel required someone pushing him in a wheelchair or by kicking his legs enough to blaze down the front driveway in his walker. Her son re-taught Kim, again and again, the hardships of life and what we can do with them.

She felt like she had lost a lot of herself when battling the "monster", those flares when the fevers and seizures and trips to A&E upended days and nights. Once Gavin stabilised and they found a nurse that allowed for a routine to fall into place,

Kim was desperate to find her next chapter. Sam supported her, encouraging her to re-find herself in this new era. She took what she knew, which was to serve, and began the process of applying to be a part of the US Army. The army had a reservist program, allowing her to travel each summer within the United States and abroad, to serve civilians and soldiers. She saw it as an adventure, a fight to do good.

On a late spring day in 2014 in San Diego, Kim was sworn into the US Army in her backyard. Hawks soared in the waxy blue sky, and a summer warmth settled. She entered the service as a major; soon to be a lieutenant colonel. Her children and husband were there in the homegrown grass. A large American flag stood, homed in the ground, next to her. The banner moved with the fresh air, carrying a distant sea breeze.

As LIFE STACKED up, it was easier to lie down and succumb to the stressors and "curve balls", as Kim called them. But she refused. Kim rebuilt her life and created a safe space for her son to develop. She fought to remember who she was, the child in her, the teen, the college freshman who testified at a murder trial, the one who, in a new post-partum state, flew halfway across the country with her newborn, so her daughter could meet her mother, so she could say goodbye. It meant something: to see who she could still become after so much loss.

Kim credited much of her resilience to a single person: Mr Tanner. She never forgot what her high school counsellor told her. She could be a victim of life, or she could use setbacks as fuel to do good. Grief would always live in her. But grief could metamorphosise, taking on different shades and shapes.

CHAPTER FIFTEEN

INHERITANCE

2018

"I'm going to run to the back for another cup of ice," I tell my mom. We are sitting next to each other on a direct flight from San Diego to Chicago.

It is the weekend before Mother's Day. We each have a child on the plane, taking over seats D, E, and F. I am with Bennett, and she is accompanied by Gavin. Because my child is still under two, he rides on my lap. Gavin, now 10, needs help sitting in the chair, so my mom props him up, leaning him against her.

"Mo ice, peez," my son says in his tiny voice.

"I got them," my mom says. "You go." She holds up her phone for Bennett and Gavin to watch a downloaded Sesame Street show together.

"Thanks," I say. I scooped some Goldfish onto the extended tray for my son to grab. My son is a new walker and wants to either play with a plastic cup full of ice or walk down the aisles on the aeroplane. The ice cup will keep him seated, and getting it for him allows me to stretch my legs.

This trip is for no particular reason, but my mom's dad is getting older, nearing 90. I am teaching at a university, but term had ended and I have time to focus on my family.

I wanted to go for a handful of reasons. To have coffee with my grandpa and step-grandmother, whom I called Grandma Barbara. To cook dinner for them, eat with them. To form new memories. These are Bennett's great-grandparents, and I wanted him to experience them. I also wanted an excuse to be back in Illinois.

My mom and I had come to Illinois the past December, and I had brought my son then as well. My sisters joined us for that trip. My mom and I had spent a day driving around. Over the Des Plaines River, past the old pharmacy, Gacy's old neighbourhood, the old banquet hall where she and my dad had their wedding reception. They were married in Des Plaines because it was easier for my maternal grandmother, the first Barbara, to attend. Because she was sick, she would not have been able to fly to a wedding in California.

We travelled to these destinations because when I became a mother, I became consumed by the murders. They had always been a part of my memory, from when I was little and I first saw my mom follow the man out in the night, with a baseball bat. When she told me, time and again, to never trust a stranger, when she wouldn't sleep unless she checked every lock in the house. Her fears stemmed from losing Rob, from facing Gacy on trial. Mothers, no matter their stories, all worry to some degree about losing their children.

In the early days of pregnancy, I began to see my mother more clearly. Before my baby ever entered this world, the moment I saw his heart beating on the monitor, his gummy bear-sized body on an ultrasound, I wanted to protect him.

At 14 weeks' pregnant, Nick and I decided to find out the biologically assigned sex of our baby. The ultrasound technician's office was in a peeling, old building in a town east of Los Angeles. The room we checked into had no windows. At reception, we paid $25. The procedure was not covered by insurance, but we figured we could afford that reasonable sum to find out a few weeks early.

A young woman invited Nick and me into a dark room. I lay back in a bed and lifted my shirt. My body tensed as the cold blue gel glazed my belly, which looked bloated, as if I'd had a little too much to eat at lunch. I anxiously squeezed Nick's hand.

In just a minute the flat-screen TV that took up the far wall of the room would project the image of our fully formed tiny human, complete with reproductive parts. On the wall, a baby moved, fluttering. A black and white grayscale of life.

"I just need one more angle, then I'll know for sure. But I have a strong idea of what your little one is," the technician said. I could tell she was used to putting on a show for couples; the reveal was supposed to be a spectacle.

I thought about interrupting her, telling her I'd changed my mind. Before I could say anything, she exclaimed, "You're having a boy!"

Nick's mouth split into a surprised smile, and he hugged me, cheering with her. The whole thing felt like a strange sporting event, a surprise touchdown. "Can you believe it?" He kissed me and began weeping. Happy, untainted, beautiful tears.

I began to cry with him, but my tears were different. I choked on them, panicking. The room teetered and swung. The ultrasound technician must have noticed because she said in a softer voice, "Little boys are great."

"Of course," I said. And I was honest when I said that. I did not know why I was crying. I slid off the bed and ran out of the room while Nick collected the images.

As I waited for him in the hallway, I tried to catch my breath, but my mind and heart had fissured. I pressed a palm to my forehead and found the stringy pieces of hair that had fallen out of my bun. They were wet, tangled. I felt as if I was in a fever dream. Nick appeared, looping his arm around me, unaware what was happening in my mind.

Once we arrived at our car, I stared upward, inhaling the smog-crowned Los Angeles air as my mind moved through disturbing scenes: my brother shaking in my mother's arms, his lips a petroleum purple, sick, fragile from a disease that calcified parts of his brain. Then he was lying limp in my father's arms, ghostlike after a grand mal seizure.

When Nick and I entered the car, I realised I wasn't unhappy that we were having a boy. I was afraid of the illness that infiltrated my brother as an infant, squeezing his body, causing wreckage and suffering. The chance of my child having the illness was about one in a million, even with a family connection. Both parents had to be carriers. It was complicated. An isolated world to walk in, but we walked anyway.

Later, I would also reflect on Rob. How I felt his loss deep in my body, inherited from my own mother. I mourned Rob Piest's life as though he was my own to love. As though I had once loved him in the flesh. The love was so real, it was painful. I could not reckon with what it would mean to lose a baby boy I already loved so much.

A boy represented so much. A boy represented an inherited past.

———

Years later, I would look up what it means to inherit trauma. Trauma leaves a mark on someone's genes, their genetic makeup, and this mark can be passed down to future generations. Trauma did not change one's DNA, neuroscientists believe, but it could alter the way your body reads your DNA. Inherited trauma, also known as generational trauma, lays down a framework in how I understand myself, as someone who once lived in my mother's body.

This research helps me comprehend my mother. And how my sisters and I respond to the terrors of the world, our concern of being taken in the night. The study of epigenetics offers methods to heal inherited trauma, beginning with advice to better understand your family history, including family stories. This dive into a genealogical past will help on the path of healing. It is in my nature to ask questions, and this advice to follow the crumbs of my mother's story causes me to walk into its history.

My interest in the Gacy case grew after the positive identification of Victim No. 26, James Byron Haakenson, in July of 2017. Gacy had re-entered the news cycle, and the attention caused me to re-read *Killer Clown*, where Rob still lived in the opening pages. I began asking my mom questions. Lots of them.

She offered me something she had never done before: the gift of her diary. My mother's words, her innocence, changed the way I viewed the murders of Rob and the others. It changed the way I consumed stories in real life.

The trauma over losing Rob is inherited, one I must walk into to find a form of meaning and healing. The fear of illness is my own, a terrible pain I witnessed. But this fear of illness, like

Rob's death, is inextricably linked to my mother. There is an intersectionality between both, creating a compounding effect. During the height of my brother's illness, I watched my mother suffer, almost give up. But when I saw her fight for my brother's life, emailing doctors around the world while he napped, and taking him to physical and occupational therapy appointments to better understand his changing body, I knew where my urge to fight came from.

"Thank you," I say to the kind flight attendant who hands me a cup of ice. I walk back down the aisle to my seat. My mom, son, and brother still sit in the seats, where I left them, with Goldfish in hand and a show on the iPhone. Bennett's eyes light up when I hand him the cup of ice.

We land a little after 9pm at O'Hare. At the rental car facility, we are able to rent a vehicle and two child seats. Gavin is still small enough to fit in a toddler-sized, forward-facing support seat.

My grandpa and grandma are waiting for us when we arrive at their quaint townhouse. They rented a cot for my son and it's waiting for us, set up in the guest room. They pull out the brisket my grandma had cooked earlier. They have old blocks they saved from when I was a kid that they bring out for Bennett to play with on the floor, briefly, as it was already nearing his west coast bedtime.

The next day I want to get my grandmother an orchid for Mother's Day and cook dinner. During Bennett's morning nap I head out. At the checkout counter at Trader Joe's, with a purple orchid and ingredients to make pesto and pancetta pasta, my eyes fall on the greeting card display. I pick out four

Mother's Day cards. One each for my mother, my grandmother, my mother-in-law, and then I grab an extra one for a mother who is never far from my thoughts: Elizabeth Piest.

By now, Elizabeth Piest is deep into her 80s. My mom has not spoken to her in decades. When I returned from the store I found my mom at the kitchen table, having an afternoon coffee with my grandpa. I hand my mom the card, saying, "What do you think about writing Mrs Piest a Mother's Day card?"

"No," she says. "I can't."

"Why not?" I ask. "I can sign it, too," I offer.

Once upon a time, they lived in the same urgent world of searching for Rob. Of enduring that first Christmas without him, when my mom made sure she sat with them at the funeral and shared their grief. I watch her face as she turns the card over, considering what to say. It is as if she is in the past, sitting at the Piest kitchen table. A softness settles into her eyes.

"Okay," she says.

We agree we will not knock on the door or bother her. The card is only meant to be a gesture, to say happy Mother's Day with no expectations of more. In the card, my mom writes how much her life had changed since 1978, with four kids, with her journey with Gavin. She says she prays and hopes Mrs Piest is well. I echo this in my own note, saying I had heard so much about her family from my mom; I feel a deep care for all of them. I wish her a warm spring and lovely summer.

We leave the boys with my grandparents and drive to the Piest house, the same one Rob grew up in. It is the first time I have seen it. A flagpole stands in front of the single-story home, in a safe and picturesque neighbourhood. I can picture young boys on banana-seat bikes riding around and exploring.

A sign is taped to the front window: "Oxygen in Use." The warning makes my throat tighten. The letters are faded, giving the sense that the sickness in this house has been ongoing. I didn't know if my mom saw the sign or could read it. My eyes can barely make out the words. We spent the rest of our afternoon sharing plates of pasta and taking the boys out to enjoy bucket swings at a park near my grandparents' house. They smiled and giggled as they soared higher. I felt a certain joy watching them. It is one of the best feelings in the world, watching your child happy.

When we return from our second trip to Illinois, I ask my mom if I can interview her. One day, everyone who was alive during the Gacy case will be dead. Only the artefacts and stories that had been shared would live on. I grew tired of the same retellings, led by men. Women, too, had been altered by the murders. Mothers of victims. Young girls who became mothers. The young girls who had girls who would become mothers. I did not want time to run out before my mother's voice was heard. She ought to have a piece of this history.

In October 2018, *Harper's Bazaar* ran my interview with my mom. It would be their first ever true crime feature. And it would run just days after the announcement of new sketches of possible unidentified victims, meaning Gacy was in the news. I hoped my article might bring attention to the unnamed victims.

The interview runs on Halloween and is entitled, "A Serial Killer, a Receipt, and My Mom: Haunted by the Murder of 33 Boys." Following the interview's publication, my mom and I receive an influx of beautiful messages from people who had also been a part of the Gacy case. People remembered. They wanted to continue to remember. To pay respect to the dead and hold space for the ones still living with the memories. Writing about this case publicly helps me process my own journey in connection to the legacy of Gacy. This is a necessary step in finding my footing in a conversation that started long before I was born.

2018 was also the 40th anniversary of Rob's disappearance and the excavation of the bodies from under Gacy's house. I share the victims' names for the *Chicago Tribune*. The paper runs my op-ed titled, "Remembering the 33 Victims of John Wayne Gacy," on the day of Rob's disappearance.

During this time David Nelson reaches out after reading my work online. His initial email slips through the fissures of my inbox, and we don't connect until after his book on the Gacy victims is published. To me, Nelson's book is a love letter to the lives that were lost. One thing David tells me about his research is this: "I always felt for the moms. To have a child that died so long ago. They're frozen in those 1970s portraits. It's strange. One mother, Esther Johnston, always stuck with me." She was the mother of Rick Johnston, a 17-year-old from Bensenville.

"She searched for him everywhere. During the trial, she kept trying to give more detail, but it was obviously too much. You just got a sense she wanted to say so much more. I also wonder what their deaths were like. Were they thinking about their sons at the end? Of seeing them again?"

When I think about the mothers, I think about my own motherhood. All the unknowns, both beautiful and painful, I'm yet to hold. Part of me wants to keep a time capsule of my children, keep them safe right here with me. I wonder how any of the parents survived the experience of losing a son. I don't know how anyone truly could.

CHAPTER SIXTEEN

WHAT SURVIVES

2022

When I return home from my research trip to Des Plaines, I don't realise what I have carried with me. But I am changed.

At the airport, it is dusk when my husband and two sons pick me up. "Mummy!" Bennett shouts from the car window. He waves so fast and enthusiastically, my heart hurts. Nick pulls the car to the curb, and I load my bags into the trunk. I turn to my two boys in the back seat, and tears drip down my face, onto my neck. After having lived in a world of examining the loss of boys, it feels like a surreal and humbling experience to be home, with my own.

The next day, I take Cal to daycare, and he wants to bring a balloon with him. Balloons remain in the house, left over from my birthday. "Boon?" he cheerfully asks. "Boon?"

I walk him into the in-home daycare and give him a tight hug and say goodbye. He holds tightly to the balloon as I hand him off to the wonderful woman who watches him while I work.

"How was the trip?" she asks.

"It was good," I say. "A lot to think about."

As I walk away, I catch the sight of the balloon and the long white string that hangs from it. On my way back home, I can focus only on the string accidentally wrapping around my baby's neck. Before I start working, I pace up the hill in front of my house. I tell my brain to stop. The image hurts so badly, it feels real. But I know this caretaker. This woman would never let my son be with a balloon unattended, so logically I had nothing to worry about.

I text David and ask if he thinks this anxiety is an after-effect of the trip. He agrees that it is. I had just deeply lived inside a case that hurt a lot of people. I was finally coming to acknowledge I was one of those people.

David's support is enough to dispel the image, make the fear float away. By understanding where the fear is coming from, I am able to let it go.

AT MY DESK, to further expel the image of the balloon, I nosedive into the internet and books, re-examining the ways the Gacy murders have affected the collective American psyche. I am curious about patterns people carry, what draws them to something as putrid as Gacy. I pick up a book from the pile stacked next to me on the desk.

I thumb through psychologist Helen Morrison's paperback book, *My Life Among the Serial Killers: Inside the Minds of the World's Most Notorious Murderers*. When I ask people why they are drawn to the Gacy case, an answer I sometimes hear is the psychology behind the murders. What made him tick? Morrison had, for some time, overseen the keeping of Gacy's brain in her basement. Later, the brain would be returned to Gacy's family.

At 3.21am after Gacy's death, Morrison was called into the autopsy suite. Gacy's family had insisted she assist in the autopsy. On an aluminium table, a pathologist and Morrison cut into Gacy. His body was blue. His trunk was opened, and his internal organs were pulled out. It was silent. No music, no speaking. Just the sound of sawing and body parts exiting Gacy's corpse.

An electric saw smoked through Gacy's scalp, removing the top of his skull. In front of Morrison, she saw the thing she had been thinking about since she first knew of Gacy, the grey matter.

After the brain was severed from the spinal cord, a swoosh. The brain was in her hands. She placed it in a glass jar filled with a special cocktail of formaldehyde gas and buffered water. The solution's chemical name is known as formalin. In this powerful fluid, the brain would become thicker, less likely to break into pieces. She sent it out to a pathologist to study for her, with Gacy's name obscured. She hoped the results would help her better understand Gacy's actions. Could a tumour or aberration help explain his crimes?

But nothing interesting about his brain was found. The killer's brain was actually quite boring.

Disappointed by the findings, or lack of them, Morrison decided analysing the brain was like examining a piece of steak, when studying the whole cow would have been better. Gacy's brain remained in the formalin solution in a glass jar. Although Morrison's book included Gacy, her book delved into over 400 hours she spent alone with multiple serial killers. Even if nothing of interest was found from Gacy's brain, there is a fascination on Morrison's part. She discusses how Gacy sent her signed art he painted and Christmas cards from death row.

Other books, too, focused on John Wayne Gacy. *Killer Clown*, of course, by Terry Sullivan and Peter T. Maiken. The first. Then *Defending a Monster* by defence attorney Sam Amirante and Danny Broderick, and *The Last Victim* by Jason Moss co-authored with counselling professor, Jeffrey Kottler, whose fascination with Gacy and other murderers became harmful to Moss. Add to the mix: televised and streaming dramas, YouTube, podcasts, TikTok, and other social media that has entered the serial killer sweepstakes. In some of these spaces I recognise a desire for an evolved way of storytelling that centres the people affected by these murders. But, of course, the tradition of shocking material, devoid of human decency, is still alive and well in the retelling of murder stories. I have seen creators use the term deep dive to promote their own slanted agenda, chock-full of conspiracy theories, while still magnifying a murderer's narrative.

I settle in front of my desk to really do some work now that I have excised the image of the balloon string around my baby's neck. My friend Sara texts me a link to Bailey Sarian's YouTube channel. She specifically wants me to see an episode titled, *Devil in Disguise as a Killer Clown – John Wayne Gacy Was INSANE | Mystery and Makeup Bailey Sarian.* It had over eight million views.

I press play.

A makeup-free Bailey begins talking directly into the camera. She places her hands under her chin and greets her viewers, wishing them a wonderful day.

Bailey sports tattoos and a single piercing above the centre of her lip. You needed only a few seconds to understand the appeal of the way this woman tells stories. She is a natural with a captivating candour about what she thought she knew. She comments that her 6.25 million and counting subscribers had asked her to do her makeup while discussing popular cases. She also admits to not being able to add anything new to the case.

"My name is Bailey Sarian, and today is Monday, which means it's Murder, Mystery, and Make-up Monday. On Mondays I sit down, and I talk about a true crime story that's heavy on my noggin, and I do my makeup at the same time."

She introduces the subject of Gacy, a regular family guy, acknowledging that people are not always as they seem. Most of her story centres on Gacy, who he was, how he lured victims into his trap, his photograph taken with First Lady Rosalynn Carter. Bailey comments on the absurdity of how Gacy got away with so many crimes before abducting and killing Rob. Near the end of the episode, Bailey says she thought Gacy received way too many chances with authorities. She says she hopes some of those people who let him slip through the cracks got fired, but she believes they likely did not. Bailey then opens up the conversation to her subscribers to see what they think.

The top comment on the video: "Side Note: If a child randomly tells you that they no longer want to/feel comfortable with being alone with a certain adult... DO SOMETHING." Another: "The fact that he has FANS almost disgusts me more than his crimes."

I understand the survival of such fans first-hand. The postman from Gacy's old street, dropping off packages from fans when there was no Killer Clown left to receive them. Over the years, that had always stayed with me as perplexing. A fan of what?

I take to the internet to search for these people who might draft a letter to a long-dead serial killer. Among the likely candidates is Ryan Graveface, who owns more Gacy artefacts, including his paintings, than any other collector. He is still active, buying estates of Gacy art and memorabilia.

In the summer of 2023, Ryan released a video discussing the world of Gacy art and the surprising world of Gacy fakes. People produce fake Gacy pieces because there is a market for it, sometimes upward of two-four thousand dollars, more than Graveface had ever paid. He has museums in Savannah and Chicago, where he charges guests 20 dollars to look at what he called his collection of "weirdo crap".

Graveface purchased his first piece of art by Gacy when he was 15 and learned Stephen King's *It* was inspired by Gacy's alter ego of Pogo the Clown. In high school, he wrote to a handful of serial killers on death row. Most of them wrote back. He was taken by how conversational and regular they seemed. Except they had done horrible things. Admittedly, I had thought Graveface to be one of those fans, but after speaking to him, I am reminded to not assume that interest in a serial killer makes one a fan.

Graveface is a Gacy scholar. If anyone was tracking the past and looking to the future regarding Gacy and his crimes, it is Graveface. He is not trying to protect Gacy. Rather, his aim is to expose him. Yes, even after death. Not only did Graveface give a home to Gacy's paintings, he also preserved Gacy's logbook. Gacy's records are extremely detailed, and Graveface could access specific facts from his life within those pages. He could authenticate letters. Know who Gacy's inner circle was.

The logbook noted the names of people to whom he sent letters and packages. Even if I didn't love the fact that Gacy's art still existed in a marketplace, I can appreciate Graveface as a historian. He serves a purpose in preserving the record.

We talked for two hours over the phone about his work. "What about the victims? How are you honouring them?" I ask. That was the question that haunted me since I learned of his active collecting of Gacy's art. There has to be a balance, I thought, between preserving history and honouring the ones who died.

"I do this mostly for the victims," he says. "For past victims. For cold case victims. For possible accomplices." He speaks of the fact that Gacy was most likely too big to fit into the crawl space during the time of his final murders. Graveface has a replica of the crawl space in his museum. At first, I wonder if this is for shock value, but Graveface makes it seem that he is someone who loves physical evidence and wants people to see him more as an obsessive investigative journalist that also hoards a lot of stuff. Not as a mega fan. He is an empathetic person. I can tell by how he mentions specific victims' names. He even brings up Rob, and how he thinks of him and his family.

He continues. "In Savannah, I have a whole wall of the victims and their images. Not just their names, but who they were as humans. What they liked, what they did."

"That's important," I say. "I'd love to see this."

"You are welcome anytime," he says.

I make plans to visit his Chicago museum location next time I am there. It opened six weeks before I made my research trip to Des Plaines and it was not on my radar. During our conversation, Graveface reminds me that it is important to see the whole story of a murder. It's okay to see the killer for who he was, and it is crucial to discern the ramifications of the crimes.

EARLIER IN 2022, before my trip back to Des Plaines, Netflix aired a three-part docu-series about the Gacy murders, *Conversations with a Killer: The John Wayne Gacy Tapes*. The producers claimed these recordings of Gacy speaking had not yet been shared. They first reached out to me in 2021, after reading my articles online. I was early in my pregnancy with my second son.

I sometimes receive emails from production companies, asking me to talk or to talk with my mom. Typically, my mom wants nothing to do with them. She endured a terrible experience when producers from a popular crime network flew her out to Chicago and interviewed her in an outlandish warehouse. Their questions, she said, felt aggressive, without compassion. They did not look for her humanity or the humanity within the greater story. She vowed never to do anything like that again. When the show aired, she struggled to watch it back, remembering how the show runner made her feel during the interview.

When I told her about the email from Netflix, she said no. I told them no. I suggested that they reconsider their angle. "All the docs and shows are all the same, with Gacy at the centre, and the police and authorities come on to retell the events. The victims' lives are often lost, as are other people involved."

They ask us to talk to them again once they refine their angle, explaining that they are merely in the research phase. A producer named Liz Hodes, from Radical Media, whom I enjoy speaking with, becomes the human behind the project for me. She is compassionate, patient, and convincing. Ultimately, my mom agrees, and the production team flies out to San Diego. Filming takes place in a $3million mansion in Del Mar, overlooking the Pacific Ocean.

My mom says she won't film without me. I am eight months

pregnant, and as with my first child, I feel vulnerable. Part of me wants nothing to do with this story at this moment, being so close to birth. I imagine all the mothers who lost children they once nurtured in their own bodies, before giving them to the world. I draw courage from my mom, who taught me to keep the faith, to not give up, and to find the meaning, everywhere.

On a lunch break, we sit with a team of at least 10, drinking lemonade and eating chicken curry sandwiches in the sun. It has been a long morning of shuttling around the different interview locations, the décor in these shots is expensive looking and plucked straight from the 1970s.

"How are you?" I ask my mom.

"I'm good," she says. "This seems better than the last." I have learned my role for my mom within the confines of this case. I am a safe space, a buffer for her to confidently share her story.

My mom opens the series by reading from her diary. Stylistically, the production was much better than any series we had seen on Gacy. It pays homage to the victims. But it is still arguably quite Gacy-centred, or at least, heavily Gacy-adjacent. Although the questions contained more empathy, we still feel, after watching, that we have a long way to go in telling the stories of what lived after Gacy died.

DEATH, OR FEAR of it, seems to follow me after my trip back from Illinois. It comes in waves, cresting seemingly out of nowhere, washing away in the business of a commute to work, decorating for Halloween, and picking out matching family Ninja Turtles costumes for the fall carnival. But also, during that year in 2022, my family grows closer. I move to the same town where I grew up. My grandparents relocate to live on my parents' property.

Sometime after Halloween and before Thanksgiving, my grandmother Barbara dies. The second Barbara. She was struggling with dementia. My grandfather, Buddy, now nearing mid-90s, was her primary caretaker, making every meal for her, doing her laundry. She would have days where she did not want to leave the couch or couldn't. She had hurt her back. The injury was slow to heal, so my grandfather took her to a hospital. Doctors there suggested a short stay at an outpatient facility, where a lot of nurses would help. We assumed she would come home. But on that fall day, my mom called and said she had passed.

"Can you go be with Grandpa?" she asks me over the phone. My husband, the boys, and I are getting ready to head out of the house for a T-ball game. I change out of my team shirt and swiftly drive to the facility. I dash through the entrance. "Byers?" I ask. A nurse points me down a long hallway. I sprint to the room and find my grandpa sitting in a chair next to her. The room feels hot, muggy. And it doesn't smell quite right. Her mouth is propped open; paramedics tried to resuscitate her. Grandpa Buddy pets her head, running his hands over her skin, as if trying to lend her some of his warmth as she grows colder. I stare at her, hoping she will move.

I am not immune to death, but I had never experienced the heaviness of sitting next to the dead body of someone I loved. It is not easy.

"What is the plan?" I gently ask my grandpa and Barbara's daughter, who was there, too, having flown in from New York the night before. She got to see her mother the night before she passed.

There is no plan. We spend all morning calling our local funeral home, asking them to take her and care for her. Well after lunchtime, someone finally comes. By then the room is stifling, my attempts to open the sliding glass door to smell the patio are thwarted by bolts keeping the door shut.

"Do you want to go get some air?" I ask my grandpa Buddy.

"I'll wait until they come to get her," he says. "Did the same thing with the first Barbara."

I imagine him coming back to the hospital, running his hand through my first grandmother's hair, after she had met me at six weeks old. Two Barbaras, two deaths; two bedsides. Death has a way of repeating itself.

When her body is finally picked up I focus on the surprisingly gentle way the funeral team handles the body, more than my sadness or watching my grandfather's grief. "I'm glad we just took her to get her toes painted," my grandpa says. Her nails were cherry red. I am glad, too.

CHAPTER SEVENTEEN

REFRACTION

2023

"He's not at school." My husband's voice sounds muffled over the phone. Nick is at work, so I am confused by his mid-morning call. "The school just called and said he is absent." He is referring to Bennett, now elementary school aged.

"You dropped him off. How could he be absent?"

"I don't know. Will you call?" I am at home, between summer and fall teaching schedules. Bennett is a first-grader. Not the tiny baby growing in my belly, but always my baby. I looked at the open takeout box leftover from my 36th birthday the night before. I can't spare a minute to put it back in the fridge. I grab my purse and keys and phone and run to my car. En-route to the school, I call the attendance office. No answer. I call again. Finally, a pick-up. I tell Betty, who knows Bennett and me, about the automated call informing us of my son's absence. I explain that my husband had dropped him off. His six-year-old body had run to the breakfast line in the cafeteria. Where could he have gone? Who could have taken him?

"That must have been a horrible call to get. Let me go check." Betty from the attendance office puts me on hold.

I drive past the pond, following the route to school. The skin around my heart tingles. My lower jaw shakes. A red light. I am about half way, listening to elevator music at a traffic signal that feels 10 minutes long. I contemplate running it, defying the laws of the world. Getting closer to finding my son is the only thing that matters.

Green. I speed past the pumpkin farm. Had my son, the one who follows the rules, been persuaded to walk here? The class had walked here for a field trip in kindergarten. Both my husband and I had been here with him on that fall day. We took a hay ride, petted baby goats, handpicked sunflowers taller than him, from a never-ending field.

I pray. Please God, let him be okay. Please God, let him be okay. Tapping my fingers on the steering wheel, I glance at the glittery purple nail polish that he chose for me last week. We had flown to Minneapolis for a wedding. Bennett had sat by me on the Delta flight. We both ate cheddar Sun Chips and drank fizzy soda water with ice.

I pass over a bridge that Bennett and I noticed, one morning on the way to school, had been built in the 1990s. Below this bridge is a small creek and hiking trail he enjoys exploring. I did not go to school here, so I get to see this town as a young child through his experience.

I turn on my blinker at the final stop light to turn into the school. I am still on hold. The hold music hums maddeningly in my ear. If no one came back to the phone before I arrived at school, I made a plan to hang up. I was going to run into the school to the front desk, quickly print out my visitor pass because I did not know how to not follow the rules quite yet, sprint to his class, scope out the cafeteria, the field, the back stairs. I would not stop looking until I found him. I imagined

I would have to file a police report. I wondered if the police would take it seriously, a missing six-year-old, or think he just wandered off.

He'll be back, I can almost hear them telling me. I would tell them he was my son, he followed the rules. He would never just wander off. My brain does not understand how to process the scenarios running through it. One day you are having a birthday party and sharing German chocolate cake. The next day you are worried about being able to tuck your baby into bed, smell his after-shower hair, again.

The music stops. "Hello? Courtney?"

"Yes, did you find him?"

"He's here," Betty says. "I'm so sorry. The teacher marked the wrong person as absent. I'll be sure to mark that he was here."

"Thank God," I exhale.

"Terrible phone call to get," she repeats.

I call my husband, who has had the same boulder building at the top of his throat. "He's there," I choke out. "He's at school." All I want to do is go in and hug my baby.

"Thank God," my husband echoes. "I had a weird feeling today. The person on duty, who is usually by the gate, wasn't there. I told Bennett to eat his breakfast and then find his friends in line. I watched him run toward the cafeteria before I drove off to work."

I picture Bennett. His outfit: blue Adidas Velcro sneakers; grey basketball shorts; a teal-blue shirt with the word Colorado on it, perched in front of painted Rocky Mountains. I imagined an interruption, an interception. I realised I was prepared to give anyone details of what he looked like, that I memorise his outfit every day before he leaves for school in case I need to know. "I just drove there, to school, panicking," I say.

"I'm so sorry."

I already feel the crystal-clear understanding of what Elizabeth Piest had felt dissolving, losing its potency. I'd be back in two hours to pick my son up. I'd see his little body, running down the back stairs, catch him when he jumped into my arms.

He would ask me if he could have some of the sour candy he gave me for my birthday. He'd hand me his backpack with the teal and navy dinosaur figures on it, the one we picked out at Target, and play with his friends while I talked to other moms. I'd chat with his teacher, who I adored, and she would apologise for the unintentional attendance error. I'd get to kiss my boy on the forehead when he was fast asleep in his bed that night, and his brother, too.

DURING MY STAY near Des Plaines the previous September, my mom had wanted to ask me what I was discovering about the murder case. I had sat next to her on the small en-suite sofa at the Hyatt Place, sipping crisp sparkling water.

"How has your perspective shifted since being back here?" she asked.

"I already had an inkling that it was challenging and strange for each individual person, but it's more clarified. Surviving is unique. There is a snowball effect in each family lineage, for the people these murders touched. You do not know about that snowball effect unless you ask and learn more."

She hummed.

"My suspicion was that these events bled into everything,

even if it was subconscious." Terry Sullivan not wanting to take murder cases again was a key example. Of course, there were endless others.

I continued. "I think that people who find meaning and healing seem to be doing better than those who have not. If you don't find meaning and healing, then it seems like you are stuck in time."

"You have to take the lesson and move on. Is that what you are saying?"

"Mmm, not a lesson." I searched for the right words to explain myself.

"Things happen for a reason, that kind of meaning?"

"I don't think the experience can be reduced. The meaning is deeper than a simple phrase."

I told her it was hard to articulate what I meant because everyone grieved differently. Everyone was affected immeasurably. Some people were private, some were loud. The place where the murders happened, and the families affected, was like the epicentre of a cataclysm.

The aftershocks rolled through, shaking up so many lives in the disaster's radius. We talked about the metaphor of seeds and a garden. In our hands, we can carry only so much before we must let the seeds take root. Become something else, out of our tight grip. The story takes root and blooms and grows differently for everyone.

"The murders affect the tapestry of your life and affect what else will be planted after," my mom responded.

"But you don't have to hold so tightly to those seeds forever, because of guilt or anger or karma. Maybe it's blame," I said.

"I think it is more of a burden. There is harm in the burden," my mom added. I nod. "When you get to the end of your life, there is no reward for carrying that burden."

"I think not everyone has the same response. Everyone digests and processes things differently. Your heart can hurt for someone who is in pain and not healed. But you can respect that their tool is to not move on. To leave everything as it was. Too hard to open the lid and deal with it." She commented on faith. "Maybe people with more spiritual or faith-based tools feel they have permission to move on."

"Yes, permission to move on, that is it," I said.

"You can't blame yourself for things you have no control over," she said, running her hand through her hair. "Probably many people, including myself, felt like you could have changed your response. In hindsight, 20/20, you would have done things differently. For me, when Rob's mom came in looking for him, why didn't I run outside to look for him? And why didn't people make phone calls earlier? Why didn't someone drive over to Gacy's house? There will always be the 'What if?' and 'Why didn't?' but we didn't. You can only self-deprecate yourself for so long for not doing things differently."

"But no one could know," I added, crossing my legs.

"Exactly. No one knew. So you did the best you could."

"No one said this young man is going to go die right now, so be on high alert."

"And back in the day this shit didn't happen."

"And not in this place."

"It was a wonderful, quiet, sleepy little community with minimal crime. It was so off the radar. What happened was just horrendous."

"And then there is the generational response," I added. "I

hope you found what you were looking for, coming back here with me." I pulled my hair up into a bun.

She said she did. "I was never coming back. It was a rudimentary, self-protective manoeuvre. Start fresh somewhere else." Kids talking loudly and laughing passed in the hallway outside our hotel room. I asked her about photography, the link between her and Rob. I asked her what the hobby meant to her. I remembered photography was something my dad had loved about her, too, as a young woman.

"Photography is art. It is meant to capture meanings and moments and try to pass on those sensations to others. Whether it is humans or nature."

"A way to share feelings."

"Yes. Quick art, really."

I chuckled. Quick art, totally a phrase she would come up with.

"You don't have to spend hours on the canvas, you see it, you take it, then you have it. And you can enjoy it to the same level of minutia."

She looked at the photos hanging in the hotel room. "Like these," she said, pointing. "You can stare at an image, and study it, or just pass it by. But then as you look, you notice the intricacies of the leaves on the plant, and it's just beautiful." In the image, the composition was split in two: the roots below the dirt, and the new life emerging into view. I told her I liked the balance of light and dark in the photo. She said that's why she loved black and white photography.

"The photograph lets you appreciate shades. And every shade contributes a different quality," she said. Life, like art, was not just black and white.

The hotel room quietened for a moment. "That's the centre of these murders, the shades deserve attention, too," I responded. "And also, what is unseen," I added, pointing to the roots of the plant, underground.

My mom smiled, having arrived at meaning in her own way. "Shades are what makes everything what it is. The black and white are just the outlines." I brought up the word meaning, curious to know directly if she thinks she found it in this case.

"Finding meaning," she confirmed, "saved me."

AT THE BEGINNING of fall in 2023, I build a couch in my driveway. It's a pleasant fall day and Bennett is off on a bike ride with Nick and Cal is taking a nap. In solitude I relish the labour of this task. Physical activity and movement have always been part of creating balance in my life. Putting my body into motion, instead of letting my mind run the show, is cathartic. My mom arrives at my house, unannounced, holding a coffee cup, and asks to hang out. She asks me what I'm thinking about.

"Mothers," I say, pushing the couch legs into the bottom of the sofa.

"What about them?"

I straighten and look at her. "Well, just thinking about the mothers of the victims, most who have now passed on."

Some victims are still unnamed. The most recent one identified was Francis Wayne Alexander in 2021. In 2023, according to the Cook County Sheriff's Office, five remain unidentified, after being buried on June 12, 1981. However, as of 2023, there is still debate around Michael Marino's identification as Victim No. 14. According to his mother, still living, there was not a positive DNA match after his body was exhumed. So perhaps that number is six. Either way, those mothers lived most of their lives without ever knowing what happened to their children.

"As I get older, I think a lot about the mothers," she says.

"It's impossible not to," I say, pushing a piece of hair behind my ear and placing the cushions onto the couch, now ready to sit on. I place my hands on my hips, take a breath. My mom takes a seat on the new couch. She pats the cushion next to her. I take a seat. We must look odd to anyone walking by, two women, sitting on a grey couch in the middle of the drive.

My mom brings up the film *Till*, which she watched recently on an aeroplane. It reminded her of the power of grieving mothers. Emmett Till's death was brutal and racially-motivated. He was kidnapped, beaten, mutilated, and killed, before his body was discarded into the Tallahatchie River. His mother decided to have an open casket for her son, to show the horrifying injuries he suffered. Till's mother would not hide the truth. People would know the love she held for son, both in life and after. My mom told me it made her think a lot about the mothers of Gacy victims.

"What do you think about the most, regarding the mothers?" I ask.

"A mother's love is immeasurable," she says. "I think a lot about Elizabeth Piest. She did everything she could as a mother, and Rob was a great kid. He shared his love for his family. Everyone knew it was her birthday that night."

I sneeze. She is so focused, though, so calm in her introspection of Rob, of his mother, she continues on without noticing. She says, "This family was so full of love. They weren't going to be pushed away. They weren't going to be told that this was some typical runaway. I think this is the common thread for a family that experiences a violent act. It's love. Love withstands all. It lasts forever. It may freeze in time, but it never goes away."

I nod.

"The love of that child, or the love of that friend, that may be the ripple effect. You never want anyone you love to feel the same pain or stress or violence." She pivots to think about me. "What if this happened to you as a mom? If you could not protect your child like you had promised?" I tell her I don't know what I would do, and that I don't like to think about it.

She turns to other mothers of Gacy victims and discusses how many had questions but often had no platforms to use their voices to find answers. "Why did those mothers not get the same service the Piest family got?" She asks me to remind her who the blonde sister was who did most of the television interviews. I told her it was Gregory Godzik's sister.

"Yes, her," she says. "What if that family had a platform back then? If they could have spoken out more about the disappearance of her brother?" She is right. On top of the issue of authorities not taking these missing young men seriously, the world did not yet have social media, the internet, and other smart technology to spread awareness.

My mom has so much to say about mothers, and all of it centres on one thing: love. Today, love surrounds the memories of the victims, who were so young when their lives were unjustly abbreviated. We remember Timothy McCoy (16), Victim No. 28, John Butkovich (17), Francis Wayne Alexander (21), Darrell Samson (18), Samuel Stapleton (14), Randall Reffett (15), Michael Bonnin (17), William Carroll (16), Victim No. 26, James Haakenson (16), Victim No. 13, Victim No. 21, Rick Johnston

(17), William Bundy (19), Michael Marino/Victim No. 14 (14), Kenneth Parker (16), Gregory Godzik (17), John Szyc (19), Jon Prestidge (20), Victim No. 10, Matthew Bowman (19), Robert Gilroy (18), John Mowery (19), Russell Nelson (21), Robert Winch (16), Tommy Boling (20), David Talsma (19), William Kindred (19), Timothy O'Rourke (20), Frank Landingin (19), James Mazzara (20), and Robert Piest (15).

LOVE. A BIG, big word. A mother's love may look differently for every mother you ask, but I know how it looks for me. When I had my second child, I realised how much my love could stretch. He was so small, his toes and foot fit in the palm of my hand. Bennett had been so excited to become a brother. He wanted to take photos of everything. Of me with no sleep, holding baby Cal in my arms. Of his Winnie the Pooh stuffed animal. One summer afternoon Bennett was jumping on a stomp rocket in the backyard while Cal rested in a bassinet next to me that I had brought outside. The pink and white roses were opening. The palm trees swayed against the blue sky.

"Can you help me, Mommy?" Bennett asked. A stomp rocket had lodged into a branch in the tangerine tree.

I walked over. "Do you hear that?" I asked.

Bennett's eyes followed my path, looking for movement in the tree. It was bees buzzing around the flowering tangerine tree branches.

"It's funny, right? You hear the bees before you see them." He nodded and ran from the buzzing whir. I scooped the rocket out of the tree and tossed it to him.

He ran inside to get something. I thought about how easily

the phrase slipped from my mouth, recollecting how I was close to Bennett's age when my mom first told me.

When Bennett returned from the house, he held our family's Polaroid camera. He put it up to his eye, pretending to take my photo, the tangerine tree behind me. I had bought him an outer space-themed photobook, where he could store his Polaroid portraits. Like his grandmother, he had an eye for how to frame, what to focus on.

"What do you like about taking photos?" I asked.

"The click of the button and pulling the photo out."

"What do you like taking pictures of?"

He smiled. "You." The camera clicked.

You. I had spent a lot of time thinking about the love mothers held for their children. But the love children held for their mothers could also be infinite. The mother-child bond was a once-in-a-universe type of love, and I felt so grateful to experience it. I hoped to teach my boys that there was a way to choose love over fear, acknowledging both, but safekeeping the truth that love weighed more. To teach them that fear was not necessarily bad. Fear was important to survival. But fear did not have to hold the whole picture. After immersing myself so deeply in the case, I'm able to understand how I have grown. It's worthy to face fear head on, to make sense of the insensible. But it's equally important to carve out moments for deep joy.

If I was asked what heaven on earth looked like for me, it would be this moment. Children, family. I'd paint a simple picture. It would be this same sky, with a crowded table below it, outside, on a patio. Sliced watermelon cut into triangles. Food on the grill. My whole family, crammed around the table, passing platters and laughing, enjoying the last waves of daylight.

Just as my mom and I carry the same fears, we also carry the same joys, same hopes. No matter how difficult life became, how murky the sky turned, we gripped our hands into the blood and flesh of love. Sometimes love looked like fighting for your life, a future, with an understanding that you may not know how things will turn out.

In a diary entry from when my mom was recovering from her surgery, after her cancer diagnosis, when two toes were removed, she reflected this same hope. In the journal she kept at 17, she wrote about finding peace and staying optimistic in 1997. She was recovering, learning to walk again.

> *I love my family and plan on staying with them for a long, long time. I continue to pray and meditate twice daily, a big boost emotionally, physically, a recharge to my immune system. I'm still walking with a limp but someday it too will be gone. All for Now.*

When my mom and I made that first trip back to the place Rob Piest took his last breath, I took a photo of the new house built on the old grave site. To this day, that photo makes me tense.

Once we arrived back home in California, I pulled up photos from our trip to show my mom.

"What do you think this is?" I pointed to the centre of the image. An orb blocked the view of the new home built on the old Gacy lot.

Our coffee cups cooled on the table in front of us, as we sat next to each other on the couch, still in our pyjamas. She slid her pink glasses from the top of her head, over her nose.

"Maybe it's Rob," she said. "It's something."

Maybe it was Rob. Or maybe it was a disruption in light.

I return to the photo whenever I need a reminder of how to be open to surprise, how to keep asking questions. One person may look at the photo and see a camera glitch. Another might look and see something like a ghost. Another might look and understand it as a lesson on how to see.

ACKNOWLEDGEMENTS

This book is dedicated to all the boys, and I want to acknowledge the 33 victims of John Wayne Gacy, their families, their friends, and everyone who loved them. I carried you with me while writing this book, and I will continue to think of you long after this book is published.

To the person I owe everything here: my mother. For your bravery, your wit, your fire. This book would be nothing without you. Thank you for trusting me, for always believing in me and my love of stories. You have taught me the power of telling the truth, and I know people will connect to your story in ways that are impossible to predict. I love you the world.

To my agent, Ashley Lopez, and the Waxman Literary Agency, thank you for having a vision for this book before anyone else. Ashley, from our early brainstorming days over the phone, to talking through the full draft, I am grateful to have a teammate and friend in you.

My editor, Michaela Hamilton, thank you for championing this book and for bringing it out into the world. To everyone at Kensington who invested their time into this book's life, all my gratitude.

To my early readers: Jacqueline Alnes, Tanya Frank, David Nelson. Writing with you by my side has made this book better.

Jacqueline, your positivity and humour light up my day. I love talking to you, about life and writing, and I'm overjoyed we found each other in the halls of Morrill. Tanya, even though we live in different countries and vastly different time zones, you bring out the kind bulldog in me. You are a beaming light, ferocious writer, and amazing friend. David, our friendship seems serendipitous.

Thank you for responding to my texts at odd hours of the day about fact-checking something for the book, and thank you for caring so much about this case, its legacy, and the victims. Thank you to the universities and creative writing programs that homed my writing education. Gratitude to the professors who saw something in me and helped me hone my craft: Chris Abani, Tom Lutz, Mike Davis, Goldberry Long, Charmaine Craig, Sarah Beth Childers, Janine Joseph, Lisa Lewis, and many others. Thank you to Anna Sicari and Joshua Daniel for helping me navigate how to carve out space for creative writing while working in academia.

Since becoming a mom, I have not had the chance to attend many writers' conferences. But gratitude for past scholarships from Squaw Valley Community of Writers and the Santa Barbara Writers Conference, which allowed me to figure out who I was as a writer.

Recognition to the *Columbia Journal* for publishing my first long-form piece, *Angel Town*, on the Gacy case, and for *Best American Essays* naming it a notable essay in 2020. Gratitude to Longreads for choosing my *Harper's Bazaar* interview, *A Serial Killer, a Receipt, and My Mom: Haunted by the Murder of 33 Boys* as an editor's pick.

Thank you to the people of Des Plaines, for being generous and kind to me. I love this town and I am humbled by having spent time in a place that means so much to this book.

Thanks to Terry Sullivan and the many others I interviewed while writing.

To the women who loved on my children while I was writing this book: Brenda and Graciela, you are like family.

To my girlfriends: Kelly, thank you for believing in me since I first declared I was going to be a writer. You are the true testament of a best friend. Jenna, our long, deep conversations help me better understand myself and the world. Ellen, your fire for life and excitement for this book is exhilarating. To my mom friends, you teach me how to do it all, and I am beyond grateful to watch our kids grow up together. Thank you to all my friends, through various walks of life, from childhood to adulthood, who have cheered me on. I see you, I love you.

To my family: I don't know if I can find the words to share what your support, love, and belief has meant to me, but I will try. My love for you all is boundless.

Grandpa Buddy, thank you for raising my mother, for giving her the tools to fly. You are the best, for checking in on me while writing this book and dropping off Bible verses in my mailbox to help me stay on the path. When I am 95, I want to be just like you.

Helene and Bill, my in-laws, I want to recognise you for raising the best guy out there and for your text check-ins and enthusiasm for the journey of this story.

Danika and Sydney, my sisters. I thank God for giving me you two. I'm full of gratitude for us sticking together while doing this thing called life. Danika, thank you for cheering me on, even when I fail. And for the margaritas when the failure felt too big. I might need a shaker or two after all of this. Sydney, thank you for sharing a love of literature with me. I love when

I find an old book of yours, with soft, dog-eared pages and underlined passages.

My brother, Gavin, thank you for reminding me about the power of small joys, especially when life can feel unbearably hard. Thank you for teaching me how to fight for stories and voices that don't always hold much space in society.

To my dad: What can I say? You have believed in me since I was a little girl. Thank you for re-reading *Killer Clown* with me during my early research days, to know where I am at each stage in the writing process. Thank you for remaining passionate for this book to launch, for reminding me of the simple task of doing the work. "Writers write," you say. Sometimes life, like writing, is just about showing up. You teach me to try my best each day. Thank you for being my earliest reader, for being my friend, and for being my dad.

To my mom, who I already thanked, but when a book is based on your life, you get double the thanks. I can't believe we did it, the book is here. I am so proud of you. Of your healing, your courage to dive back into this story, and for trusting your intuition. You are truly one of a kind. Your grandchildren are lucky to have you. I'm so lucky you are my mother. Thank you for always encouraging me to raise my bar.

To my husband, Nick, all my love. It's safe to say this book was written because of your love and unending support. If I could nominate you for America's Best Husband, I would. I know you would win. Thank you for helping me carve out quietness and space to write, for taking the boys to Legoland and the San Diego Zoo on long writing days. Thank you for all the home cooked meals and hand-delivered coffee. As a life partner, you take the cake.

To my boys, Bennett and Callum, know that my life changed for the absolute best the moment you arrived in my arms. Your laughter, spirit, cuddles, and kindness are my fuel to keep writing. To the boy in my belly, Theodore, whom I have yet to meet, thank you for dancing and kicking and keeping me company while writing this book. I was truly never alone. My love for you three shines as bright as the sun, the moon, and the stars.

To Simple Minds, who sang, "Don't you, forget about me". The song appears at the end of *The Breakfast Club*, a film about five students from different walks of life who get a chance to connect during Saturday detention. It seems serendipitous that this movie, this song, holds a connection with Des Plaines and my mom. She used to walk the same halls as the characters in the film at Maine North High School. When I play this song, it's easy for me to see the characters in this book come alive. Thank you, Simple Minds. My dad tells me you didn't want to record this song for the film. I'm glad you did.

Thank you to the readers who find this book. Stories like this one live on because of you.

And finally, I want to acknowledge Robert Jerome Piest. You were the last one on a long line of terrible murders and I will never forget you. Not now, not ever.

Kim Byers began writing in this diary during the fall of 1978.

Kim in her teens.

Rob Piest's yearbook photo, 1978.
From the collections of the Des Plaines History Center.

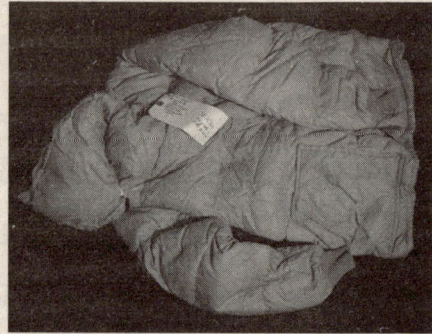

The parka Rob wore on the last day of his life was later found at John Wayne Gacy's home.

Kim Byers and Cory Litza, Homecoming 1978. This photo was part of the batch Kim packaged for development on December 11, 1978.

Acting on instinct, Kim slipped her film receipt into the pocket of Rob's jacket. It became a crucial piece of evidence.

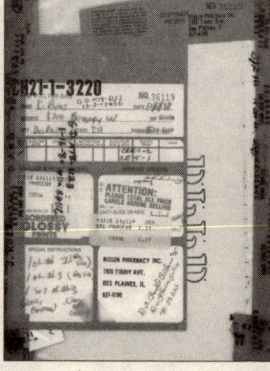

Kim with Nisson Pharmacy co-workers, having a fun ski day in 1978 before Rob went missing.

Inside Nisson Pharmacy. Kim took this photo of her boss. It is glued into a scrapbook of hers from 1978.

The snow piled high in Des Plaines, Illinois, in the winter of 1978–1979.

Kim Byers, 17, Maine North High School senior.

Gacy's house at 8213 W. Summerdale Avenue in unincorporated Norwood Park Township at the time of his arrest on December 22, 1978. *Photo by William Yates/*Chicago Tribune/*TCA.*

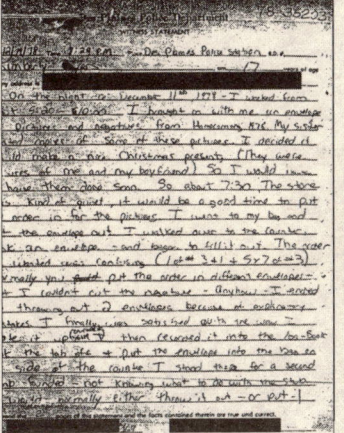
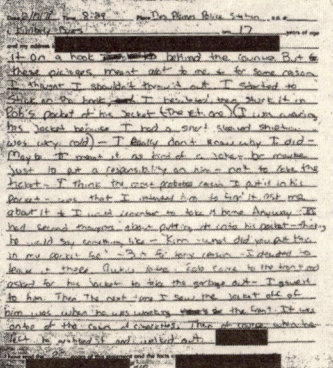

Kim's two-page witness statement, written at the Des Plaines Police Department.

Family members and friends searched tirelessly for Rob and posted flyers throughout the community.

Bodies being pulled from Gacy's house, December 1978.
Photo by Karen Engstrom/
Chicago Tribune/*TCA.*

On the Des Plaines River near Morris, Illinois, firemen from the Channahon Fire Department searched for bodies in the John Wayne Gacy case on December 23, 1978. A helicopter assisted in the search.
*Photo by Frank Hanes/*Chicago Tribune/*TCA.*

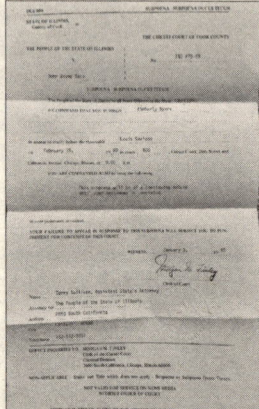

During her freshman year of college, Kim was notified of her assigned day in court, where she would testify against Gacy.

Kim's calendar during the month of Gacy's trial.

The entrance to the crawl space in Gacy's home was brought to court as evidence. Kim sat next to it while waiting to be called to the stand to testify.
Photo by Erin Hooley/
Chicago Tribune/*TCA.*

At the Richard J. Daley Center on January 8, 1979, Cook County State's Attorney Bernard Carey spoke at a press conference announcing the indictment of John Wayne Gacy for the murders of seven young men. Behind him, from left, are Assistant State's Attorneys Lawrence Finder, Robert Egan, and Terry Sullivan and Chief Deputy State's Attorney William J. Kunkle, Jr.
Photo by Chicago Tribune/*TCA.*

The jury en route to court at 26th and California in Chicago on February 8, 1980, for the Gacy trial.
Photo by Karen Engstrom/
Chicago Tribune/*TCA.*

Elizabeth and Harold Piest arrive for the funeral for their son Robert at Our Lady of Hope Church in Rosemont on April 18, 1979.
*Photo by William Yates/*Chicago Tribune/*TCA.*

Workers demolished Gacy's house on April 10, 1979.
*Photo by Arthur Walker/*Chicago Tribune/*TCA.*

Cook County Medical Examiner Dr. Robert J. Stein, left, and sculptor Betty Pat Gatliff speak during a press conference at the Cook County Morgue on July 14, 1980. Gatliff made facial reconstructions for Gacy's nine unidentified victims.
Photo by Walter Kale/Chicago Tribune/TCA.

On June 12, 1981, more than two years after their remains were pulled from the crawl space, services were held for Gacy's nine remaining unidentified victims at the Abbey Chapel in Oak Ridge–Glen Oak Cemetery in Hillside. Everything for the burials was donated by area cemeteries.
Photo by James Mayo/Chicago Tribune/TCA.

Kim saved the flyer that announced a benefit for Rob Piest and other victims.

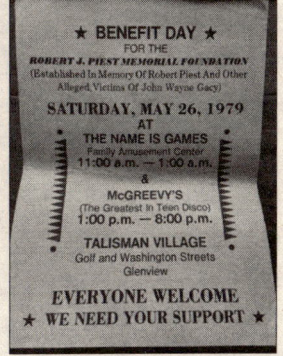

Kim visiting the site of the old Nisson Pharmacy for the first time in almost 40 years.

The Des Plaines River Bridge, where Gacy drove to dispose of Rob's body.

Kim in front of her family's old apartment on Gregory Lane.

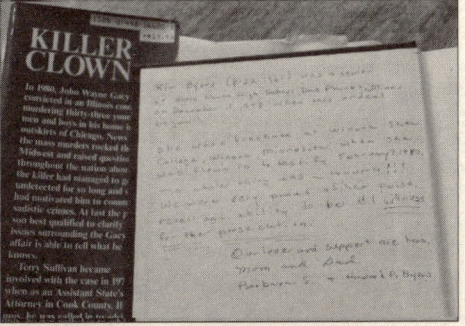

Killer Clown by Terry Sullivan and Peter T. Maiken was the first book published on the Gacy murders. The first two words in the book are "Kim Byers." Kim's mom wrote a note for her to find in this copy.

Kim's senior yearbook and commencement program, 1979.

Detective Lt. Jason Moran, of the Cook County Sheriff's Office, looks through evidence from the Gacy case on December 4, 2018, at a warehouse in Chicago. *Photo by Chicago Tribune/TCA.*

High tension wires near Kim's childhood home in Des Plaines, Illinois.

Kim as a student at Maine North High School.

Kim as an adult revisiting the old Maine North High School, which was the setting for the film *The Breakfast Club*.

A new home, shown here in 2017, was built on the site where John Wayne Gacy once lived.

Kim stands next to the double doors through which her friend Rob left Nisson Pharmacy to meet with contractor John Wayne Gacy.

Fresh concrete marks the property line where the new home was built on Gacy's former lot.

Courtney Lund O'Neil driving, with the old Nisson Pharmacy seen out the window.
Photo by David Nelson.

Rob Piest was laid to rest at All Saints Catholic Cemetery and Mausoleum.

Courtney stands outside Our Lady of Hope Church, where the Piest family held Rob's funeral.
Photo by David Nelson.

Kim and Sam, outside Kim's childhood home in Des Plaines, Illinois, 1984. It's Kim's 23rd birthday.
Photo by Howard Byers.

Courtney and Kim before filming takes place for a Netflix documentary.

Kim using Courtney's Canon camera to take photos at a nature reserve in Des Plaines, Illinois.

At Maine West High School, many things remain much as they were in 1978.

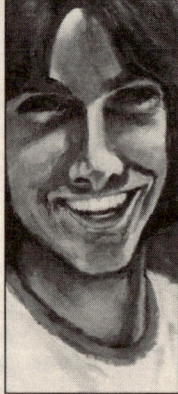

Painting of Rob Piest by Jennifer Given.

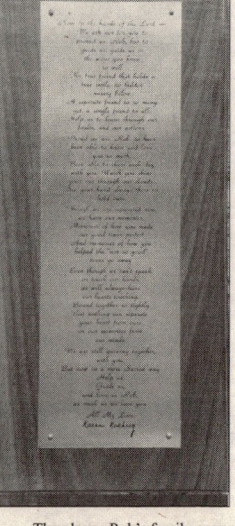

The plaque Rob's family gave to Kim at his funeral, to thank her for helping to lead them to their son's killer.

Sketch of Rob Piest by Brianna Thomas.